VANISHING POINT

Vanishing Point

*The Search for a B-24 Bomber
Crew Lost on the World War II
Home Front*

Tom Wilber

Three Hills
an imprint of
Cornell University Press
Ithaca and London

First published 2023 by Cornell University Press

Printed in the United States of America

Library of Congress Cataloging-in-Publication Data
Names: Wilber, Tom, 1958– author.
Title: Vanishing point : the search for a B-24 bomber crew lost on the World War II home front / Tom Wilber.
Description: Ithaca [New York] : Three Hills, an imprint of Cornell University Press, 2023. | Includes bibliographical references and index.
Identifiers: LCCN 2022036224 (print) | LCCN 2022036225 (ebook) | ISBN 9781501769641 (hardcover) | ISBN 9781501769665 (epub) | ISBN 9781501769658 (pdf)
Subjects: LCSH: Airplanes, Military—Accidents—Ontario, Lake, Region (N.Y. and Ont.)—History. | Airplanes, Military—Accidents—Investigation—Ontario, Lake, Region (N.Y. and Ont.) | B-24 (Bomber) | Aircraft accidents—Ontario, Lake, Region (N.Y. and Ont.)—History—20th century. | World War, 1939–1945—New York (State) | World War, 1939–1945—Aerial operations, American.
Classification: LCC TL553.525.N7 W55 2023 (print) | LCC TL553.525. N7 (ebook) | DDC 358.4/28309747—dc23/eng/20221003
LC record available at https://lccn.loc.gov/2022036224
LC ebook record available at https://lccn.loc.gov/2022036225

To Trish, Alex, and Julie, whose love and support inspire me, and to veterans and current members of the armed forces dedicated to our freedom

On February 18, 1944, eight American airmen aboard a B-24 Liberator bomber disappeared over upstate New York while on a training mission during World War II. They remain lost to this day.

CONTENTS

PREFACE

Lost Tomb

Everybody knows about the Tomb of the Unknown Soldier, and many have seen it. The white marble mausoleum at Arlington National Cemetery occupies a spot of solemn import atop a hill overlooking the nation's capital. Here some three million visitors a year pay respects to "an American Soldier Known but to God," under the watch of honor guards in meticulous and unceasing ceremonial drill. The tomb was created in November 1921 when, following an act of Congress, the remains of an unidentified soldier from World War I were exhumed in France and reinterred at the monument, to rest "in Honored Glory." Later the remains of Unknowns from World War II and the Korean War were reinterred in tombs adjacent to the original. A fourth tomb, honoring those missing in Vietnam and other foreign wars, symbolically remains empty.

Few people know of the tomb of the forgotten soldier—an unrecovered plane fuselage resting somewhere in upstate New York. The few who know about it are not even sure where it is. At face value, it's the result of tragic yet understandable mishaps when a B-24 Liberator bomber and its crew of eight were lost in a snowstorm while training for battle during the Second World War. Yet, like its celebrated counterpart in Arlington, it represents something greater.

Relatively few of the men executing wing-to-wing bombing raids that filled skies over Europe and the Pacific during World War II came to the job knowing the first thing about flying, let alone in ponderous synchronized formations under unimaginably pressing circumstances. For much of their young lives the science of flight had been in its infancy; it's safe to say most had not even been on a plane. Yet with victory dependent on air superiority achieved largely through strength in numbers, they had little choice but to learn in a hurry. Or die trying.

More than fifteen thousand of them died trying. They crashed, burned, fell from the sky, or simply disappeared with their planes. In 1943 alone 2,268 fatal accidents claimed the lives of more than fifty-six hundred airmen (and in some cases women) on the American home front—an average of more than fifteen noncombat deaths *every day*. To put it in another perspective, the US Army Air Forces lost forty-five hundred planes fighting Japan over the course of the war, and seventy-one hundred planes in stateside accidents.[1] It was a time when, in the service of freedom, death quite literally rained from domestic skies. While these fatalities might appear inglorious next to battle deaths, they are products of the same devastating burden of risk that came with advancing an air campaign, the scope of which has never been equaled, and on which victory was staked at all costs.

The magnificent tomb in Arlington offers fitting remembrance of otherwise unheralded sacrifice overseas. The story of those who died while training on the home front, by comparison, registered so little on the public consciousness at the outset that it's hard to consider them forgotten. The Army's search for the bomber lost in upstate New York—presumably in Lake Ontario—was discontinued less than three weeks after the plane disappeared and never officially resumed after the war. Yet a handful of war buffs and amateur divers are keenly aware of the tomb, and a few have spent a considerable part of their lives looking for it.

Working individually or in small alliances, they have brought different outlooks and expectations to the search: an idealized past, a conspiracy, a travesty, a potential tourist attraction, a treasure hunt. Some are said to be compelled by the lucrative market for rare World War II artifacts. Others are inspired to complete the record of the plane's disappearance while keeping alive a remote hope of returning the remains of the crew to their hometowns with military honors. All tend to be wary of the motives of others. Some believe the relic has been found, its coordinates kept secret to allow it to rest in peace . . . or provide pillagers exclusive access. Inquiries placed with military offices about the status of the plane hardly clear things up; they produce only generic warnings of the physical perils and legal consequences of diving war graves.

In the absence of fact, the seeds of myth are nurtured, and the story of the lost tomb provides fertile ground. There are reports of the wreckage having been spotted by parties not fully appreciating what it was, only to be lost again, moved by currents, forgotten with time, or buried by sediment. One old-timer remembers with certainty, during the summers of his youth in the 1950s, the outlines of the plane being clearly visible from a remote promontory overlooking the lake when the sun reached a certain height on clear, calm days. He and his boyhood buddies made regular efforts to reach it on inner tubes. They always failed; distances were greater and depths deeper than they appeared from shore, and the form was invariably lost in reflections as the youths paddled closer.[2]

Another lakeside resident—since moved to South Carolina—keeps a small brass hydraulic coupling said to have come from a piece of the wreckage that washed up a week after the plane was lost. The keepsake, connected to an event he knows to be important yet defies anything beyond hazy recollection, has been passed down through three generations.[3]

As a native of the area where the plane was last heard, I long harbored a latent and incomplete idea of its history. For years, what I knew was nothing more than a memory of a memory, briefly and imperfectly recalled by previous generations. The disappearance of an Army bomber and crew over my family's cottage at the height of World War II invited youthful wonder. How could it be that, after all this time, nobody had found it? In the absence of a guarded mausoleum or even a simple plaque to ground this memory to actual events, I set about collecting random fragments of oral history and tangible record. Over time, this information grew to include military files, newspaper accounts, correspondence with distant family members, contextual history, and information shared by divers and detectives, some now deceased, who have been at it far longer than I. From these elements a story emerges—one that reconciles memory with written record and, perhaps, stands as tribute to those who died before making it to battle.

VANISHING POINT

1

DEEP DIVE

The craft arrived at its destination on a summer day in 2016 guided by science, folklore, and intuition. Tim Caza pulled back the throttle, and his twenty-five-foot research vessel, *Voyager*, powered down and began idling toward the coordinates. The water that day was calm, making the task somewhat easier. So, too, did the help Caza had enlisted for the mission: John McLaughlin, a retired volunteer fire chief and body-recovery diver, who was climbing around the cuddy and onto the bow. Caza, with an eye on the GPS, shifted into neutral. As the boat drifted over the designated point, he signaled to McLaughlin, and a moment later the anchor was overboard, the rode running from the chain locker. Caza cut the power, and the engine noise gave way to the patter of wavelets against the hull and a general sense of stillness. They were within sight of the southeastern shore of Lake Ontario in only ninety feet of water, even though generations of conventional wisdom placed the object of their search somewhere to the west and in much deeper water.

Caza and McLaughlin, both broad at the shoulder, moved about the crowded little boat with practiced steps, the conversation turning to the task at hand. Caza ducked below and reappeared a moment later with his diving kit. McLaughlin, in his mid-seventies, was still a capable diver but knew well the hazards of uncharted wrecks, even for individuals in their physical prime. The plan was for McLaughlin to remain in the boat and spot Caza, who was twenty years younger, with a drop camera. McLaughlin had gear if the need arose, but he was happy to leave the frogging to a younger man. Above all he was there to witness the discovery. For the occasion he had brought an American flag, pristinely folded and sealed in clear immersible plastic.

It was early July, and along the shoreline, some miles off, occupants of seasonal cottages were in the midst of a weeklong celebration of Independence Day. Flags were in abundance, both those stirring languidly in the offshore breeze and the dollar-store variety that seemed especially suited to the clutches of small children. Though it was still only midmorning, the heat was building, and youths were dragging inflatables down to the water, over pebbly beaches, past remnants of campfires where on previous evenings parents, uncles, aunts, and neighbors had set off fireworks. Adults—those not joining the children on the beach—would now be drawn to porches and lawn chairs with coffee or iced tea or maybe a bloody Mary.

The cottages—locally known as "camps"—were for the most part built in the post–World War II boom years, some of them styled after two-story beach houses but most little more than bungalows or trailers with decks and awnings. Harking to an era when waterfront property could be bought on a working-class salary and developed on fifty-foot lots by a generation flush with victory, they remain remarkably unchanged to this day, sharing an eclectic charm, general mustiness from being shuttered from Labor Day to Memorial Day, and an unbroken view to the horizon. That view—as sensational as the camps are modest—is an ever-changing flourish of light on water: fireworks, sunsets, lightning storms, constellations parading around the North Star or, on days like this, the sun burning colors from a vast empty sky into ponderous depths. It's this stunning view—sometimes serene, sometimes sensational—that captivates generation after generation, though few are aware of the wreckage it conceals. Caza's boat, roughly the size and shape of a sport-fishing charter, might have been observable on this clear day for anybody who cared to look through binoculars. Still, it would have registered as no more than a speck on the horizon, its singularity of purpose lost on the observer.

It was at this point on the horizon, on a previous outing, where the long train of empty lakebed visible on Caza's sonar screen had yielded to something of impressive dimensions. As the image scrolled into view, Caza had known immediately it wasn't a shipwreck. And while ill-defined and obscured by sediment, it was too uniform to be a natural feature of the lake's bottom. Geometric shapes amid shadowy features suggested parity of form. With much to cover that day, Caza had taken several screen shots, logged the coordinates, and continued with his survey.

It wasn't until after Caza had returned home that he began to fully grasp the potential of his discovery. McLaughlin, a friend and neighbor, had stopped by to have a look. After examining the sonar image, McLaughlin produced a folder with diagrams of a four-engine aircraft. He placed one illustrating the aircraft's proportions viewed from above next to the sonar image. As he rotated one image to align with the other, the confusion of shapes depicted in grainy monochrome on the lake's bottom took on sudden coherence. The exposed section of its centerpiece and, most vividly, a lattice pattern on its top matched the nosepiece and cockpit canopy of the aircraft in the diagram. McLaughlin pointed out shapes protruding from the sediment—engines at the leading edge of the wing.

"Looks like the Twenty-Four," McLaughlin had said, returning his reading glasses to his shirt pocket. Discoveries did not tend to inspire demonstrative enthusiasm in the body-recovery diver. A find isn't a find, he is fond of noting, until "a diver can reach out and touch it."

The object they were trying to reach was a B-24 Liberator bomber that had vanished with a crew of eight after taking off from the Westover Army base in Massachusetts at the height of the Second World War. "The Twenty-Four" was last heard circling low over Oswego County in a snowstorm in the early morning hours of February 18, 1944. For seventy-four years it had defied searches from the Adirondack Mountains to the depths of Lake Ontario, first by the US military, later by recreational divers, and, in an apparent attempt to exhaust all possibilities, a group of dowsers and mystics enlisted by private parties to channel the aircraft's whereabouts.

The Liberator is fabulous both for what it was and what it represents. There is arguably no item that more singularly illustrates the country's rise

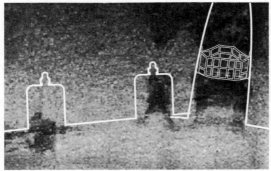

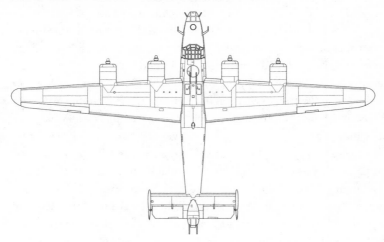

Figures 1.1–1.3. A sonar image recorded by Tim Caza in 2016 matches outlines of the front section of a B-24 possibly buried in sediment in eastern Lake Ontario. Sonar record courtesy of Tim Caza, collage by Mike Bechthold.

to engineering and manufacturing prominence while leading, in more than a figurative sense, the war effort.[1] Engineered by Consolidated Aircraft under urgent deadlines for a war where, for the first time in history, air supremacy was counted as a deciding factor, the Liberator could go farther, faster, with more payload than other bombers of its day—attributes that would carry the fight in Europe and the Pacific well behind enemy lines. "It would be an exaggeration to say the B-24 won the war for the Allies," writes historian Steven Ambrose. "But don't ask how they could have won the war without it."[2]

The plane's capabilities were unique, though its legacy ultimately rests with an unprecedented manufacturing feat. As the American home front tooled up for war, the Liberator became the centerpiece of aircraft development. Between 1941 and 1945, some 18,500 were produced, more than any other military aircraft in history. Rosie the Riveter rolled up her sleeves and got busy on B-24 lines, including a Ford Motor Company

Figure 1.4. At the height of the war, Liberators roll off the line at Willow Run, the converted Ford Motor Company assembly plant in southern Michigan. More Liberators were produced than any other military plane in history, but few exist today. National Archives and Records Administration.

factory a half mile long and a quarter mile wide near Detroit where Henry Ford's auto assembly line was scaled up for production of the thirty-six-thousand-pound bomber. To be sure, the Liberator was not the only famous warplane to carry the day.[3] But if the war was said to be won in the factories, the B-24 was exhibit A.

With so many of them rolling off the line back then, it is striking how few exist now. Like most of the country's prodigious surplus arsenal that survived the war, the B-24s were valued mostly as scrap. Only thirteen are known to still exist; of those, two are airworthy.[4] Yet the story of the unrecovered plane in upstate New York, no more than a dusky memory at best, was possibly less preserved than the plane itself by the time Caza and McLaughlin prepared for the dive. Few possessed reliable knowledge of the circumstances under which it disappeared, and fewer still pretended to know anything about its crew.

McLaughlin had seen a lot of things and people who had come to a tragic end at the bottom of rivers, quarries, and lakes, but the Twenty-Four remained in a league of its own. The plane itself, however, was the lesser part of an ambition—a pilgrimage may be a better way to put it—that he had been pursuing for close to forty years.

The military had called off the search over upstate New York on March 3, 1944, two weeks after the airmen were last heard from and by which time it was all but certain, wherever they ended up, they had not survived. None of the bodies of the craft's eight crew had been recovered. At the time, many tens of thousands of men were dying and disappearing on multiple fronts of the war, and tens of thousands more were urgently needed to replace them. All those men required training. The military had neither time nor resources to continue the search then, and apparently lacked incentive to do so later. The lost airmen, but for one exception, were young and single; they left behind grieving mothers and fathers from all regions of the country, but no direct descendants to pursue their precise fate and final resting place. Now the mothers and fathers of the crew were long dead and gone. So were sisters, brothers, and cousins. McLaughlin and Caza, returning to the site on that July day with a folded flag, were, in a way, surrogates.

As *Voyager* tugged at her anchor, Caza prepared for the dive amid an assortment of gleaming tanks and regulators. The air bore the aroma of sun-warmed neoprene and rubber. Underwater visibility is best with the sun high overhead. A clear day like this one, only a few weeks removed from the summer solstice, offered an extended window for their mission; Caza would be in no rush. He had been on many hundreds of dives exploring vessels lost to time, each with its own weight of anticipation counterbalanced by the protocol of safety. He would need only one tank for the reconnaissance, perhaps a thirty-minute enterprise. He would survey the wreck and return for the camera and flag.[5] He checked the sheath for his knife. At ninety feet, the relic would likely be festooned with lures and streaming with fishing line. A diver could quickly burn through his air supply trying to free himself, like a hooked salmon, from a line snagged on his back or an entanglement with the remains of a net. It was a hazard common to all wrecks. But this spot was notorious, and McLaughlin knew a story behind it. Local legend held that the nets of a commercial fishing trawler once became snagged hereabouts—an unremarkable event, except, as the captain finally pulled his gear free, an ink-black cloud boiled up from the depths. Within moments, the trawler was floating in an oil slick. The incident, the story goes, had gained the attention of military officials, who sent divers to the area. When exactly this happened was not clear, but it was a long time ago; the tale had circulated in Oswego County divers' circles since McLaughlin could remember.

Like fishermen, divers tend to have a propensity for spinning good yarns and, even more so, relishing their pursuit. Just because a story seems far-fetched, unsourced, apparently amounting to nothing, doesn't mean it isn't true. Myth is built in the absence of fact. Where there is myth, there is the making of a quest for a diver. McLaughlin had been on the quest for the lost bomber since he first learned of the plane while training for his diving certification with the Brewerton Volunteer Fire Department in 1969. As a much younger man, he tried tracking the rumor of the oil slick to its source. His inquiries with fishermen from nearby Port Ontario yielded plenty of rich speculation but nobody apparently with firsthand knowledge. For years, the story remained no more than a fish tale.

As it happened, the image Caza had captured on sonar appeared off the same shore as the fabled oil slick—a fact that inspired McLaughlin to revisit the old story while waiting to investigate the site with Caza. This time his archive search, now aided greatly by digital search engines, uncovered either a wild coincidence or a material bit of history. It appeared on page eighteen of the *Oswego Palladium-Times* of June 15, 1944.[6]

> After two days of dragging, Coast Guard-men from the Oswego Coast Guard have contacted a submerged object that may prove to be wreckage of the B-24 Liberator bomber . . . lost on a routine flight from Westover Field last February. After the Coast Guardsmen's grapples had been released from the derelict, a buoy was put out and there will be no further activity until arrangements have been made for the services of a diver to descend to the floor of the lake, 90 feet below the surface, and inspect the wreckage.

This information was sourced to US Coast Guard and Army intelligence officers. The Coast Guard hooked into the object "directly at the place where Earl Wood, Port Ontario Fisherman, discovered a slick of oil on the surface of the water after his fish nets became fouled in the wreckage." The report also noted that "doubt has been expressed" that officials had found the bomber, and "regardless of whatever adverse opinions are held, it is apparent that Army officers intend to complete the job and determine definitely what the submerged object is."

McLaughlin, as it turned out, had been onto something. Yet tracking down leads to the lost bomber, he had learned, inevitably amounted to prying open a box and finding another box inside, and this time was proving no different. Enough oil to make a small slick could, for sure, have come from any one of the B-24's four engines, each with a capacity of thirty gallons and prone to leaking even under ideal circumstances. Yet exhaustive searches of the *Palladium-Times* archive yielded no follow-up account of the promised dive to investigate the mysterious derelict, let alone what a diver may have found.

McLaughlin could only guess the reasons for this gap in the record. Maybe the Army's probe found something so mundane that it wasn't newsworthy. Could be, but it was hard to believe that a newspaper editor would pass up such a what's-in-the-safe moment. Even if the result of a subsequent dive had been anticlimactic, the reveal alone would surely draw readers.

It's feasible that delays led to eventual abandonment of the plan. Diving was a specialized endeavor in 1944, and people and resources were hardly in abundance. The reporter covering the story may have lost interest after earnest intentions were put off. There was, after all, no shortage of other news to pursue at the time.

A third scenario came to mind: officials discovered the wreck and didn't publicly share the outcome—cynical but plausible. The search for the plane had been called off four months earlier, and though Army officers intended "to complete the job and determine definitely what the submerged object is," as the article noted, they might have been in no position to divert resources for a salvage if it turned out to be the plane. Nobody would be the wiser. The B-24—soon to be in such surplus that the government would be hard-pressed to deal with them all—was not yet coveted by collectors. Diving technology was limited and not widely accessible. The wreck was now technically a grave by maritime custom, and the chances of it being disturbed were remote.

McLaughlin has the gift of a deep, sure voice, an air of authority suited to a fire chief. Yet he is likely to contemplate each new unopened box with a chuckle, followed by an invitation to "draw your own conclusion." Invariably there are plenty to choose from; considering them is an exercise of which McLaughlin seems to never tire.

Going through the safety checks on that summer day in July 2016, Caza and McLaughlin had no way of knowing if Caza would be the first to visit the resting place of the bomber and her crew, but they were determined to open the final box.

"It was a dream," Caza later reflected. "Our plan was to video the heck out of it, place the flag on it, and notify authorities."

Growing up in the 1960s and '70s, Tim Caza spent summers not far from where he was now anchored, in a family camp on a sizable inlet off the lake's east shore known as Sandy Pond. The relatively warm and shallow waters of "the Pond" yielded finds—old Coca-Cola bottles, crusty anchors, mossy fishing lures, and various discarded or lost artifacts that only an imaginative youth rapt with the quest for discovery, or an encouraging parent, could count as treasure.

Though now in his late fifties, Caza's youthful exuberance remains unchanged as he explores deeper and more expansive waters. Living in the golden age of consumer electronics makes it possible for him to work more in the boat than out of it, his Kmart snorkeling gear of yesteryear replaced by a network of transducers, screens, cameras, and diving drones, most of which he assembles himself out of electronic components ordered online and things lying about in his garage. He is typically joined by his friend, Dennis Gerber, a retired electronics engineer in his mid-seventies who once specialized in radar and sonar systems for General Electric, among other firms. Gerber's enthusiasm for both electronics and diving is a rare match for Caza, such that the two can spend sixteen-hour days on *Voyager* talking about their hobbies, drinking coffee, and keeping vigil over, for the most part, an endless procession of sand, rocks, submerged logs, and fish on their sonar screens.

Caza tried to encourage his wife Tammy's interest in diving earlier in their marriage by building a submarine from a mail-order kit—a three-person craft intended as a family activity. But it has seen only limited use. His two sons are now grown, and ever since a harrowing experience when the vessel got hung up on an underwater ledge and began flooding, Tammy has strongly preferred golfing with her friends. It's not a bad arrangement, they both concede; he's not a golfer, Tammy is not a diver, and they have been happily married for more than forty years.

Caza has tousled, sandy-brown hair and the physique of a man who earned a living moving packages, toiling on loading docks, and working construction. A favorite T-shirt depicts divers, backlit with sunlight knifing through depths of teals and majestic blues, swimming toward a treasure chest spilling from the ruins of a sunken ship. The words "FORTUNE FAVORS THE BRAVE" float above the image. Though Caza is yet to find any treasure in a chest, he once found a slot machine—a likely remnant of Prohibition gambling—near what is now known as Casino Island on the Saint Lawrence River. He didn't immediately recognize it for what it was, but while freeing it from the bottom and swimming it back to the boat, he sensed some pieces falling off. It wasn't until he was loading it onto the back of his truck that he realized, as one final piece pinged off the truck bed, so the story goes, that the bits now hopelessly strewn over the channel's bottom were actually Indian-head nickels, some of them possibly rare and worth more than the rusted shell of the artifact itself.

That was sometime after Caza earned his diving certification in the late 1970s, back in the days when a freebooting ethic prevailed with underwater finds. In years since, honoring a look-but-don't-touch policy that has become the legal and ethical standard of diving, he has invested countless dollars assembling the gear for DIY campaigns to be the first to view wrecks that have long eluded divers, or surprises that nobody knew existed to begin with. His noteworthy finds include a Durham boat—identical to the heavy open rowing craft that famously ferried George Washington across the Delaware. Caza was first to set eyes on a Durham boat—the primary workhorse of commerce and travel in the eighteenth century—since they disappeared from the timeline of maritime history with the development of railroads in the early nineteenth century.

Caza knew that his discovery, in forty feet of water in Oneida Lake, was old and probably rare. But he didn't know exactly what it was until he attended a lecture in Oswego by a marine archaeologist who was explaining how little was actually known about the physical characteristics of the Durham boat because none were known to exist anymore. After the lecture, Caza approached the professor—Ben Ford of Indiana University of Pennsylvania—and said he was pretty sure he could show him one. Caza took a skeptical but game Ford, who was working on another project in town, to the Oneida Lake site, and the two dove it on a stormy day.[7] The rest, as they say, is history.

Word of Caza's skill and passion has since gotten around among marine archaeologists, who have recruited him, at times with no compensation and little recognition, on projects to survey New York State's waters for clues on how the nineteenth-century canal trade steered the economies and sociology of the day. Caza likens his diving with "going into outer space and discovering something new . . . except it's history."

Any given day from May through November, when he is not towing *Voyager* from his home in Oswego County to the Finger Lakes, Lake Champlain, or various points on the Erie Canal system to find old things that are new, he and Gerber are bobbing in the wake of salmon fishing charters and the occasional ocean liner, bouncing signals off the bottom of one of the world's largest and deepest lakes, yard by yard, mile by mile, all day and often into the night, drinking coffee from a thermos, swapping tales, the mere thought of the sustaining rush of discovery carrying them through long stretches of finding nothing at all.

Calling Lake Ontario a lake is like calling the Florida Everglades a glade. Occupying some 7,154 square miles straddling two countries, Lake Ontario is a primary link in the international seaway connecting the Atlantic

Figure 1.5. Tim Caza (*right*), at the helm, and Dennis Gerber track GPS and sonar monitors aboard *Voyager* during an excursion in eastern Lake Ontario. Photo by Tom Wilber.

Ocean to the US heartland and the largest freshwater system in the world. Like its sister Great Lakes, Lake Ontario is capable of producing waves that can swallow ships without a trace, which it does on occasion, along with countless smaller vessels and sundry objects, structures, and sometimes people swept from its shores during storms.

Peering into the depths of Lake Ontario is like probing obscure realms of history; shapes begin to emerge for those who want to look long and hard. But even then, plenty is left to the imagination. Most of the lake drops well beyond the 130-foot limit for recreational divers, with the deepest sounding registering at more than 800 feet. So removed are these subsurface nether regions that the water temperature remains below forty degrees Fahrenheit through blistering summers and frigid winters. It's dark down there, and remote. Sturgeon nearly the size of telephone poles lurk about but are rarely seen. Sometimes schools of baitfish are picked up on sonar. But Caza's scans, hour by hour, month by month, mostly show stretches of featureless bottom occasionally giving way to ill-defined shapes, natural and manmade, that have settled over the eons.

Caza is able to penetrate these depths with breakthroughs in sonar, which bounces sound waves off the lakebed to chart its contours, and transducers, which digitize the signals for imaging. The technology, originally developed for military functions in the mid-twentieth century, was later adapted for fish finders in the 1980s and 1990s. Their components, once formidably expensive and limited in function, are now powerful, accurate, and accessible.

Over the years Caza and Gerber have modified the equipment to suit their needs by taking the guts of fish finders, typically mounted on the hull of a boat, and transplanting them into torpedo-like drones—"tow fish"—they make from PVC piping and other material. This unit is towed behind the boat at various depths. The tow fish allows the signals to project across the lakebed at an angle for greater range, while sweeping closer to the bottom to minimize distortion and wave-induced motion that impede hull-mounted units. On board, Caza and Gerber have added systems that track navigation and even steer the boat, high-resolution screens that display results, computers that store all information for later retrieval, and necessary interfaces to make the system run reliably and seamlessly.

The technology is effective but not especially speedy. The sonar can map swaths up to four hundred feet wide as the boat idles along at two or three knots—a brisk walk or slow jog. Much of the trick involves navigational challenges to ensure the sonar tracks systematically over the lakebed. Overlapping routes by too large a margin wastes valuable time and resources, and gaps can miss targets. They call it mowing the lawn, an analogy that aptly conveys the principle of the endeavor but not the scale. It's more like searching for a needle in a hayfield by cutting it with a pair of scissors and finding various other things in the process. Caza once mused he would be two hundred years old before he mapped Lake Ontario's floor, let alone the other upstate New York water bodies that are commanding the interest of archaeology teams.

Some finds, on first pass, may register as an anomaly. Any number of things can distort the image—the motion of equipment in currents and waves, layers of zebra mussels, decay, unfavorable angles or, depending on how the item sunk and came to rest, an unexpected orientation to the lakebed. Multiple passes, different angles, and some fine tuning can sharpen images. Because sonar gear is not exactly easy to deploy or retrieve, when a promising image appears—a target—Caza typically logs its coordinates, takes a screen shot, and continues mowing the lawn. He returns later to confirm and film targets with a scuba dive or, in deeper water, by employing a submarine drone—known in the diving world as an ROV, short for remotely operated vehicle.

So it was with the conundrum of granular form that was later found to fit the shape of the B-24. Sometimes, though, sonar images can be dramatically clear on first pass, especially over targets that settled with little trauma in deep, cold water devoid of oxygen and light and other agents of decay. Even then, verifying historic finds requires a rigorous confirmation process. The longer they have defied searches, the more skeptical their reception among qualified authenticating parties.

One of the most sought-after legends in the Great Lakes, a British Revolutionary War ship, was discovered in 2008 by two engineers who, in their free time, adapted electronic diving technology to the challenges of Lake Ontario. Jim Kennard and Dan Scoville had all but grown old on a quest to find the HMS *Ontario*, a twenty-two-gun brig sloop claimed by a gale while under way from Fort Niagara to Oswego on October 31, 1780. Some 130 souls went down with the ship, including 60 British soldiers and various family members, 40 Canadians, and several dozen American prisoners.

Kennard, a fellow of the famed Explorers Club, has earned somewhat legendary status among Great Lakes shipwreck enthusiasts. A septuagenarian flush with the charisma of a lusty adventurer, he had been looking for the *Ontario* off and on since the 1970s and lists "a touch of madness" as a quality necessary to sustain such a quest. Indeed, a nearly compulsive focus seems hardwired in those drawn to Kennard's idea of fun.[8]

As with McLaughlin and the lost B-24, many elements of the search for HMS *Ontario* were predicated on years of land-based poking around. In the case of Kennard's team, this included consultation with historians, development of submarine technology, and research of newspaper microfiche and documents from British and Canadian archives.[9] Kennard began pioneering homemade sonar equipment well before commercial fish finders were available. With groundwork laid and relaid, he and Scoville spent countless hours over a span of years surveying the ship's last known route. Each time, they returned to port with little to show for their efforts other than a hard-won knowledge of where the vessel was not.

In early May 2008, the team ventured into a deeper part of the lake, and there, finally, she was, making the years of effort immediately worthwhile. The eighty-foot vessel rested wholly and neatly intact, listing slightly to port, where she came to rest 228 years earlier in five hundred feet of water, two seventy-five-foot masts with telltale crow's nests registering spectral shadows over the otherwise empty lakebed. The team returned to the site with an unmanned submersible craft, which Scoville had developed with students from the Rochester Institute of Technology, to document and authenticate the find. Some eighty minutes of video show stunning details, including unbroken windows of the brig's officers' quarters. They have no plans to return and have vowed to keep its coordinates a secret.[10]

While the discovery of a fully intact British Revolutionary War ship in upstate New York—the only one of its kind in the world—is hailed as "an archaeological miracle," it's but one of Lake Ontario's many captive wonders spanning the age of sail to the age of flight.[11] Innumerable aircraft ranging from weather balloons to top-secret Cold War–era military projects are known or thought to be lost in the lake. Among the most intriguing, apart from the B-24, are test models of the Avro Arrow CF-105, a delta-winged supersonic craft developed by the Royal Canadian Air Force in the 1950s to intercept Russian bombers that could attack North America over the Arctic. The Arrow, shaped as its name suggests, was capable of speeds nearing fifteen hundred miles per hour at fifty thousand feet, placing it at the limits of aerospace technology at the time. After five years of top-secret development culminating with a series of impressive test flights in 1958, the Arrow was ready for full-scale production when, to the astonishment of many, the program was abruptly scrapped by Prime Minister John Diefenbaker in 1959. Some fifteen thousand workers were fired on the spot—many of them subsequently recruited for the burgeoning space program in the United States. The Arrow's blueprints were destroyed and prototypes dismantled.[12] With the elimination of all technical data and even the tooling used for production, the program was history, so to speak, nearly before it got off the ground.

Certain aspects of the program did, however, get off the ground. And they happened to fall, quite literally, beyond the reach of military officials charged with wholly eliminating them. Unmanned models of the Arrow tested over Lake Ontario in the early phases of the program ended up, either by design or by accident, at the bottom. Some sixty years later, one of these, encrusted with zebra mussels and slightly crumpled from its impact with the water—was raised by a privately funded team in 2018 and was said to be under restoration for display in the Canada Aviation and Space Museum in Ottawa.[13] The others, most likely in Canadian waters, remain of incalculable value to any bootlegger or permitted institution with the wherewithal to find and retrieve them.

The wreckage hidden below the shimmering view of sunsets and fireworks can be thought of, among other things, as points on a timeline of warfare spanning centuries: the supersonic capabilities of the Arrow representing seismic leaps in aviation technology in the decade after the prop-driven B-24 went down; the heavy bomber emblematic of twentieth-century firepower that appears surreal compared to the twenty-two-gun brig sloop guarding the interior of the colonial world.

Some finds on this archaeological timeline represent far more than material artifacts, however, and they transcend any moment in history. These are, in traditional military parlance, "Soldier Dead"—remains of military personnel who perished in the line of duty. Protocol and custom governing the handling of Soldier Dead have evolved over the centuries with official policy, inevitably complicated by wartime limitations, priorities, and consequences; postwar jurisdictional matters; natural and physical hurdles; and, most compellingly, expectations of survivors dealing with the burden of uncertainty regarding the final hours and ultimate resting place of their sons, daughters, fathers, and husbands who suffered premature and typically violent deaths.[14]

The remains of countless Soldier Dead famously rest in Arlington National Cemetery or lovingly tended hometown plots. Others—more than eighty-two thousand in twentieth-century conflicts—lay undiscovered and unaccounted for where they fell or were hastily buried on foreign battlefields spanning oceans and continents: frozen mountain passes in North Korea, tropical jungles in Vietnam, sparkling atolls in the Pacific, or the gray roiling waters of the North Atlantic.[15] The memory of their sacrifice is kept alive with MIA and POW flags, tributes and memorials, on the grandest of government buildings and arenas, and the humblest of woodsheds and garages. Yet one would hardly expect to unknowingly snag an unrecognized tomb of fallen soldiers while fishing somewhere in upstate New York.

Depending on the outcome of Caza's dive, what once amounted to no more than long-forgotten tales of fishermen had the makings of a national news story. Standing on the deck of *Voyager*, caught in the anticipation of discovery, McLaughlin thought only in vague terms about where it might lead.

The twenty-first-century American military, yet to be engaged in the kind of wars that killed soldiers and hindered the recovery of bodies on the scale of twentieth-century conflicts, and equipped with powerful technology to find and identify remains missing for generations, has gone to visible lengths to recover Soldier Dead overseas, especially in certain notable instances. McLaughlin, himself a veteran, had been lately struck by accounts of lost soldiers being recovered and returned home to their families in flag-draped coffins borne by white-gloved honor guards. These ceremonies were moving and fitting. The crew who went down with the B-24, he believed, were no less deserving. The fact that there may be little if anything of the bodies to be recovered was not lost on him. Dog tags, personal items, and bone fragments were fitting stand-ins for corpses and in no way diminished the honor of a military burial. A bigger obstacle might be the lack of obvious parties to receive these remains, or provide motivation for the exceedingly expensive, painstaking, and disruptive tasks of collecting them.

As it stood, the wreckage, wherever it was, ultimately fell under the jurisdiction of the US military. If officials did nothing upon learning of its whereabouts, the secret must be Caza and McLaughlin's to keep. Kennard guards the coordinates of the HMS *Ontario* even though it is in water too deep for any but the most well-outfitted and skilled divers. Both Kennard and Caza report they have been followed on their excursions by divers with possibly good but more likely bad intentions. The B-24—if found in shallow and far more accessible waters—could become an attractive target for a range of parties, from curiosity seekers to pillagers. There is a rich international market for World War II memorabilia, especially from warplanes and particularly those, like the B-24, that are both famous and now rare.

These darker considerations would come later. At the moment, the day was brimming with the promise of discovery. The sun rose higher, and the parts of Caza's boat not shaded by the Bimini grew hot. Still, a mild breeze freshened and wavelets sparkled. Gulls flittered and bickered. Caza, now fully suited, swung his tank over his shoulders, positioned his goggles, and took the plunge. He descended into a realm that was silent, except for his breathing. The temperature dropped and the light faded with each fathom.

It was sometime later that McLaughlin and Caza reflected on the broader ramifications of the lost tomb. "The bodies may or may not be recovered," McLaughlin said. "What's important now is recovering their stories. Who were these guys?"

2

A Boy's Dream

What, exactly, has been lost, and what stands to be gained by finding it? The answer, in part, rests with the soul presumably in the foremost position of the forgotten tomb.

The story of Wendell Keith Ponder's life, obscured by time and discarded by memory, is almost as elusive as the precise circumstances of his death. Enlisted in the Army Air Forces—the AAF—at the age of eighteen and dead by the age of twenty-one, Ponder, as with many of his peers, had no spouse or children to preserve and pass on his letters and personal items. He fought in no battles that would serve as intergenerational touchstones to glory. After his widowed mother died, family photos, a few pins, and newspaper clippings of his disappearance eventually came into possession of Ponder's nieces and nephews and, later, their children. His letters, once cherished by his mother, now defy searches through attic drawers and crawl-space trunks.

Who was he? A search for other clues yields, first and foremost, evidence of an ambition cultivated since childhood that would guide his fate.

It appears, by chance, in a column of endearing holiday notes—in vogue for papers of record at the time—in the *Jackson Clarion-Ledger* on December 16, 1932:

> Dear Santa Clause
>
>   As Christmas is drawing nearer and times are hard, I won't ask for much . . . an aviator suit, six boxes of torpedoes, four boxes of fire crackers, candy, nuts, fruit and some Roman candles. Also, two sky rockets.
>
> Please don't forget my mother, sisters, brother, dad and my little niece and nephews. And above all, don't forget my little sister's teacher, Mr. Blumie Duncan, for he is very nice . . .
>
>   Love 'til Christmas Eve night,
>
>   KEITH PONDER
>
>   P.S. I forgot to tell what size aviator suit. It will take a size 13 or 14.

Keith Ponder's wish for an aviator suit serves as apt starting point to his story. Yet the framework of his short life can be resurrected more broadly from the Depression-era Mississippi landscape bearing the roots of his pioneering Baptist ancestors and a large extended family—including a great-nephew who bears his name—trying to understand his fate to this day.

When he made his pitch for an aviator suit and skyrockets, it's known that ten-year-old Keith lived with his parents and siblings on a homestead nestled in the fork of Forkville—the confluence of rutted country lanes bisecting rural Scott County. Keith's father, Bennett Compton Ponder, was a grandson of a traveling mail carrier instrumental in settling the area in the mid-nineteenth century. Subsequent generations of Ponders had staffed a small post office serving a community of yeoman farmers eight miles north of the larger hamlet of Morton.[1]

Bennett Compton, better known as B.C., was himself a rural letter carrier working for his father, the postmaster and tax assessor. He made the rounds to tin-roofed granges in a horse-drawn buggy as a young man, a vocation that likely played a role in his acquaintance with and courtship of Keith's mother, Lucy Caroline Davenport, the eldest daughter in a large Scott County farming family. Lucy married B.C. when she was twenty, he, twenty-four. Over the next seventeen years, she would give birth to seven children and lose two as infants. After that, she would lose her husband

Figure 2.1. B.C. Ponder was the third-generation member of a family that delivered mail in Scott County since pioneering times. Courtesy of Eddie Evans and descendants of Lucy Ponder.

to a premature death, lose a breast to cancer, and lose Keith, her youngest, to war. She would never remarry and live to be ninety-eight.[2] The essential aspect of the scant record of Lucy's life suggests an embodiment of stoicism girded by faith.

During Keith's youth, the hub of domestic activity was a seven-room, single-story shotgun house in Forkville. Though now vacant and boarded for the past many years, the house remains in the extended family to this day. With shared sleeping quarters and living space off either side of the center hall it was, in Keith's day, a place that would have smelled of biscuits, frying pork, panfish, or fresh game mingled with soot from kerosene or coal oil, depending on the time of day and season. A family Bible sat on a corner shelf in the small kitchen in the rear corner of the house where Lucy, most likely with one or more of Keith's older sisters, would have been a regular presence. The kitchen afforded no room for those who weren't there to work; food was served, along with instruction for place settings and meal timing, through a pass-through to an adjoining room with an eating nook and table. In this part of the house old church pews had been repurposed as benches, and sturdy hooks and racks held hats, coats, and shotguns in a vestibule that opened to the rear porch.

Outside the door, next to a cistern that supplied the kitchen with water, a weighty steel bell hung from a post to alert family members in nearby woods and fields of mealtime. Or crisis. It made a pure, piercing sound that never failed to turn heads near and far, and at one time or another during his youth Keith would have resisted or failed to resist the temptation to needlessly ring it at the peril of disciplinary consequences.

Whereas the rear of the Ponder homestead conveyed an aura of domesticity, the roadside view suggested a regard for presentation. A series of broad wooden steps ascended to an ample porch spanning the modest width of the house, ushering visitors to a single door flanked by two large windows. Posts supporting the porch, though not fashioned for ornamentation, appeared sturdy enough to give the structure an extra touch of dignity. Inside, the first room to the left doubled as a parlor for receiving guests on formal occasions, including viewing a deceased family member prior to a funeral. Accident, illness, and infant mortality would touch the Ponder homestead as they did the rest of the community, but in 1932, ten-year-old Keith was too young to know tragedies that came before him and yet to experience those that would come later.

Keith's comings and goings would have been primarily through the back. On weekends, when not busy with chores, homework, or attending church and related functions, he might be found bounding off the porch, hounds at heel, toting a sixteen-gauge shotgun. He would likely set an eager pace past the smokehouse, an outhouse, chicken coop, hog pen, stables, pastures, and a corncrib that was said to have sometimes doubled as guest room when not serving its original purpose. Depending on his quarry and the nature and training of his dogs, he would settle into a more tactical advancement as he skirted stands of loblolly and sweet gum and scouted lush understories and frequent clearings from logging and farming and well-trodden paths leading the back way to cousins' and grandparents' homes. This would be sport for Keith, but also something more. Given the practical and cultural importance of hunting in Depression-era Mississippi, the dogs would be quite capable, and

Keith—frequently joined by another family member—would have command of the drill at a very young age.[3]

The record shows his full name as Wendell Keith Ponder, though, as evidenced by his letter to Santa and later clues, he eschewed the use of Wendell. Reasons are unknown, but a possible explanation would be the name conjured a certain bookishness incompatible with his personality and peer group. While Keith's personal items and letters, with a few notable exceptions, have eluded search by distant relatives, fragments of a few stories—passed on long ago by his late brother Amos—survive orally. They depict Keith in various stages of youth: dispatching a water moccasin, raiding a watermelon patch, or engaged in some teenage hijinks, details of which defy memory except for the part about the relocation of an outhouse to the schoolmaster's front yard.

Keith was, judging from a single surviving photo album, most at home with friends, relatives, and classmates on a football field or a basketball court as existed in Forkville at the time—raked earth rolled flat and lined

Figure 2.2. Keith (*second from left, bottom*) as a high school freshman at Forkville (prior to attending school in Morton) with his basketball teammates. Courtesy of Eddie Evans and descendants of Lucy Ponder.

with chalk. When asked to say cheese, he reliably produced an under-stated smile that could be taken as shyness if not for eye contact that was direct, knowing, and confident—body language that reads *you want me on your side if you are choosing teams.*

Keith's later achievements would reflect a keen regard for schooling and especially for math-related prerequisites to physics, aeronautics, and navigation. Long-limbed, square shouldered, and among the tallest in whatever group he was with, Keith would be well adapted to the rigors of Depression-era farming and heartily acquainted with the kind of phys-ics amply applied in his daily life: leveraging a stump, rigging chain falls, shooting a gun, repairing an axle, or launching a skyrocket.

His request for fireworks to light up the 1932 Mississippi Yuletide sky stemmed from a tradition in the Gulf Coast states dating back to French colonial times. Yet for Keith, this celebration would still be a novelty at a time when the public was no longer just gazing at objects launched into the sky but actually beginning to fly in them. It would have been whimsical to imagine young Keith, within the life span of one of his hunting dogs, piloting an aircraft longer than the house in which he came of age and incalculably grander than even his boyhood dreams. Yet, in hindsight, it's plain to understand how the time and circumstances of his upbringing provided the raw material for his fortune and ultimate misfortune.

When Keith sought an aviator suit, flight was more than a staple of child-hood dreams. It was a national obsession. The barnstorming exploits of World War I veterans would be fixed in Keith's earliest memories and the memories of country folk who grew up in the 1920s. These "aeroplane circuses"—encouraged by a surplus of primitive military aircraft and a cadre of young people trained to fly them—became regular attractions on the open fields of rural America after World War I.

Farmers relished the spectacle of low-altitude races and daring stunts involving planes and aviators buzzing throngs of spectators, waving from a wing, or tumbling from the sky—most often but not always re-covering control or employing parachutes in the nick of time. Before or after the aerial exhibitions, pilots would offer rides to the public, which meant that in out-of-the-way places like Scott County, Mississippi, it was conceivable some folks rode in an airplane before an automobile. Most abundant of these aircraft was the Curtiss JN, a two-seat biplane used for training during World War I. Affectionately known as the Curtiss Jenny, it was the most widely produced plane of the time, and a large surplus remaining after the Great War played a defining role in the rise of civil aviation.[4]

Flight was much about the magic and mystique of the Wild Blue Yonder, but the aeronautical interests of farmers were rooted also in down-to-earth pragmatism. The boll weevil was decimating cotton crops throughout the Mississippi Delta, and farmers were eager to eradicate the pest. Now a once-unimaginable aerial assault on the critters was at their service. Early crop-dusting businesses—notably Huff Daland Dusters, forerunner of Delta Air Service—were establishing markets throughout the South. There were also plenty of enterprising freelancers, and the barnstorming events would have been a natural source of networking between farmers interested in horticultural breakthroughs and fliers looking for work.

While crop dusting was one interest at the fore of aeronautical advances, postal delivery was another. Mail pilots took even greater risks than crop dusters or stunt pilots as their journeys spanned impressive distances in all kinds of weather, over all kinds of terrain, sometimes in darkness, with no reliable forecasting or assurances for a safe place to abort when things went wrong.[5] For the most part, the aircraft that landed and sometimes crashed in farmers' fields in the late 1920s had not advanced significantly from a decade earlier; one periodical aptly described them as "a nervous collection of whistling wires, of linen stretched over wooden ribs, all attached to a wheezy, water-cooled engine."[6] Reliability was an issue. "Never forget that the engine may stop," one manual advised, "and at all times keep this in mind."[7]

It was these circumstances at this moment in history that gave rise to a twenty-five-year-old midwestern barnstormer and mail pilot who would unexpectedly lay claim to the most celebrated aeronautical achievement prior to the moon landing. Charles Lindbergh was a latecomer to a challenge for the first nonstop flight to link New York City and Paris. The prize, offered in 1919 by New York hotelier Raymond Orteig, was $25,000. But the stakes were much higher. The feat would prove to be nothing less than the sword-in-the-stone of aviation history.

Over the course of nearly eight years, renowned adventurers and aviators with large sponsorship and development teams met costly and humbling failure and sometimes death trying to claim this prize. Many skeptics reasonably considered it beyond the technical means of the day when Lindbergh arrived on the scene in 1927. His plan to undertake the challenge flying solo in a much lighter, simpler, and cheaper aircraft than that of his competitors drew skepticism and even scorn. Lacking in age, experience, and backing, Charles Lindbergh was in every sense an underdog. Yet thirty-three hours after takeoff in his *Spirit of St. Louis*, a monoplane so laden with fuel it barely cleared telephone wires at the end of Roosevelt Field in Long Island, Lindberg circled Paris, searching for a clear spot amid more than one hundred thousand people gathered at Le Bourget field to receive him. The moment he landed, throngs rushed his plane and carried him from the cockpit.

The prize that had for years eluded the best fliers in the world was his. The fact that he did it was sensational, and the way that he did it was more fantastic still. It's hard to overstate Lindbergh's impact as American cultural icon and standard-bearer of the country's global preeminence in the aviation industry that stands to this day.

Keith Ponder and hundreds of thousands of his contemporaries destined to become aviators in World War II were young boys when Lindbergh made his flight. The subsequent spree of tickertape parades, celebratory tours, and ceremonial keys to cities, including a thoroughly reported visit to Jackson (a short train ride from Morton), would have left a lasting impression.[8] The greatness of the feat set against the modesty of Lindbergh's background as a mail carrier would have cast him as a particular hero in the Ponder family. Though outward pride had no place in Keith's Southern Baptist upbringing, his family's vocational connection to the Lindbergh legend must have thrilled and inspired Keith. He would, indeed, someday fly.

This aspiration was greatly encouraged by the fact that Keith's father served as secretary of the Scott County Fair when the country's fixation with flight reached a climax in the years leading up to and immediately following Lindbergh's flight. By the late 1920s, regulations and obsolescence were bringing the Curtiss Jenny's postwar heyday as a barnstorming favorite to an end. Yet there were still plenty of them in service, and they would still show up as featured attractions at country gatherings. So it was at the 1929 fair held in a large clearing a short run and skip from Keith's home.

The fair was grand in every sense and occasioned visits by the governor and the Speaker of the Mississippi House of Representatives to hold forth on topics of agriculture, infrastructure, and education. It was, it might be said, the twilight of the golden age of oration; and Keith came from a home that would have valued a good speech and, to an even greater extent, a fine sermon. On that August day, Speaker Thomas Baily, champion of the "roads and ways" of Mississippi, might have delivered a commendable address on the topic of infrastructure, most likely including the state of the eight-mile stretch of rutted road that connected Forkville to Morton, and rail and roads from Morton to Jackson. Yet, as distinguished as the dignitaries and their speeches were, they would have little chance competing for the boy's attention against the yodelers, female impersonators, vaudeville acts, baseball, horseracing, and boxing contests that had sprung up virtually overnight like some fantastic boyhood fantasy almost in Keith's backyard.[9]

Amid all this, one attraction quite literally soared above all others, its arrival announced with a waxing drone from the sky. A biplane—possibly painted primary red or yellow to suit its repurposed role as a public attraction—appeared above the horizon, circled lower, and settled with a bounce or two on a hoof-pocked field before its engine idled down and sputtered to a stop. By every measure, the aircraft would have embodied Keith's passion for things spectacular, bright, loud, and sky-bound. There was little doubt, given his father's standing at the fair, that Keith would ride in that plane.

The sort of visceral sensations that make passengers hate or perhaps love flying would be acutely amplified for anybody strapped into an open-cockpit biplane of that period. Keith would have found the Ferris wheel ride mundane by comparison as the craft accelerated, lifted, dropped, pitched, and rose, tilting one way and the next, exposing the windswept cockpit to the widening gulf between earth and sky.

With the rush of air brushing aside the humidity of a late summer Mississippi afternoon, Keith, searching for reference points, might miss the rutted road to Morton—little more than a faint scar running through the quilt of field and forest. The serene white steeple of Bethlehem Baptist Church, however, would be visible, rising like a humble prayer over the single-story brick building, framed by picnic grounds and rows of simple markers in the carefully tended cemetery. From the sky, as from land, the church was Forkville's most distinguished landmark.

If the pilot wanted to impress his passenger, he might fly toward the state capital thirty-five miles due east. In this case, Keith would observe the rail line that led from Morton to Jackson remarkably reduced to the size of a toy train set in the catalogs his father delivered. Plantations along the way would impress, but nothing compared to the dome of the capitol building, topped with a gilded eagle, that would soon come into view in the distance.

However long the flight was, it would seem too short, the reappearance of the church steeple signaling the trip's end, Keith's disappointment offset by the thrill of landing. The engine pitch would soften as the pilot throttled back and began dropping toward the impossibly small target of open field adjacent to a riot of activity in an otherwise placid landscape. There would be the customary attention-seeking pass over the crowd of upturned faces. Minutes later, the critical moment would arrive with Keith clutching the cockpit combing, resisting forces of deceleration as the plane bounced off the earthen landing strip.

Flight had arrived to Forkville even before electricity and indoor plumbing. The freedom, adventure, and self-sufficiency of life in the Mississippi countryside provided Keith with all the raw material to shape and nurture his calling. When Keith hopped down from the plane, he had glimpsed his future.

By December 1932, when Keith's request for an aviator suit became a matter of record with the Jackson newspaper, the cumulative ravages of diabetes were taking a toll on his father.[10] Keith's brother Amos, thirteen years his elder, would have taken over much of the responsibility of running the farm. Despite help from a close and large extended family, the hardship and frustration of B.C.'s convalescence would have been compounded in a time and place where a farmer's sense of worth, regardless of his administrative skills, might be largely tied to his physical ability. Times would be tough and getting tougher with the deepening Depression.

Mississippi was one of the poorest of states to begin with, and the bank failures and economic implosion that came after the market crash in 1929 would decimate its fledgling industrial economy.[11] Still, Scott County's yeoman farmers were less vulnerable than plantation owners, whose fortunes depended on the price of a commodity that was quickly losing value; or sharecroppers and tenant farmers, impossibly indebted even in the best of times; or dustbowl famers driven from their homes by drought and over-farming. Living off the land was more or less hardwired into the Ponders' pioneering heritage. This proclivity, absent significant debt and helped by the lush and prolific Mississippi countryside and, above all, faith, would be their saving grace.

Faith would be a birthright assimilated into every aspect of Keith's upbringing. The discipline required for a boy to sit through multiple Sunday services at Bethlehem Baptist Church following a week of schoolwork and chores would be rewarded by feasting. Advent and Christmas would generally coincide with hog-killing time, when men of the church, sleeves of their Sunday dress shirts rolled up, turned spitted meat over a fire pit, sending the sizzling promise of roast pork wafting thickly on white smoke around the church steeple. Women of the church, also in their Sunday best, adorned tables with platters of biscuits, corn bread, sweet potatoes, black-eyed peas, and pies.[12]

Periods between these gatherings would be marked by austerity and untold difficulty, but in December 1932 Forkville and indeed all Mississippi was lifted by a prevailing optimism. President-elect Franklin D. Roosevelt had campaigned on a New Deal to restore the economy with government programs and policy favoring commoners and farmers. It is hard to convey in words how singularly Mississippians supported Roosevelt's vision, but numbers tell the story plainly. FDR won 95 percent of the vote—nineteen of every twenty voters—statewide, and a like number in Scott County.[13] In short, expectations were high.

The paper that carried Keith's request for an aviator suit on page sixteen featured a report on the front page about how the new administration might handle crop and milk surpluses driving down prices. While news of the new president's plan would likely be a primary topic of conversation for B.C. Ponder and fellow civic patriarchs at the post office, general store, Masonic Lodge, and barbershop, other news items might warrant mention: a good-size audience braved an icy rain to attend a charity concert by the Francis Ewing Gordin Circle of the International Order of Kings Daughters; a bill to make beer legal, sponsored by Ways and Means chairman James Collier from Mississippi, had passed out of committee; state lawmakers deemed anti-lynching legislation unnecessary, as the number of reported lynchings in Mississippi had dropped and "differences of opinion exist sometimes whether the killing of an individual is or is not a lynching." While prevailing social forces shaping Keith's upbringing in Scott County were in some ways unique, they also spoke of ideals to be cast as American archetypes: times were hard but faith was strong; a sense of righteousness ran deep though not always true and sometimes tragically errant.[14]

Coverage in that day's *Clarion-Ledger* had little in the way of certain international developments festering beyond the reach of any single paper or the anticipation of any individual. Fear, anger, ignorance, hunger, repression, and disillusionment—no strangers to the darker narrative of world history—were reaching a critical mass in Europe and beyond. Amid want and privation, the threat of Marxism, and a hue and cry over lost national identity, millions in Germany were fervently pledging loyalty to the party of young Adolf Hitler and his promise to return Germany to greatness.[15] On the other side of the world, Japan—lacking land and natural resources to sustain a population whose industrial trading economy had been devastated—rallied under the vision of militants also exploiting dire need coupled with nationalistic fervor to advance their own power.[16] In mid-September 1931, while the League of Nations took little notice and less action, Japan had invaded Manchuria to secure raw material and resources to enable its plans for regional conquest.

When the *Clarion-Ledger* arrived in Forkville on December 16, 1932, Keith might have noted with satisfaction that his letter, appearing in a column directly below Ripley's *Believe It or Not!*, was printed as he wrote it (if this in fact was the case), and in any event been happy it included his reminder that the aviator suit would need to be a size large. It would also be reasonable to expect that his mail-carrying father would owe him an explanation of how the letter got to the North Pole; a reasonable answer would be, by airplane. It's not far-fetched to imagine that Keith, like many ten-year-olds with some residual belief in Santa, feigned or genuine, would have fallen asleep on Christmas Eve dreaming of snow. And flight.

It could be taken as tragic irony that events in Europe and Asia enabling Keith Ponder's swift ascension to flight officer in the US Army Air Forces ten years later would also bear the germ of his fatal destiny. In this respect Keith was typical of tens of thousands of other airmen of his generation, soon to be cast from the Eden of youth into the rush to war.

3

READYING FOR WAR

When Keith Ponder fell in love with flight, the Curtiss Jenny biplane dancing over the fairground was a wondrous and novel attraction. At the height of World War II, US factories were turning out some ninety thousand military aircraft a year—more than double the rate of any other country, allied or enemy.[1]

On a dreary late afternoon in February 1944, Keith and seven other men in shearling aviator suits walked across the tarmac at the Westover Army Air Forces base in Chicopee, Massachusetts, to one of these planes. Slung over their shoulders were canvas duffels with accoutrements of survival at twenty-seven thousand feet in an unpressurized cabin: parachute harnesses, headgear, oxygen masks, over-suits. Ponder, the tallest in the group, wore an officer's cap, lending to his person an added air of distinction. Other than that, he looked more or less like the others—able figures suddenly diminished by the contours of the craft they were approaching.

At sixty-seven feet, the B-24 Liberator bomber was the length of a large whale—a comparison made more apt by its tall, blunt nose and broad fluke-like stabilizers. It was a "heavy bomber," the biggest of the planes of its day, weighing thirty-seven thousand pounds, another twenty thousand pounds loaded. For all its bulk, a 110-foot wing passing through the top of the fuselage lent the craft an incongruous grace when airborne. It had no doors, so the crew had to enter from underneath, through the nose-wheel well or bomb bay. They stooped down with their kit and, one by one, like a magic act, disappeared from beneath as they climbed up into the belly of the ship. Ponder, tending to some inspection and signing off with ground crew, would be last to board.

Though Flight Officer Ponder and his crew were expecting to join the war in Europe in the imminent future, he was not well acquainted with this model of the aircraft, so he might have taken a little longer in the pre-flight walk-around inspection.[2] He would be focusing on mechanical and structural systems, though a lavish if not lurid distraction painted on the broad front side of the fuselage would invite appraisal. Nose art on World War II warplanes, reflecting sensibilities of the time as morale boosters for the men who maintained and flew them, commonly featured pinup girls, but not always. This one was *Gateway Gertie*, and whether she was ravishing or warlike, or even the meaning or source of her name, must be left to the imagination; there are no surviving photographs or descriptions of what she looked like. But given the dimensions of the craft and depictions that typically graced the broad, boxy noses of B-24s, she had plenty of space to be big.

Gateway Gertie was officially aircraft 41-29047E, known to flight controllers and maintenance crews simply as 047. She had seen her share of action and was ready for retirement, though as of now she was relegated to the role of a trainer while crews awaited the arrival of new planes. Regardless of what Ponder made of the artwork on 047's broad side, she may have inspired consideration of what he and his crew would christen their own plane, now in some stage of assembly at one of five factories dedicated to B-24 production and scheduled for completion before they received orders for deployment.[3] Meantime, the war-weary *Gertie* would have to suffice for today's exercise.

As large as the B-24 was outside, inside it felt cramped, with most of its space reserved for bombs and armament and mechanical systems for their deployment. Stripped to the essentials for making war and, to a lesser degree, surviving it, it smelled of solvent, grease, and gasoline.[4]

The crew made their way to stations consisting mostly of benches, safety harnesses, controls, and chart tables—austere concessions to human ergonomics amid a universe of ribs and rivets, cable and conduit, tanks and valves, and sliding and pivoting hardware. Ponder climbed to the flight deck and settled into the pilot's seat on the left side of the cockpit amid a constellation of dials, levers, and pedals. Copilot Raymond A. Bickel, a man of medium build with a round, pleasant face and a dimpled chin, took the seat to the right. Eighteen months earlier Bickel had been a factory worker for a company in Chicago that made barber chairs and shoeshine stands. His age, twenty-eight, made him something of an anomaly, as none of the other crew were older than twenty-one. Bickel was also hitched; just three months prior, his accelerated courtship with the much younger Marion Hardeis, also from Chicago, had culminated with a military wedding. The couple was no different from countless others of the time, cementing bonds, by marriage or otherwise, before being separated by war.

After a few minutes organizing their gear, Ponder and Bickel donned headsets and began audibly working through preflight checks and sequentially flipping switches to batteries, generators, hydraulic pumps, and superchargers before powering up each of the craft's four twelve-hundred-horsepower engines.[5] The rest of the crew settled into their stations and plugged headsets into switch boxes to allow necessary communication and perhaps a well-timed wisecrack or word of encouragement. The flight engineer stood through an overhead portal on the flight deck to visually check that the propellers were optimally synced and elevators, ailerons, and rudders fully operational as *Gertie* roared to life. Minutes later, as the plane—now an animation of noise, vibration, and exhaust—began its taxi, the engineer took a final look at the systems, ducked inside, and closed the hatch.

A B-24 on the ground is very much a whale out of water, and despite a light touch on the throttles to starboard or port, it lurched with each directional change to the runway. There it stopped, nose to wind, seemingly gathering itself as Ponder communicated with the tower. Given the nature of the exercise—formation flying in local airspace—he was cleared for takeoff under visual flight rules, meaning visibility was above the threshold to allow navigation without instruments. *Gertie* shuddered like a sentient creature as Ponder throttled up. Bickel released the brakes, and

Figure 3.1. Ray Bickel, the only crew member who was not single, with his newlywed bride, Marion Hardeis Bickel. Courtesy of Amber Rhea Simmons and descendants of Ray Bickel, Marion Hardeis, and Ed Buckley.

the craft charged heavily down the runway, with Bickel holding the four throttle levers wide open. A few protracted moments passed as the end of the runway drew closer; finally Ponder pulled back on the yoke with both hands, and the craft parted from the ground.

It was 5:01 p.m. Minutes before and minutes after, crews were going through similar drills in five other B-24s at the Westover base. On this day, they were to practice coaxing the giant crafts into a tight defensive formation twenty-five thousand feet over western Massachusetts before breaking up and returning to base in sequence. It was a short exercise, and they would indeed have to be quick. Night was coming, and the forecast was calling for snow. When they had been briefed, at noon, they still had a reasonable weather window. But, as many of the crews at Westover often found themselves, they were behind schedule.

Allowing aviators to train in substandard craft in threatening weather might seem patently unsound to generations that never faced imminent

Figure 3.2. Workers rivet a wing section for a B-24E bomber at the Willow Run plant. National Archives and Records Administration.

threat of hostile takeover by foreign armies. Yet the risks were unexceptional by the standard of the day.[6] The US Army Air Forces and England's Royal Air Force Bomber Command were days away from launching the largest air offensive to date on interior Germany. Operation Argument—later known simply as Big Week—would target Germany's airplane factories and manufacturing centers, which were known to be fiercely defended. The intention, aside from blowing up factories, was to provoke the Luftwaffe into terminal battle. At a devastating cost, Big Week would decide air superiority over Europe essential to success of subsequent ground offensives, beginning with the Normandy Invasion.[7] Success counted on AAF reinforcements as quickly as the factories and air bases back home could turn them out. To this end, the frenetic rate of aircraft production in the United States had been outpaced only by recruitment. In a few short years, the AAF had grown from one hundred thousand personnel prior to Japan's attack on Pearl Harbor to 2.4 million, with other military branches expanding on a similar scale. When Ponder enlisted a year and some months prior to this day on February 17, 1944, the US war effort was nearing its peak, with twelve million soldiers. They all had to be trained and trained quickly. Ponder and his crew were the merest of specks in the most monumental war mobilization in modern history.

In ways unexpected, Ponder had become the embodiment of his boyhood dream by age twenty-one, and it had been a pretty good run up to this point. After completing junior high, he had transferred from the single-room school in Forkville to the high school in Morton. It was an impressive upgrade, with multiple classrooms and playing fields. Based on the old photo album Keith's mother kept, Keith's high school years suited him just fine. He and his buddies got around in somebody's old Ford sedan and wore varsity letters and pleated trousers and patent leather shoes. The boys were sometimes accompanied by well-coiffed schoolgirls smartly attired in jackets and skirts or dresses with blousy shoulders. On these special occasions—dances or picnics in the park— the gang happily mugged and struck poses in the manner of period matinee idols. None appeared camera shy, and one, a laughing girl with tumbling waves, factored heavily into the photographic record with Keith. She had reason to be happy. Louise Richie, the only daughter of a sawmill foreman in a nearby lumbering town, was popular and pretty, and was said to be Keith's belle.

Life when Keith was younger was much as it had been for generations, but it changed dramatically during his high school years when electricity came to Scott County along with improvements to roads and cars. Not all the changes were good. Keith's father endured his last days as an amputee with failing vision. Though he held on long enough to see his youngest graduate from high school, B.C. Ponder would not accompany his family through the momentous changes to come. His burial site at Bethlehem Church was still mounded with raw earth on December 7, 1941, the day Japan's attack on Pearl Harbor shook the country to its roots. The call to war effectively precipitated the ending of the old way of life on the Ponder homestead and many other places across the country.

Two of Keith's older siblings immediately enlisted. Amos, who had been working for the Postal Service in Jackson, became a Navy fleet mail worker in New York City; Sallye would serve as a Navy nurse in the Pacific. Though too young to enlist, Keith registered for the draft and found work in a Jackson foundry that forged agricultural tools, now being retooled for military production. In this role, Keith was no different from many others who left the farm after the Pearl Harbor attack to, in effect, hammer plowshares into swords.

It was only a matter of months before Uncle Sam found that able-bodied males of Keith's age would better serve the country in uniform. In 1942 Congress lowered the draft age from twenty to eighteen. At the same time, looking to boost recruitment of pilots, the AAF waved the final barrier to Keith's ambition to fly—a college requirement for flight cadets.[8] Now six weeks shy of his nineteenth birthday, the kid who so desired an aviator suit fell in line, most likely accompanied by some high school buddies, at a recruiting station in Camp Shelby. If the lofty vision he had as a youth remained intact, it would soon be well-tempered by the very real prospects of dying a violent death at war.

Keith's war journey would begin in classrooms and labs, shoulder to shoulder with waves of other recruits, newly homogenized in crew cuts and khakis, facing a battery of tests with simulators, training aids, in low-pressure chambers, or seated at school desks with test booklets and no. 2 pencils. Not surprisingly, most air cadets wanted to be pilots. They would first learn, as informed by a lieutenant by the name of Ronald Reagan addressing them in an orientation film, "If there's any single little nerve you've got hidden away in the middle of your spine that makes you jump this way, instead of that, Uncle Sam will find out which way it jumps and use it in the way he says will end the war quicker. Which is why we're all here."[9] Over the next week, approximately half the class with the best reaction time, dexterity, steadiness, coordination, vision, leadership potential, and scholastic aptitude would be selected for pilot training. Others with good scores, but not good enough, would be selected to train as bombardiers and navigators. The lowest tier would retain their starting rank of private and be reassigned elsewhere.[10]

Having made the initial cut, Keith still had plenty of opportunities to "wash out" from the program. He immediately began nine weeks of basic training and academic courses in mathematics and physics applied to avionics and navigation. His flying at this stage would be mostly on a simulator, although "flight indoctrination" involved a ride-along in a two-seat training craft—possibly a Stearman trainer biplane, more advanced than the Curtiss Jenny but similar in appearance—that left cadets sick, terrified, or ready to advance to the next phase of training. The kid from Forkville passed that test and all the others. He was ready to take to the air.

In that pursuit, Keith soon became well-traveled if not worldly. He would get his first crack as a pilot at an airfield in Montgomery, Alabama, in a two-seat single-engine trainer. After nine weeks, he would move on to Freeman, Indiana, to learn to fly farther and longer on multiengine planes. There he would earn his wings and advance to the final phase—transitional training—at a base in Pueblo, Colorado. But first, he was granted a short leave.

Hog-killing season would be approaching in Forkville, and no doubt there would be some good living in store with friends and family when Keith returned to his hometown as Flight Officer Ponder.[11] His mother's scrapbook carries a picture of her and her youngest taken at this time. Lucy stands erect in an aproned housedress, the top of her hair bun barely reaching the smart crease of the Windsor knot in Keith's tie. She is looking straight at the camera with an expression suggesting something between annoyance and amusement—her countenance possibly explained by Keith's own. Impressively attired in uniform, Keith towers above his mother with one hand clasping her shoulder. He is not looking at the

Figure 3.3. Keith with his mother, Lucy Ponder, likely photographed a few weeks before his death. Courtesy of Eddie Evans and descendants of Lucy Ponder.

camera but gazing dramatically skyward, a pose inspired either by his own clowning or perhaps encouraged by the photographer, possibly one of his uncles.

While the trajectory of Keith's life can be traced within a long thread of family history and a handful of personal records set against events of the times, an accounting of his final hours must be derived from declassified military files and, less precisely, a smattering of newspaper reports. The known record, sparse as it is, depicts events that began with vivid clarity before degenerating—quite literally—into static. Though it comes as no surprise that there is no *happy* ending, the enigma and tragedy of Keith's story are that, essentially, it has no ending at all.

Soon after the takeoff of 047 from Westover, the view aboard dissolved into drifting haze. The aircraft gained one thousand feet in elevation and four miles in distance every minute. The air thinned. Temperatures dropped. After nine minutes the aircraft broke through the overcast.[12] The sun, still off the horizon, would be casting light horizontally across cloud cover now below the plane, offering the kind of view so larded with form and color that any facsimile of it might be dismissed as banal; a twenty-first-century traveler might well sleep through it. For Keith and the others, the sight might still be regarded as extraordinary. Regardless, the vision would be fleeting, and the last sunlight any of them would see.

Flight engineer Sergeant Thomas C. Roberts took in the view over the pilots' shoulders. The engineer's station at the rear of the flight deck, by design, afforded a panorama from which to track the status of mechanical systems inside and outside the plane and flag telltale signs of malfunction. Roberts's watch encompassed the cockpit's gauges and indicators, as well as the wings, motors, props, and, below, access to manual overrides to landing gear. Critically, Roberts was also charged with metering twenty-three hundred gallons of fuel—more than seven tons—distributed in four fuel tanks built into the wings. This task required, at certain points, opening and closing valves to draw down the supply evenly and prevent an excess in tanks on either wing from compromising the plane's trim.[13]

Having completed only two years of high school, Tommy Roberts had come a long way, as they say. Fifteen months prior, at the age of eighteen, he had quit his job in a metal fabricating shop to join the war. He would likely now take a fair level of pride in his charge as engineer.

At the station next to Roberts sat another newly minted specialist. Sergeant Joseph Michael Zebo had just been promoted after eighteen weeks of training to operate the radio systems and ensure all equipment was in working order. Zebo shared with Roberts, at least broadly, a coastal New England background—Roberts from South Boston and Zebo from Providence, Rhode Island—that may have fostered an affinity for cultural touchstones beginning with their Yankee accents and provincial turns of speech. Both were five feet, seven inches, with compact builds. In uniform, they might at first glance have been mistaken for each other. Unlike Roberts, however, Zebo was not a volunteer. He had been working as a clerk at a shipyard in Pawtucket when he received his draft notice a year prior. And while Roberts had dropped out of high school to seek a payroll job, Zebo had been, according to his East Providence

Figure 3.4. Flight engineer Tommy Roberts. In addition to handling engineering responsibilities, including metering gasoline and checking mechanical systems, engineers would be trained as gunners. Courtesy of Cheryl Allen and Karen Mickler.

High School yearbook, a "truly studious, plugging pupil . . . who never fails to make the honor role."

Zebo's training would be grievously tested on this flight. In addition to providing the means to communicate with other craft and controllers on the ground, radio guided ships to homing beacons at landing fields and navigational reference points along routes. Accordingly, radio operators were charged with helping pilots and navigators with positional fixes. On this mission, however, there was no navigator onboard. Nor was there a bombardier—a position also qualified to help with navigational duties. Perhaps this was because there would be little opportunity for either to practice his job on a local formation flight, with no particular destination or target, guided by sight rather than instruments. Or maybe the missing crew were victims of a bug going through the overcrowded barracks. On this day, Zebo and Roberts had understudies, however. Aubrey H. Alexander, from Muscle Shoals, Alabama, was listed on one record as assistant engineer, and Private First Class Phillip R. Walton, from the San Francisco Bay area, was assistant radio operator.

They were, in effect, students teaching students, and they had a lot to learn in a short time. Engineers and radio operators, in addition to assisting the pilots, would be counted on to join the ship's gunners to ward off attacks from smaller, more maneuverable fighter planes. This meant quickly refocusing attention from consoles of instruments at their respective stations to M2 Browning .50 caliber guns mounted in the nose of the craft—a paneled, Plexiglas compartment below the flight deck where the bombardier and navigator worked—and the dorsal turret, a bubble on the top of the plane just aft of the flight deck. While it looked like a simple matter of taking aim and letting 'em rip, the guns' slender barrels belayed an outsize ferocity and bruising recoil, capable of eliminating armor-plated fighters with a short burst and prone to jamming in unfamiliar hands.

The final two members of Ponder's crew—Corporal James O. Cozier and Sergeant Kenneth N. Jonen—were gunners stationed in the plane's waist, forward of the tail. Separated from the flight deck by a harrowing twelve-inch-wide catwalk over the bomb bay, they were among crew members neither directly nor indirectly engaged with the flying of the plane. They sat within reach of their parachutes, twenty-two-pound flack vests, and other kit, and a short pounce away from the waist guns—M2s situated at openings the size of living room windows in the plane's flanks.

Corporal Cozier, a reservist who had been called up eleven months prior, was a slender six-foot-one with fair hair, blue eyes, and the kind of disposition that sought fraternal bonds. Shortly after being called to war, he had pledged Phi Kappa Psi as a freshman at the University of Oklahoma. His father, according to census records, worked for a trade magazine for the oil and gas industry; it would not be far-fetched to imagine Cozier also drawn to that field, which was an intergenerational way of life in his hometown of Tulsa.

Perhaps Cozier spent a few idle minutes after takeoff counseling his less-experienced companion while they were still unencumbered by oxygen masks, at least to the degree that they could carry on a conversation over the engines. Jonen, drafted fresh out of high school, was listed as an assistant gunner. He had lived with his parents, grandparents, and two younger siblings in a working-class neighborhood in Milwaukee where his father and grandparents owned a moving and furniture repair businesses. Barely nineteen, Jonen was the youngest of Ponder's crew and, in contrast to Cozier, possessed the compact physique necessary to occupy the belly turret, an oscillating capsule not much roomier than a rain barrel, vulnerably suspended in a retractable substructure below the ship's fuselage.

Any scraps of conversation that carried over the throb of engines would not be deep or long and less so as they gained altitude. The crew, prepared to climb to twenty-five thousand feet after the rendezvous with the other planes, would have factored in clothing adjustments before takeoff. If worn on the ground, their flight suits, designed to keep occupants warm for extended periods at thirty below zero, would cause profuse sweating and a layer of moisture next to the body that would only add to misery if not danger later into the flights. Now, as the plane ascended into thinning air, over-suits would be zipped; heater cords, which sometimes worked, plugged into control boxes; and outer garments and accessories secured: heavy gloves, to prevent fingers from freezing instantly to omnipresent metal surfaces; goggles to prevent frostbitten faces; and oxygen masks to prevent hypoxia.

While all crew had to suffer the elements, Cozier and Jonen faced exceptionally harsh duty. When the waist guns were deployed, the windows would be open, subzero temperatures brutally intensified by the air jetting into the rear of the fuselage as the plane cruised along at 220 miles per hour. Any body part exposed even briefly would be flash frozen. Moreover, accuracy surely mattered, as errant shots by waist gunners would not only fail to discourage the enemy, but also risk hitting a tail or wing of the plane that carried them, or another in their formation that fell within the sweeping arc of the guns.

Learning how to work in these conditions was part of the drill; surviving them, an exercise rich in negative reinforcement. Airmen risked calamity with each mistake or sometimes through no fault of their own. Oxygen masks occasionally froze or came unplugged from tanks, the effects unnoticed until a man dropped or failed to respond to a radio check.[14] Limbs or torsos might get pinned in doors of turrets that rotated before they could be fully occupied or vacated. Engines or electrical systems were prone to catching fire. Heated suits malfunctioned.[15] More commonly, eardrums ached or rang from frequent and radical pressure changes, the din of engines, and the concussion of gunfire. Sinuses swelled. Minor head colds hastened into raging infections. Crews had to be inured to these hardships in training before hoping to succeed on twelve-hour missions into battle, collectively enduring the same maladies, and more, in unfamiliar territory, flying wing to wing under a barrage of enemy fire from ground and air.

The primary assets to overcome these hardships—robust health and youth—were by no accident foundational criteria for selection into the armed service; and Uncle Sam drew heavily from this fountain. They were commonly called "boys," a reference so enthusiastically applied to American soldiers in World War II that the endearment has become engrained in popular culture. To their parents, their girlfriends, and their wives; to the press, makers of newsreels, and cinema; to politicians and commanding officers even, they were "our boys."

The moniker could well apply to soldiers throughout history. Many who fought in pre-twentieth-century wars—the Civil War and the American Revolution to name but two—were no doubt boys, in many instances younger even than those who served in World War II. But to the American mind in the early 1940s, the characterization embodied, in addition to an element of literal truth, a broader projection of values on the home front: innocence if not naïveté; high-spiritedness; and, above all, a nascent potential for great achievement. Though the personal stories of those aboard the bomber that took off from Westover in the winter twilight remain for the most part unrecoverable, we know for sure they shouldered a sizable measure of inexperience, their own and the nation's, coupled with weighty expectation.

At ten thousand feet, the point of rendezvous, they were to fall into a box formation, designed to concentrate their collective bombing payloads and defensive firepower from the turrets and waist guns while minimizing chances of shooting each other. They would fly to twenty-five thousand feet before breaking off and returning to base. The mission was not a long one, but it would provide pilots with practice joining and breaking from formations. The gunners would develop a feel for working within constraints of the alignment; radio operators and engineers would gain proficiency with sundry supporting roles.

On this and other missions, crews were to keep a keen watch for identifying landmarks on the ground—for navigation and bombing purposes—and for spotting friend or foe approaching from the air. Sometimes they made a contest out of it, and all would be now peering out windows from their respective stations as the point of rendezvous approached. Bickel and Ponder—qualified for their jobs in part because of their keen eyesight—would likely be the first to see a leading plane when they reached the clearing at nine thousand feet, and Roberts, the engineer, keeping lookout through the dorsal turret, may have seen one break through the overcast behind them. But another bank of clouds prevented them from initiating the drill. As minutes passed, the clouds got denser. At this point, a decision had to be made. Like a cat stuck in a tree, they reflexively climbed higher.

While the hallmark of a bomber crew is unity—World War II history is flush with this theme—there is no evidence that Ponder's crew had been together long. The absence on this flight of a bombardier and navigator, the presence of three assistants, and the fact the men were barely settled into the overcrowded Westover base suggests they were still acclimating to new roles and relationships.

The crew was part of the 471st Bomb Group—a training unit for reinforcements recently arrived at Westover after a hectic transfer from Pueblo, Colorado.[16] Strangers cast together by the luck of the draw and whims of bureaucracy, they would share more togetherness and less privacy than they had with their own families and, like family, come to know and be compelled to accept the best and worst of each other. A man's whistling, accent, singing, banter, or flatulence could be a source of amusement or irritation. Small gestures—an offering of a smoke or sharing of a parcel and news from home—might encourage the passing of some carefully considered or random confidences: who was a good egg, who was a prick, or the clearing up of some misunderstanding regarding such judgments. The state of their new living arrangements and, above all, the food would certainly provide fodder for empathy.

At the time of the transfer, the crew's training was in its last phase and their battle assignment weeks away. The men had earned their wings. Now they were mastering them. The final phase of training joined pilots with crews and planes they would take to war. At six-foot-two, Keith was too tall for a fighter plane. But he was a natural fit for a heavy bomber, which required strength, endurance, and a steady hand. The B-24 was the largest, heaviest, and, by all accounts, the most difficult plane to fly. The pedals and yoke were connected to controls by cables rather than hydraulics, making for heavy going. Charles Lindbergh himself, by that time a consultant at Ford's Willow Run factory, reported the Liberator's controls "the stiffest and heaviest I have ever handled."[17] None of the craft's handling characteristics were helped when it was loaded with twenty thousand pounds of bombs, fuel, gear, and men. Designed by Consolidated Aircraft under do-or-die wartime deadlines to carry the greatest number of bombs possible the greatest distances possible, the B-24 was, in short, the maximum amount of aircraft allowed by the engineering and manufacturing capabilities of the day, with minimal concessions to what is now thought of as "user friendliness."

While World War II pilots enjoyed something akin to celebrity status, no additional prestige came with flying a B-24. In fact, the Liberator—or "Lib"—provoked a kind of chauvinism among those who flew the B-17 Flying Fortress, the other prominent workhorse in the AAF's fleet of heavy bombers. Both planes carried a crew of ten to twelve men, and the crafts' capabilities were not vastly different. The Fortress was sleeker, somewhat more maneuverable, and, according to conventional wisdom, better able to stand up to enemy fire. World War II aviation culture is rich with jolly disparagement of the Liberator. The B-24 was a flying coffin; a constipated lumberer; the cargo container that the B-17 came in. But with superior speed, bomb capacity, and range, the B-24 better suited the needs, at least on paper, of an air campaign that in 1944 and 1945 would depend increasingly on the ability to cover longer distances to drop greater quantities of bombs deeper into Europe and the Pacific.[18]

Preparing for these missions required an intense and condensed period of target practice, formation flying, and drills warding off attacking fighters. The bombers would fly high and low, on practice missions long and short, pinpoint targets over land and sea while adjusting to all conditions and variables. This transition training was as close as the aircrews could come to a dress rehearsal for war, and it was not off to a great start for the 471st at Westover.

The larger story of operations at the base in February 1944 is one of improvisation and workarounds in the face of shortages and unbending schedules. Ponder and crew may have first sensed this when they carted their footlockers into an overcrowded barracks and headed to the mess hall, where their eager appetites would be greeted by the aroma of cube steaks and gravy competing with whiffs of garbage and vermin. The facilities were "overburdened," a status report explained, to the point "it was almost impossible to maintain proper sanitary conditions." Overall, base morale was further suffering "from the accelerated schedule."[19]

As members of the 471st began their dress rehearsal for war, they would quickly learn the base lacked sufficient gasoline, spare parts, flying suits, classroom space, training aids, and instructors.[20] Most significantly, it lacked fully functional aircraft. Some 150 crews shared thirty-five Liberators. Fewer than two dozen of the planes were in commission on any given day, while the others were grounded owing to shortages of parts and ground crew.[21] Many of the planes, as characterized by one officer, were "clunkers."[22] A "complicating factor," according to a report from the base supply officer, involved inventorying parts for the battle-worn fleet. "We operate four models, the D, E, H and J, each of which contains items that are not interchangeable with the others. Since many of the D and E models have seen combat service, they require much in the way of replacement parts." The base, he added, expected to "be relieved of all the Ds and Es in the near future" with the arrival of new planes.[23] *Gertie* was an E model. The "near future" would not come soon enough for Ponder and crew.

The deficiencies at Westover might provoke complaints among the rank and file, but no amount of grousing would result in delay. Rushing training was dangerous, but so was putting it off. A pilot and crew ill prepared to charge into battle in tightly packed, tiered formations of many hundreds of planes could be a catalyst for disaster for the entire mission. Using resources at hand, the men would have to learn to work seamlessly with one another and with other crews in rigid operational windows, sometimes in lousy conditions, coordinating operations down to the second. To this end, classroom learning went only so far. Real experience was gained in the air, and time was running short. "Most crew members are unfamiliar with B-24s," the group schools officer reported. "It's necessary to teach them B-24 SOP"—standard operating procedure.[24] Yet a lack of training aids, classrooms, and planes would present the type of paradox familiar to readers of Joseph Heller's World War II novel *Catch-22*: The men could not expertly fly planes with which they were not familiar; they could not become familiar with planes they could not fly.

A provision from One Bomber Command, a training arm of the First Air Force, responded to the problem by bestowing on flight officers what today might be euphemistically called "empowerment": "Although . . . directives set certain minimum requirements which must be accomplished, higher headquarters has permitted considerable latitude in method and manner of execution. It is also the policy of the Commanding Officer to permit free exercise of judgment and initiative on the part of staff and subordinates in carrying out the training program."[25] Put another way, command was leaving it up to staff and subordinates to get 'er done. And while this departure from the "Army way" was surely intended to ease the restriction of red tape in the interest of expediency, it also caused accountability issues when things went wrong.

When the 471st transferred from Pueblo to Westover, plenty was going wrong. Nearly 40 percent of the missions taking off from Westover in early 1944 were aborted.[26] The reasons were vast and varied. Crews had to turn back when guns wouldn't fire, bomb bay doors wouldn't open, radios malfunctioned. Breakdowns were partly responsible. Yet presumably faulty equipment sometimes checked out fine back on the ground in the hands of experienced instructors and mechanics who understood its quirks. Radios were especially glitchy. Overcrowded frequencies compromised efficiencies of entire networks. Individual units were liable to be thrown off by the vibration of engines laboring at altitude. "Radio operators are supposed to be trained to adjust these discrepancies," one communications officer complained, "but they often don't recognize them as such."[27] Even radios in experienced hands, however, tended to be rendered useless by weather interference when they were most needed. The only surefire safeguard was to avoid flying in rain, snow, and fog. Working against this safeguard was the most limited resource of all—time.

Though a necessary function of safety protocol, aborted missions— "abortives"—whether the fault of equipment, inexperience, weather, or negligence, were a bane to training schedules. Crews operated under constant pressure, both tacit and explicit, to limit them. In early February, days before the 471st began flying at Westover, an order was passed down from One Bomber Command "to recognize, tabulate and analyze all of those factors which impede the accomplishment of training." The primary tool for this was a form to be filled out by pilots and passed up the chain of command noting "reason for abortive missions, including ship type and number, the unit and the missions assigned."[28] The information was tabulated and sent daily to the commanding general. Such reports "increase the pilot's sense of responsibility for completing his training missions," one commander noted. "The knowledge that he will have to explain in detail the reasons for aborting causes the crew commander to be more diligent in disciplining his men and himself, both before and during the flight. In this manner, he spares himself unpleasant discussions."[29]

By 7 p.m. on February 17, three hours after Ponder and the other five crews had taken off, it looked like six more abortives would soon be chalked up at Westover. Some "unpleasant discussion" would surely ensue. Standing in the control room, one Lieutenant Price, the operations officer on duty, looked out past the reticulation of runway lights reflecting off the wet surface of the tarmac. There wasn't much to see in the darkness, though it would be natural to expect the lieutenant would be searching for lights descending from the sky. If the crew and its squadron leader had seen heavy weather coming in the preflight briefing, which they should have, they had grossly miscalculated its arrival. And its impact. Weather might be blamed, but unless there was some fudging, this mess would properly be chalked up to a scheduling delay. The crews had been briefed at noon, when there was still a workable window.

All that would be somebody else's problem to sort out at another time. Price's problems were just beginning. With weather moving in and visibility and radio communication deteriorating, all local flights had been called in at 6:30 p.m., and for the past half hour the tower had been on the receiving end of sporadic one-way communication with several of them. With frustrating redundancy, pilots were requesting weather information and clearance to land. Each time the tower reported overcast three miles, light rain, haze, and requested the planes' respective positions. The crews apparently failed to copy.

Behind Price, several uniformed individuals sat at stout desks with phones, headsets, a teletype machine, and ashtrays.[30] From time to time one of them might move to a chart table, glance at the oversize wall clock, or consult a nearby console of weather gauges. The weather instruments confirmed what one might guess looking out the plate glass windows: the barometric pressure and temperature were falling; surfaces would soon begin freezing, and snow would come.

The Westover contingent was exchanging communications by interphone with traffic controllers in New York City and Boston, who were, in turn, in touch with radio operators in navigational towers and landing fields near and far. It was the radio operators who were (ideally) directly in touch with the pilots. Much of the attention at Westover, at the moment, was devoted to the overdue local flights cleared earlier that day under visual flight rules. Though the parties did not use the term "flying blind," that was in fact what circumstances now boiled down to. Boston Air Traffic Control was reporting calls from multiple Army planes that did not appear on any of Boston's flight plans. Over the course of the last half hour, a certain edge had been creeping into the transmittals along with a tacit understanding: the planes out of Westover, having wandered from local air space, were a threat not only to themselves but to other traffic being directed along flight paths to and from the hubs of Boston and New York City.

The pilot of 042, it had been reported by Boston, had "one engine out and one fixing to go out."[31] The controller did not know how much fuel the plane had or where it was exactly—probably in the vicinity of North Scituate, southeast of Boston. . . . An update was now being phoned to Westover: "Apparently everything is all right. But he is still flying around and they have lost him again. . . . He keeps contacting us but he hasn't given us a position. He has been unable to read us."

There was more back and forth along these lines pertaining to 042 and several other planes, none of it conclusive, when, at 7:10 p.m., one of the subordinates in the Westover tower approached Lieutenant Price and reported: "He wants to speak with the operations officer." At that point, a few heads may have looked up.

The officer took the phone: "This is Lieutenant Price."

"Well, Lieutenant Price," the voice on the other end began. "This is Poe with ATC." Poe, from Airway Traffic Control in Boston, got right to the point: "About these B-24s that are out. It seems we haven't gotten any flight plans on them, and they are all up on top [of the overcast] on instruments and everything else and request clearances down." It cannot be certain what "everything else" meant, but Poe was not happy with any of it. "We can't give them clearances because we don't know what you have out or where they are."

"I see," Price answered. He informed Poe there were six planes out, adding, "They were all flying locally. Then this came up and they went above it. I don't know the circumstances, myself." Poe provided the circumstances: "One of them showed up at twenty-seven thousand feet and wanted to come down, and we have this 042 floating around somewhere and one or two others and we can't give them any kind of clearance other than to descend with three miles forward visibility."

"Yes," the lieutenant said. "Well, we're trying to get them down as best we can." Then, perhaps aware that others in the room were following his end of the conversation, he added, "You understand the circumstances. . . ."

"Yes," Poe said. "We know how it is with no flight plans. You probably don't know any more about it than we do."

It was surely a dig, though Price merely responded, "That is right. If I get anything, I will give you a buzz." The call warranted no further explanation. Poe well knew local flights cleared under visual flight rules do not require flight plans. And Price well knew the Westover planes had strayed into the domain of regional traffic controllers. Lost in heavy weather, they would have to return to the base, from wherever they were, on instruments. Navigating by instruments with no flight plans, they were not only in explicit violation of federal rules, but an outsize risk for midair collisions.

Price returned to his work. Outside, massive hangars standing back from the taxiway were visible in intermittent sweeps of light from the rotating aerodrome beacon. Snowflakes began falling in the thickening mist.

As flight officers, Ponder and Bickel were required to know the jobs of each and every crew member; and as pilot, Ponder was accountable for all. In the developing crisis, he would have his hands full trying to troubleshoot problems while flying the plane. At that point in his short career Ponder had logged 468 hours flying—a respectable number when gauged by the standard of the day. But 90 percent of his training had been in smaller planes, in fair weather, during the day.[32] None would have been in a developing storm with no flight plan or reliable radio.

Despite Bickel's relative maturity, the copilot was subordinate to Ponder and technically less qualified in getting them out of the jam. As second in command, he would be doing what copilots typically do—reading instruments, providing extra hands on controls especially during takeoff and landing, checking and confirming sequences, logging everything, communicating with the crew on the flight deck, checking on the boys in the back, and taking the helm if Ponder had to take a leak or was otherwise indisposed.[33] After they lost touch with the other planes and the ground, Ponder would likely have asked Bickel to help Zebo sort out the radio problem if he hadn't taken on that task himself.

It would be no consolation that crews on the five other planes were having a similar time of it. Unable to assemble for the formation, they would have no way—at least within their ability and experience—of continuing in an orderly fashion. They had, in fact, lost track of each other. Visibility at designated landmarks from the airfield had dropped to something less than three miles—likely far less at certain points in the air—not good for multiple Liberators, difficult to maneuver in ideal conditions, flying somewhat blindly at two hundred miles per hour, presumably in the same vicinity. The best Ponder could do to minimize risk of collision was maintain a steady hand at the helm and remind crew not working the radio or tracking fuel to keep a sharp eye out, though they would be in no need of encouragement.

One of the men, likely Tommy Roberts, would be afforded a panoramic view above the plane from the dorsal turret behind the flight deck. At least two others, probably Alexander and Walton—the gunners listed as assistant engineer and assistant radio operator—would be watching from the Plexiglas chamber at the plane's nose below and in front of the flight deck. This offered a sweeping view directly beneath and in front of *Gertie*, though there would not be much to see in these conditions. If lights of another plane appeared out of the darkness, they would give a shout.

While several of the planes, in Poe's words to Price, were "floating around somewhere" over the Boston area one hundred miles east of where they belonged, Ponder, at some point, had managed to pilot *Gertie* on a westward heading. A principal aid to navigation in early 1944 was a cross-country network of communication towers that broadcast homing signals. This was "the beam," and "flying the beam" meant the crew had picked up the signal and was following it to a designated point.

Sometime after 9:30 p.m., Ponder, likely conferring with Zebo and Bickel, picked up a faint sequence of Morse code that gained clarity and intensity as Ponder subtly adjusted course. At this point there would be some urgent checking of instruments followed by confirmation. The frequency—272 kilocycles—matched Westover's signal; they were approaching from the northeast. It's not hard to envision the body language and expressions of the crew on the flight deck, sighs of relief, perhaps with a chosen utterance or two, as the signal grew loud and strong. It could be expected that Ponder, as commanding officer, would feel the most relief and greatest reservation in expressing it. At the very least, he would interphone Cozier and Jonen in the waist and the men in the nose to let them know they were on the beam back to Westover. At some point, the status of the other ships would surely cross Ponder's mind. Had any made it back to the base? There would be hell to pay, but they would have a story out of it.

Finally locked onto the beam, Ponder called the tower to report his altitude and request clearance for an approach. Given the circumstances, a voice on the other end of the transmission might ask him to repeat that, and a moment of confusion would ensue before the responding voice clarified matters: 047 was approaching a communications tower in Wilkes-Barre, Pennsylvania. There was no landing field. Ponder was to stand by.

4

INTO THIN AIR

When they picked up the signal from Wilkes-Barre, Ponder and crew had been flying four and a half hours and were more than three hours past due. By the standards of their training—some missions lasting twelve hours—this would ordinarily be no big deal. But circumstances were making it so. Ponder was expecting to arrive at a landing strip at Westover. Instead, he was nearing a radio range in central eastern Pennsylvania. It was merely a navigational waypoint, transmitting beams to guide pilots to other destinations. Yet it happened to be broadcasting a homing frequency—232 kilocycles—identical to Westover's.

Now, at least, he knew where he was, though subsequent minutes would be weighted with a new set of tensions. As Ponder stood by, it took only a moment for controllers working from La Guardia in New York City to check the slip board—a wall organizer holding cards representing the progress of each flight—and see nothing to reconcile a report that Army 047 was northeast of Wilkes-Barre at thirteen thousand feet and seeking a place to land.[1] La Guardia, in turn, phoned controllers in Boston to see what *they* might have on "this Army 047." Boston controllers also lacked a record, though they had some ideas (possibly formulated by Poe) soon confirmed by a series of queries relayed back to the plane via the Wilkes-Barre tower: Did 047 have a flight plan? No flight plan at all? Was this a B-24 out of Westover?

The flight would be put on course, but first controllers needed 047's fuel status. The answer Ponder gave—two hours—would have come from Tommy Roberts, the engineer, but here, too, there would be creeping uncertainty. Landing fields in New York City, one hundred miles or so to the east, would have been the most immediate choice for safe harbor, but controllers apparently could not shoehorn an unplanned flight into the mix with a now menacing low-pressure system churning up the coast. After some deliberation they advised Ponder, via the Wilkes-Barre tower, to proceed to the Syracuse Army Base some 150 miles due north.[2]

Banking north and again nosing the plane up through the overcast, Ponder acknowledged the advisory and confirmed he was heading "directly to Syracuse." With that decision made, he would check in with the boys in the back and in the nose, where the latest turn of events would surely be testing morale.

Cozier and Jonen would have had plenty of time to dwell on the situation in the cramped quarters of the plane's waist. They sat idly next to windows drawn closed and guns folded upright on their pivoting stands; the men's features, apart from their considerable difference in height, would have been lost in the bulk of flying suits and headgear. The ride so far, at changing altitudes through the flanks of a gathering low-pressure system, would have been jarring by today's standards. And if not airsick, the men would certainly be hungry. Crews were responsible for packing their own provisions—maybe a baloney sandwich and an orange grabbed from the mess hall along with a few chocolate bars—but given this was supposed to be a short flight, at altitude nonetheless, eating would not have factored much into the plan; they anticipated being back in time for a hot dinner anyway. Now, by the time they got rerouted to Syracuse it was 9:50 p.m., and it would be another hour, at best, before they were on the ground.

Under other circumstances Cozier, the fraternity brother, might have passed time with yarns about college life, and the younger Jonen might have proven a rapt audience. Such stories, one might reasonably suspect,

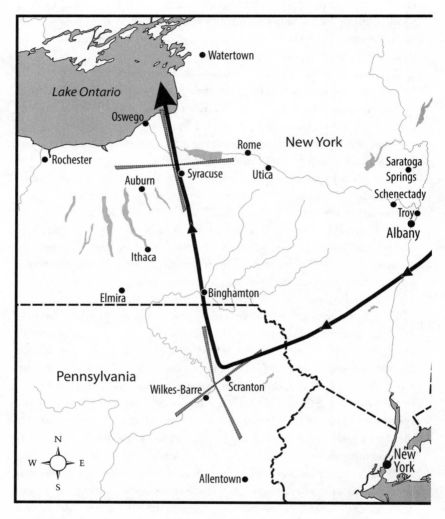

Figure 4.1. After taking off from Westover at 5:01 p.m. on February 17, 1944, *Gertie* was lost in a developing storm over New England. Her precise route is unknown, though several other planes in her group, also experiencing limited radio contact and poor visibility, were reported wandering blindly over eastern Massachusetts. At 9:45 p.m. *Gertie* mistakenly followed a radio homing signal to Wilkes-Barre, Pennsylvania, and was subsequently directed north to Syracuse. Lines emanating from each airfield show radio tracking beams that guided aircraft prior to modern navigational technology. Map by Mike Bechthold.

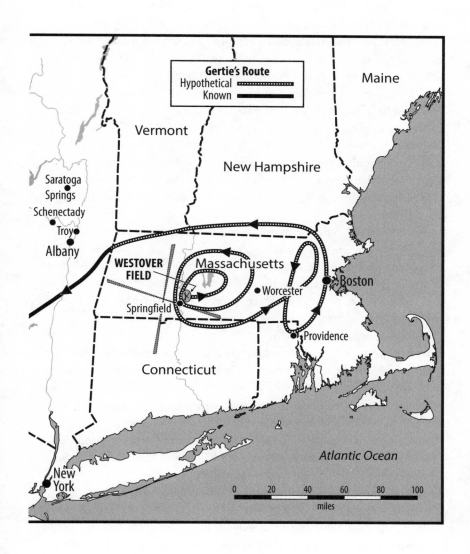

Gertie's Route
Hypothetical
Known

Maine

Vermont

New Hampshire

Saratoga
Springs
Schenectady
Troy
Albany

WESTOVER
FIELD

Massachusetts

Boston

Worcester

Springfield

Providence

Connecticut

Atlantic Ocean

New
York

0   20   40   60   80   100
miles

would be woven by the whims of male youth: nicknames, appearances, hygiene, appetites, sports, shenanigans, girls, scraps of family life in Tulsa and Milwaukee. But enveloped by engine noise, oxygen masks, skullcaps, and goggles, there would be little in the way of continuing any budding fellowship they shared on the ground beyond body language and an occasional declaration or expletive. An interphone system connected the crew, and though it might be used to pass on orders, updates, or a word of encouragement now and again, it would not be used for idle chat. As the plane again climbed above the weather, the two figures would pass time seeking any modicum of comfort to be found in worn and temperamental heated suits that allowed parts of their body to become too warm or too cold or both at the same time, and hoping for the best with the chow situation in Syracuse.

Alexander, the assistant engineer, and Walton, the assistant radio operator, would be enduring similar conditions in the nose. Here, at least, the mullioned Plexiglas compartment allowed the best view in the house. When in the thick of the overcast, that counted for little. But now, as Ponder leveled the plane above the weather at twenty-five thousand feet, a sphere of celestial patterns sprawled vividly over the horizon.

The view would be equally spectacular from the flight deck, where defrosters provided enough warmth to keep the windows from icing over and, though the air was still frigid, allowed the crew to handle controls without bulky mittens.[3] Roberts would be mindful of gauges and toggles to keep fuel balanced evenly in the wing tanks. Zebo, perhaps with Bickel's help, would be trying, without success, to dial in the beam of their new destination. When confirming his intention to fly to Syracuse, Ponder had also reported 047's "radio compass out." There was no elaboration about this in the message later relayed from the Wilkes-Barre tower to controllers, other than Wilkes-Barre "had trouble reading him." Regardless of the cause, it would be up to the crew to fix the problem. Or do without.

Here, on the flight deck, the exigencies of trouble shooting would crowd out thoughts of discomfort or missed dinner, or even much discussion of the stunning view of the cosmos, beyond their relevance to the urgent matter of route finding. Ponder, who had spent the first half of his life in a place without electricity and eyes frequently cast to the Mississippi skies, would likely be familiar with the primary constellations and their positions relative to the North Star long before learning to apply them

Figure 4.2. Copilot Ray Bickel, training at an unidentified base while earning his wings. As a flight officer, Bickel, like Ponder, was required to know the jobs of all crew members. In addition to helping fly and navigate, Bickel would likely be helping with problems of radio communication and fuel management that grew dire throughout the night. Courtesy of Ray and Jean Vanasek.

to chart the course of an airplane. When traversing oceans, which would soon be expected, celestial navigation would become acutely relevant. For this reason, and given the hard lesson they were now receiving, Bickel or Ponder may have taken a shot with a sextant, or at least referenced their orientation to the stars. Their primary method of navigation, however, would be dead reckoning, which required tracking heading, drift, and ground speed against their last known location established with the help of radio signals and a catalog of charts.[4] With whatever method they used, a bearing of 350 degrees would bring them from Wilkes-Barre to the Syracuse range; the North Star would at least confirm they were heading in the right direction.

At 10:41 p.m. Ponder reported that he was forty miles out on the south leg of the Syracuse range at twenty-one thousand feet, "on top of the overcast." Three minutes later, the Syracuse tower cleared 047 to begin descent to ten thousand feet. Within minutes, the stars were swallowed by a smoky haze and then snow, wildly animated in the glare of landing lights.

About the time 047 was being rerouted from Wilkes-Barre to Syracuse, other pilots in the group were still finding their way back to Westover. The first of them successfully chanced a landing with no radio contact. Others, deciphering static-laced instructions from Boston and the Westover tower, eventually found the beam to Westover and also managed to land.[5] Once on the ground, while squaring away their planes and tending to post-flight paperwork, each of them would certainly receive a message to report to the captain's office.

At twenty-three, Captain Paul Lewis Mathison, the squadron leader, was barely older than the crews he commanded, and in some instances a good deal younger. Yet in experience and qualification he was beyond his years. While attending the University of Wisconsin as an engineering major, he had been selected "on the basis of academic standing, personality, physical qualification and aptitude" as one of fifty-five students to begin training for a pilot's license through the Civil Aeronautics Administration.[6] He left college in November 1940 to join the AAF when it was still a fledgling operation. Though Japan's attack on Pearl Harbor was more than a year away, it was probably no coincidence that Mathison, whose grandparents were from Norway and who grew up in a small neighborhood in Madison populated by Norwegian immigrants and their immediate descendants, enlisted not long after Germany invaded the homeland of his ancestors. Shortly after the US entered the war, he was awarded the Air Medal for destroying German U-boats in the Atlantic.[7]

Now, Mathison's message to his charges, if anything along the lines of the clipped responses the captain would later provide to a panel investigating the day's occurrences, would be short and explicit. He would remind them that this had been a local flight. Under no circumstance were they to have left the area. He might add, if the matter of radio communication came up, that each pilot was responsible for the readiness of his crew, ship, and situational awareness of the weather and all other factors. Everyone's lives depended on it. No matter how short the flight, it was inexcusable to leave the base without calibrating fuel gauges. And they should have damned well turned back at the first sign of bad weather.

After tending to their gear and any additional post-flight matters, undoubtedly relieved to have the matter behind them, some of the pilots would likely be drawn to the officers' club for a late meal, maybe a beer, and momentary refuge from the appraising eyes of their crews. It was Thursday night, and while that counted for little on base at this stage of the war, it was becoming a certainty that weather would limit operations the following day. At the bar, there would be inescapable talk of developments on the war fronts.

Two days prior, Allied forces had bombed the Monte Cassino monastery in a German-held province of Italy. Wire reports on the front page of a local paper had claimed a decisive victory, a "drumfire of death" that "knocked out the powerful German defenses."[8] History would show the destruction of the thousand-year-old Benedictine abbey and 250 civilian inhabitants taking shelter within was not only a tragic miscalculation but an enabler of a prolonged and exceedingly bloody German entrenchment among the prodigious skeletal ruins atop a strategic mountain overlook. Yet the wire report of the day fed public eagerness of any news that might pass as victory in the aftermath of crippling losses.

Monumental setbacks in the second half of 1943 included a raid on the Ploiesti oil refineries in Romania in which more than one in four of 178 bombers and eighteen hundred crew that set out on the mission on August 1, 1943, failed to return. It was a day to be known as "Black Sunday."[9] Ten weeks later, a similar casualty rate awaited twenty-nine hundred men and 290 planes sent to bomb a ball-bearing factory in Schweinfurt, Germany, on October 14, 1943—a date now known as "Black Thursday."[10] The astounding losses raised doubts whether Allied forces had the men, planes, and stomachs to sustain such costly offensives. Though the Monte Cassino monastery was an undefended target in Italy, its obliteration might be a clear signal of the thinking of the generalship: air superiority was foundational to victory on the ground and would proceed at all costs.[11]

At some point, talk in the officers' club might touch on the day's aborted mission, and word would come that Ponder's ship was yet to return; the ground crew had been called by the operations officer, who wanted to know exactly how much fuel 047 had when it took off. It is conceivable there would be some reference to the "clunkers" the men were flying, or the problems other crews had gauging their fuel that night, or the scarcity of fuel of sufficient octane for high-altitude training. As the night wore on with no word of *Gertie*'s status, the mood would darken.

While the men were preparing for the devastation of battle, they already lived with daily fatalities across the home front. Rescue parties, perhaps including some of those now assembled around the nondescript tables and bar at the cheaply paneled officers' lounge, had just spent weeks searching for wreckage of a B-24 carrying eight of their colleagues that disappeared after losing radio contact over New Hampshire. As they fruitlessly combed the White Mountains for any sign of the ill-fated plane, another disaster involving planes from Westover unfolded over the skies of Utah. War is said to be long periods of tedium interrupted by moments of terror, and that certainly would apply in this case. Flying cross-country in a formation of five, one of the bombers, encumbered by icing, clipped the wing of a neighboring plane, sheering off an engine. Before crew in either plane could react, both were spinning out of control, carrying all twenty-five crew members to their deaths.

There was nothing extraordinary about these accidents in late December 1943. They fell eighteen days apart, and during that period 228 other men died in ninety-four crashes elsewhere in the US.[12] In the end, the numbers would bear out what those who eagerly aspired to be pilots after Pearl Harbor may have strongly suspected by early 1944: the chances of safely completing a full tour of duty over the Pacific or Europe were grim. Chances of surviving training necessary to begin that tour were not a whole lot better.

Regardless of what tomorrow might bring, the pilots recharging their morale at the officers' club would have neither the time nor energy to linger there. Exiting the clapboard building, heads bowed against a wet snow that plastered their caps and coats, they might find escape from their cares, at least briefly, with a full stomach, the prospects of a night's rest, and the feeling they were not in it alone.

There were no such comforts aboard Army 047.

The weather moved in, and the snow came hard. The low-pressure system was morphing into a full-scale nor'easter as it spiraled along the jet stream. The saturated overcast that had blanketed New England hours earlier was changing to a driving snow in upstate New York, and nowhere would it be worse than where Ponder, Bickel, Zebo, and Roberts were trying to land *Gertie*. Syracuse, thirty miles south of Lake Ontario, lies within the infamous Great Lakes "snow belt" where prevailing winds drawing moisture from the lakes produce turbulent whiteouts as they push over frozen inland terrain. The lakes can be thought of as a limitless fuel reserve for a perpetual snowmaking machine. During an average winter, more than ten feet of snow falls on Syracuse. Areas southeast and east of the lake receive, on average, between twenty and twenty-five feet.

Lake-effect storms can be highly localized affairs, dumping snow by the foot in one spot and virtually nothing thirty miles away. But sometimes they are offshoots of a much larger weather system—storms within a storm, like tornadoes spun from hurricanes—and their paths were widely unpredictable with the forecasting tools of 1944. Soldiers at Army bases in Watertown, Rome, and Syracuse would be all too familiar with abrupt whiteouts between late November and early April. Pilots could avoid localized snow bands in otherwise fair weather. But their danger was compounded by nor'easters. As the weather moved in, airports throughout the region shut down. Planes that were on the ground stayed on the ground. Those in the air went someplace else.

At 9:50 p.m., minutes after 047 had been rerouted to Syracuse, the Army meteorologist at Syracuse issued an advisory—visibility was "coming down"—prompting a reassessment of Ponder's destination among parties on the ground. Rochester, eighty miles to the west, was no better than Syracuse. Conditions further west, however, were expected to hold up for another two to three hours. The question of fuel again came up. Ground operations at Westover reported 047 "should have" taken off with a supply of ten to twelve hours. Yet nobody was certain, and apparently, because it was a "local flight," it had not been duly considered. If Ponder could reconcile the discrepancy, they might direct him to Ohio. That, at least, was the upshot of the conversation on the ground, and it would remain speculative, because 047 was again out of contact.

Up until now, perhaps, Ponder would see the rash of mistakes and bad luck that took them so far off course less as a threat to the safety of ship and crew than an ill-afforded training setback and certain invitation for an "unpleasant discussion." Now, he would realize, the situation was dire.

With snow accumulating faster than it could be cleared and visibility dropping, Army 047 would be the last flight into the Syracuse base, and crews stood by for its arrival. The expected sequence would begin with a call from Ponder seeking clearance to land. The typical exchange would include an update on conditions, and information to set his instruments. Of particular importance was the altimeter, which measures distance to the ground and must be calibrated to account for a landing field's height above sea level as well as the ever-changing barometric pressure that affects the reading. Precision in this regard is less essential when a pilot can visually judge distances. But when the view is obscured by weather, and fluctuations in barometric pressure are not accounted for, two bad things can happen, and both involve being out of sync with a runway that is either further or closer to the landing gear than expected, sometimes by fatal margins. In short, the worse the visibility, the more a pilot's dependence on an accurate setting to gauge the landing. As things stood, Ponder and Bickel were flying into an airport they didn't know and couldn't see. And now, as they anticipated their approach, the reply to their calls for clearance would be little more than unintelligible bursts of static.

With the moment at hand to begin his final descent and unable to contact the tower, Ponder either decided to abort the landing or simply missed the base altogether. At 11:35 p.m., Westover called Boston requesting the status of 047. "He isn't on the ground yet, Westover," came the reply. "We don't know where he is."

There's no telling what happened to *Gertie* after she overshot the airport. Did Ponder climb back above the storm to try to reestablish radio contact? Did he power down an engine to conserve gas? Were the wings icing? These are all reasonable guesses. Later reports from various points in northern New York suggest he continued north after passing over Syracuse on a somewhat random path over land and water. What is known, for sure, is the fuel supply held out longer than expected.

At 1:45 a.m., some three hours after his previous radio contact and almost nine hours after taking off, the Syracuse tower picked up a call from Ponder. He was approaching on the east leg of the range, "very low on gas and would like to land," according to a controller at Syracuse, who was now relaying that information to Boston. "Any instructions, Boston?" the controller asked.

The transcript of ground operations identifies controllers only by their initials. From this, one can gather that Poe, the chief traffic controller at Boston during the earlier dispatches, had been relieved by someone identified as A.C. As eager as Ponder was to get the plane down, A.C., perhaps familiar with too many bad outcomes of landing attempts in storms, or merely, in Army parlance, covering his ass, was disinclined to give clearance into an airport that was now technically closed.

"Did you give him the weather?" A.C. asked the Syracuse tower.

"Yes I did," came the reply. "I didn't get him back after that."

"He was on the east leg of the Syracuse range?"

"He was on the east leg of the Syracuse range," Syracuse repeated.

"Right. See if you can raise him, and see how much gas he has got."

"He said he was very low."

"Very low?"

"That's right."

"He is very low on gas?"

"Roger, that is what he said."

The Syracuse controller stood by while A.C. called Westover, where the news that 047 was on the Syracuse range was greeted with a burst of exuberance: "Yeah!" Price was heard shouting.

"And what do you want him to do?" A.C. asked.

"Well tell him to get down," Price responded. "That's all we can do, I guess."

"Try to come into Syracuse?"

"Try and come into Syracuse."

"I'm trying to ask him how much fuel he has left to see if he can get someplace else."

"Yeah. See if you can get any answer on how much fuel he has," Price said.

"I have asked that already. I will try to get an answer on that and otherwise the only thing to do is to let him try and get into Syracuse."

"That's the only thing."[13]

As it turned out, a good deal of other things, and people, soon entered the picture. Ultimately, it was up to Boston to clear the plane, and there was more discussion to be had on that point at the control room at Logan Field. The initial instruction—relayed from Westover, to Boston, to Syracuse—was "try and come into Syracuse." But apparently there was some second-guessing on this point when, minutes later, A.C. from Boston called the Syracuse tower and told the controller there—as of yet unable to reconnect with Ponder—to "delete any instructions to him and just give him the weather."

Approaching the field at about 120 mph, 047 would be covering a mile every thirty seconds. Neither the plane's altitude nor precise location was known, though Ponder was heard calling for data to set his altimeter. The Syracuse tower radioed the information but received no legible confirmation. Though closing in on the Syracuse field, the plane was technically still on standby for clearance.

At 1:56 a.m., eleven minutes after the tower picked up Ponder's request to land, A.C. was again rehashing the situation with Price. It is certain only that confusion reigned, and neither of them was eager to be the person of record to clear the landing. "There is no place . . . where there is any [acceptable] weather, and I don't think he has too much gas," A.C. said. "Of course, I can't direct him to go into Syracuse unless you want me to on your authority." Price asked if he could "call back in two seconds."

Moments later, there was another voice on the line from Westover asking the same questions and receiving the same answers: Army 047 was approaching on the east leg, seeking clearance to land, fuel "very low," and, at the moment, out of contact.

"They better order them to bail out," the voice snapped.

"You ordered them to bail out?" A.C. asked.

"They better order them to bail out if they think they don't have a chance of coming into the field."

"Is that on your authority you want them to bail out?"

"If they can't come into the field there, if they don't have enough gas to get any other place, they will have to bail out, if they can't make the field."

"You are ordering them that, that they will have to bail out? Are you ordering them to?"

"No, I am not ordering them to. I would like them to get into the field if they have enough gasoline."

"That is up to the pilot if they want to bail out or not, right, is that the idea?"

"That's right. . . . I hate to give an order from here to tell a man to bail out without knowing exactly the weather." A.C. promptly provided the weather: Syracuse was closed, ceiling six hundred feet, visibility one-half mile, snow and fog. With that, the man on the other end of the line made the decision. "Entire crew bail out. That is on my orders. Bail out."

"Orders of whom?" came the reply.

"Colonel Banks."

"Colonel Banks of Westover Operations?"

"That is right."

The stature of Colonel Clyde Girard Banks would have been easily recognized by those who saw him enter the Westover tower. There were few men on base who were not in their early twenties. The exceptions, as with the fifty-year-old Banks, would be career military men with a distinguished bearing. Banks no doubt had seen plenty of life-and-death moments in his thirty-year career, which began as a young officer with the Army's Second Infantry in the trenches of World War I. The outcome of the decision he made now would hinge on the men's training, equipment, and a liberal measure of blind luck. At best, it would result in twenty tons of unattended plane and an unknown quantity of fuel crashing in an unpopulated area and eight men scattered unharmed somewhere in the storm. Still, Banks favored the odds of the men successfully parachuting to safety and letting the plane crash where it might over the consequences of trying to land it in a snowstorm before gas ran out. The order was broadcast at 2:01 a.m., sixteen minutes after Ponder had radioed the tower for clearance.

When radio did work in bad weather, it was notoriously random; sometimes a receiver might pick up messages from far away, while nearby signals were lost in interference. For this reason Banks's order was broadcast from airfields and towers between Cleveland and Albany. Some sixteen towers were instructed to send the message out blind, which meant it would repeat every few minutes in the absence of a response, and to standby on 6210, the frequency that Ponder was using. Banks would connect with 047 one way or another.

His order to bail out came with another simple directive: "Advise intentions." Pilots, like captains at sea, are exclusively in charge of their ships. Protocol gave Ponder discretion to refuse a command if circumstances warranted, and it gave officers on the ground protection from the consequences of issuing an ironclad directive in the absence of relevant information. Banks, with only an imprecise knowledge of all the factors, had gone with his gut.

Sometime after the order was issued, based on subsequent reports from northern New York residents, 047 was flying low over Oswego County, north of the airport. Ponder and his crew would have been peering out windows, searching for physical landmarks during lulls between irregular and ever-moving snow bands streaming off the lake. Reading foreign landscapes from the air was engrained in their training, especially railroads, factories, cities, schools and churches, and topographical and other natural features. Distinguishing between targets and non-targets, places to crash land or parachute, navigational benchmarks, and any number of other factors would require an accurate and immediate study of the ground. In normal training, this exercise might take the form of a game to keep the crew engaged on long flights, perhaps with some friendly wagers. Now it was a matter of life and death.

One of the most commanding views, other than from the nose compartment from which bombing and navigation were done, would be from the tail turret, and it's possible that Jonen took up station there. Flying below the six-hundred-foot overcast, the crew may have caught glimpses of lights and other features of the ground as they passed over Syracuse, or minutes later, the port city of Oswego on Lake Ontario, with any visible form falling away to darkness when the plane circled over the lake.

The ground temperature had recently dipped below freezing, and the air was thick with humidity and fog—optimal conditions for the formation of ice, inhibiting lift, and requiring precious fuel to regain altitude. To have a reasonable chance of surviving a bailout, the crew would want at least one thousand feet of altitude, preferably above land. If they hadn't already done so, they would don parachutes over bulky flying suits—an awkward process made more cumbersome and time-consuming within the cramped chambers of the aircraft. They would have drilled for such an event on the ground, but if they were like most crews sent into battle, none of them would have actually jumped from an airborne plane before.

Or maybe Ponder had already committed to ditching the plane or simply lacked altitude for a bailout. In that case, the crew would be strapped in their seats, now anticipating the end with dreadful certainty without knowing where or exactly when it would come. The plane should have been equipped with a life raft and "Mae Wests"—inflatable life vests. The men's final thoughts might have been trying to visualize a drill they had, as with the parachutes, covered only in an abstract and cursory manner.

At 2:05 a.m., four minutes after Banks's order was broadcast, a controller in Rochester standing by on 6210 could hear Ponder calling Syracuse to acknowledge, but his reply was cut off in static. All that can be known from the record is: "He was asking something."

It was the last anybody heard from the plane.

The People's Story

When *Gertie* overshot the Syracuse airport she would have ventured over a region not only remote, but topographically manifold. If circling on a clear day, Keith Ponder and crew would have seen, to the east, Adirondack peaks reaching five thousand feet amid a sweep of mountain wilderness. To the west, near sea level, Lake Ontario's steely blue void would be visible to the horizon, featureless, save for whitecaps and pack ice piling into frozen banks rimming the near shore. To the north, the Saint Lawrence River, before the days it was developed into an international seaway, would appear as a frozen ribbon of white defining New York State's border with Ontario, Canada.

Between the water to the west and the mountains to the east, and more or less below the wandering aircraft at some time or another, sprawled the Tug Hill Plateau—ten thousand square miles of mostly featureless woodland and scrub interspersed with farms. Other than US Route 11 traversing north to south, the region had minimal infrastructure and was notorious for the frequency and intensity of lake-effect snowstorms that sometimes drifted and buried farmhouses and barns to their rooflines.

How far did *Gertie* stray, and in which of these places, if any, did she end up? With no flight plan, no radio contact or any other means to track the plane, the only clues are from leads—some vague and some vivid—from people who heard her or are said to have heard her circling.

The population density throughout the northern reaches of upstate New York was low, clustered mostly in villages, towns, small cities, and military bases tucked among expanses of water and mountains, fields and woodland. When high above these areas, the low-frequency thrum of the bomber's four twelve-hundred-horsepower engines might have been felt as much as heard, tentative and distant, gaining in substance only to fade again as the plane circled. It might cause one to stir from bed and cock an ear. A figment of slumber? A farmer in Saint Lawrence County fancied he heard "a big tractor," he later told investigators, inexplicably approaching and retreating sometime in the night, perhaps between 2 and 3 a.m. It wasn't until he read the paper a day and a half later that he realized what he had heard, or thought he had heard.

That report came from one Robert Hall of Morrison Road in the hamlet of North Gouverneur, nearly one hundred miles north of where Ponder was reportedly trying to land in Syracuse. In and by itself this was not exactly a hot lead. But the notion that 047 had wandered that far north, crossing the east end of Lake Ontario before circling back inland over the Thousand Islands, the Adirondack Mountains, and Tug Hill Plateau, gained traction with other reports that came into the offices of deputies and troopers after the news of the lost plane broke.[1]

A lookout at the Coast Guard station on Galloo Island, a residence at nearby Henderson Harbor, and a dispatcher for the New York Central Railroad in the town of Philadelphia, northeast of Watertown, reported hearing an aircraft between 2 and 3 a.m. These points, within thirty miles of one another, form an arc over northern New York near the border with Canada. It is plausible 047 ventured this far north after initially missing the Syracuse airport around 11 p.m. Yet the timing of the reports was confounding; they suggest the plane was high aloft and well to the north minutes and even hours after it was thought to be nearly out of gas coming into Syracuse, when Banks gave the command to bail out at 2:01 a.m.

Conversely, reports from Oswego County, adjacent to Onondaga County where Ponder was trying to land, were vivid and frequent. Their timing, between 1:30 and 2:15 a.m., cogently fit Ponder's last garbled attempts to contact Syracuse. Unable to communicate, unable to see, and running out of fuel after missing the airport on multiple passes, he would have been circling back, again trying to pick up a signal on the problematic radio compass as his crew searched for reference points or landmarks. By then, prospects of ditching the plane, if he could find a spot to bring it down, must have at least crossed Ponder's mind. By all accounts, when passing directly over Oswego County, the aircraft was low, perhaps two hundred feet. At this height the peal of the engines would come suddenly from nowhere—rattling dishes, sending dogs cowering and hearts pounding. *Gertie* might be heard, or felt, doubling back, her erratic flight and trail of disquiet leaving little question that this was a large craft and she was in trouble.

At least there was no question in the mind of one now-sleepless Mrs. Perkins, who sometime before 2 a.m. picked up her phone and asked the operator to connect her with the police. A moment passed, and then she was speaking with Officer Mathius O'Toole in the city of Oswego.[2] She was startled awake by a low-flying aircraft, she explained, and, as phrased in the newspaper the next day, "feared the pilot had gotten off course and was in distress." Mrs. Perkins lived in the town of Scriba, thirty miles north of Syracuse and just east of Oswego. The drone of planes overhead on any given day would have been mere background noise for her or anybody else who lived in upstate New York during World War II. Military craft of all kinds took off and landed at bases in Rome, Syracuse, and Watertown and conducted exercises over the lake. But there was nothing routine about a heavy bomber buzzing homes in a blinding snowstorm.

Within minutes after its sonic affront in Scriba, the plane neared a point where patrolman John Howley happened to be walking across a bridge over the Oswego River. The temperature was dropping; bands of snow were streaming brilliantly in the lighted sphere of streetlamps and erasing freshly made footprints. A quarter mile downriver the gale would be heard driving a procession of breakers and pack ice crashing into the frozen mouth of the river and adjoining breakwater. It would be unpleasant, but nothing out of the ordinary for a beat cop in Oswego working the midwinter graveyard shift.

Though Oswego was well adapted to lake-effect storms, the night would have been busy for public safety crews as they dealt with the weather on top of their normal wartime rounds and watches for sabotage and other shady business. With some twenty-two thousand residents, Oswego was a small city, but larger and far busier than the postindustrial place of antiquated charm today. As with the rest of the country, Oswego had been transformed by total war. It had lost thousands of young men who left to prepare for war in faraway places, but it gained many thousands more stationed at nearby bases. By day, soldiers drilled, factory workers built tanks and boilers, and, from April through November, dockworkers loaded ships with aluminum ore, newsprint, and other wartime commodities moving between Canada, New York City, and points beyond via the Erie Canal system. The place bustled with energy—not always wholesome—of young men primed for war and ancillary business that catered to their desires, boredom, and bravado.[3]

What stopped Howley in his tracks halfway over the bridge, however, was a quaking rumble rising from the opposite direction of the lake and suddenly upon him as a heavy bomber came in low and unseen. And then it was gone. Reflexively conscious that this was an event to be logged, Howley's first reaction was to look at his watch: 1:40 a.m.[4] As the patrolman hustled over the bridge to the nearest call box, a lookout at the Coast Guard station near the mouth of the river—on what would have been an otherwise mundane night possibly involving a pack of cigarettes, a pot of coffee, and a deck of cards—was also shaken to a state of high alert. A record of exactly who was at the station is lost to history, but a surviving report suggests the bomber swung over the lake before circling back inland in a southeasterly direction.[5]

By now, switchboard operators in Oswego were busy connecting more calls reporting what those at the police headquarters, on the ground floor of a lofty wood-and-brick municipal building by the river, would clearly hear for themselves. Only sheer desperation could account for the plane's random passes so low over the city. Officer O'Toole, an Oswego native and thirty-year veteran with the department, would know the city and its inhabitants as well as anybody. He had raised a sizable family here, and his vocation provided a unique vantage point to witness monumental changes that came with wartime mobilization. The graveyard shift— though always capable of spawning a certain kind of adventure—was not as restful as it used to be, and this was certainly the case tonight. A man in his mid-fifties and of formidable size—a dependable advantage in his line of work—O'Toole crouched over a teletype machine and pecked out a dispatch notifying local and state police agencies of a plane in distress over Oswego. A colleague at a nearby desk was on the phone with a Walter Moyer, of Porter Street, who was alarmed by the plane's latest pass low over the Diamond Match Factory on the river; it sounded like an engine was "cut out." Moyer, a pilot himself, was certain of this.[6] With the bulletin completed, O'Toole picked up a phone and was connected with the police station in Fulton, a city about half the size of Oswego, approximately between Syracuse and the lake.[7] Judging from reports, the plane's circling might take it over an airport operated by the Civil Air Patrol in the nearby town of Volney. Though the airfield was closed, O'Toole's report of the unfolding emergency in Oswego, as well as reports now coming in from Fulton residents, would initiate a hasty sequence of calls from the Fulton police chief to local heads of the Civil Protection Unit and Civil Air Patrol. In subsequent minutes, a dispatch was passed up and down the chain of command: the Volney airport must be lit.

Back in Oswego, Captain Conger Brown at the Public Affairs Office at Fort Ontario—the nearby Army base—was now on the phone with O'Toole. Army officials were in regular and not always cordial contact with police, mostly about jurisdictional issues entailing conflicts between soldiers and civilians—often originating with men fighting over women at bars—and other matters of public safety.[8] On this occasion, however, Captain Brown was keenly interested in O'Toole's briefing. While the nearby communication towers of Rome and Syracuse were connected to the network of traffic controllers and Army bases that had been fruitlessly attempting to track 047 for the last eight hours, Fort Ontario, with no communication tower or landing field, would be out of the loop. Though unaware of circumstances of the lost aircraft, where it was from or who was looking for it, Brown knew the sound of a multiengine bomber, and he sensed impending disaster.[9]

The CAP airport in Fulton was closed, but chances of a safe outcome would be better there than wherever else the plane might end up. The men were in agreement on that. Yet O'Toole's report that the Fulton police chief was drumming up CAP officials to turn the lights on apparently did not inspire confidence. A bonfire at the end of the runway, Brown suggested, would be the quickest and surest way to signal the crew.[10] Though Brown lacked jurisdiction in the matter, O'Toole assured the captain he would relay his advice to authorities in Fulton.

As the storm gathered in the early hours of February 18, residents of northern New York slept, with the usual exceptions: police, snowplow drivers, shift workers, switchboard operators, watchmen, and rail workers. Rail travel, both freight and passenger, was still in its heyday, and the New York Central line was a massive and critical piece of infrastructure moving personnel, passengers, and freight throughout the Great Lakes and mid-Atlantic region. All those functions were now augmented by the business of war.

Earnest Spink, a worker at a switching station in Richland, twenty-five miles east of Oswego, held a position known in railroad argot as trackwalker. While trackwalkers did, in fact, walk sections of track as part of their daily inspections long before computers automated that job, they were also responsible for myriad other tasks related to functions of a given length of rail. In addition to the usual schedule of maintenance and lookouts for signs of failure and wartime sabotage, Spink would be focused on any number of ways the sudden and unexpected storm might affect operations on his watch.[11]

A sign that things were amiss came not from any of the tasks related to infrastructure and switches, however, but from a low-frequency dissonance from the east. Spink well knew the sound of an approaching locomotive and perhaps would have been seized with alarm or confusion before realizing this was not one. It might take him an instant more to place the sound as that from a multiengine plane. And maybe another moment to ponder briefly why it was so damned low. As with Officer Howley on the bridge in Oswego, not being able to see the plane as it bore down would be nothing less than unnerving. Perhaps resisting the instinct to duck or run for cover, or perhaps simply frozen, he looked up and saw the wink of navigation lights, red and green, pass directly overhead, or so he later reported.

That report places Spink with his colleague Edward Martin, though it does not preserve whatever oath or profanity might have passed between the two. The plane would have come and gone before they had much time to react, let alone process what was happening. Aside from the craft's alarming proximity to the ground and Spink's later report that the engines "were laboring," the most enduring memory from this event—a point later fruitlessly studied and analyzed for generations—was that it came from the east, the vicinity northeast of the Syracuse airport, near Rome. It was flying west or northwest, which, if it maintained course, would have taken it over eastern Lake Ontario. It was 2:15 a.m.

Where the plane flew from there or how long it stayed in the air is anybody's guess. But no consideration of the question would be complete without accounting for a tale passed down in eastern lakeshore communities.

Approximately ten miles west of Richland, in the general direction *Gertie* flew after passing over the rail workers, a stone lighthouse overlooks the mouth of the Salmon River at Port Ontario. Built in 1838 during a maritime boom in that region, it had served as a guide to countless vessels and desperate captains seeking safe passage. As the lost plane circled over Oswego County, a final fantastic chapter in the structure's functional history, latent with the possibility of disaster or triumph, hinged on the outcome of an argument between the keeper and his teenage son.

Figure 5.1. The Selkirk Lighthouse, built in 1838 at the mouth of the Salmon River at Port Ontario, is a landmark at the southeast end of the lake. When a large airplane was heard circling blindly overhead, an argument was said to have flared between the keeper and his son as to whether to light the lamp in hopes of providing a reference point for the pilot and crew. National Park Service.

Though the lighthouse had been decommissioned, it was well kept by the owners, the Heckle family, who had converted it to an inn and maintained the light as a distinguishing attraction. Sometime in the early hours of the morning—the exact time is not known—Joseph Heckle was roused from sleep by the approaching plane. Heckle, seventeen years old and a year away from entering the service himself, quickly arrived at the conclusion others had reached that night: the craft was low and in trouble. But where Oswego residents sensed pending disaster, Joseph felt a rush of ambition. Ports were closed in midwinter, and lighthouses were not generally lit. Over the undeveloped eastern end of the lake, the pilot would be lost in a literal inland sea of darkness and snow. Unless Joseph Heckle lit the lamp.

Heckle's father, also wide awake and quick to surmise the situation, agreed the lamp would provide a singular reference for pilot and crew. For that reason, he could not allow it. Not at all. It would do no good, his father said. It would give the lost flier a bearing, the son argued. It would only serve to confuse, the father insisted. There was no place to land. More words were exchanged. The sound of the plane's engines faded and then perhaps grew louder as it circled, provoking urgency in the son's argument. Surely the light could be seen from some distance in the air, even in the snow.

"By God," the father said with finality, "if you light that lamp that plane is liable to end up right here in our kitchen!" The conversation ended.[12]

Had it been lit, Ponder or his crew might have seen the beacon and recognized it for what it was—the last point overlooking a vast water body. It could have been precisely the kind of reference for which the crew searched, illuminating their error, putting them back on track. Then again, the lighthouse lamp operated on the same principle as a rotating aerodrome beacon. Ponder or one of his men, by now thoroughly disoriented, judgment worn by fatigue and desperation, and maybe hypothermia, might well mistake it for a signal from an airfield, and the wide frozen mouth of the adjoining Salmon River, a landing strip. In that case, what the crew might take as their last best chance could have indeed led to an outcome resembling the lighthouse keeper's fears.

The light remained unlit. The lost plane flew on.

While the elder Heckle prevented his son from attempting to signal the plane, a team of rescue workers gathered near Fulton to do just that. The Civil Air Patrol field in the town of Volney was the pride of Oswego County, built by the local workforce and staffed by instructors at Oswego State Teachers College to augment the wartime pool of aviators. It represented a $500,000 public investment, $8.4 million in today's dollars, with a control tower and offices overlooking two four-thousand-foot runways—large enough to accommodate any plane of the time. Most impressively, it had runway lights. As with other wartime projects across the home front, it was a showcase of community esprit de corps. Some thirty thousand people had gathered at its grand opening that fall for a parade and air show, parachute jumps, and airplane rides offered to the highest contributors to a war bond rally.[13] Now, in the middle of a storm in the dead of night, the field was dark and still, save for the swirl of snow and reflection of oscillating red-and-yellow lights projected from a plow and several emergency vehicles filing into the parking lot. From the vehicles came men who set about their assignments while casting occasional glances to the sky. A bonfire had been suggested, and hasty preparation may have been under way with discussion of wind direction, optimal location, and a source of gasoline. The execution of any plan, however, would await sanction of a Civil Air Patrol officer now being driven to the airport in a squad car equipped, as later reported by the local newspaper, with two-way radio. Soon that person, Ray Green, stepped out and trudged through the snow.[14] Green was an electrician by trade and the plant engineer at a large paper mill—qualifications that no doubt brought him to this place at this moment—and gasoline and fire had no part in his intentions. Fiddling with a ring of keys, he unlocked the door to a utility building and flicked on its lights. After brief study of an array of control boxes, and with confident movements, he threw several impressive-looking switches. He may have heard a shout of approval over the potent hum of transformers as the aerodrome beacon flashed on, followed by a dim glow along the four-thousand-foot runways that gradually intensified as the lights warmed through the snow.

Inside the control building somebody was dialing in radio frequencies, and after some minutes, Green and the supporting team began piecing together the circumstances of the lost aircraft. It was now well after 2 a.m. Colonel Banks's order to bail out was still being broadcast blind every few minutes. Cigarettes were lit. Coffee was made. For the next three hours the rescue party listened for the drone of engines and awaited their cue for a heroic moment in local history.

It never came.

Whether in imagination or fact, 047 would make appearances over points farther north late into the night. When reports of the missing plane hit newsstands in the following days, local and state police agencies began accumulating leads from more people with a story to tell. The reports from Galloo Island, Henderson Harbor, the town of Philadelphia, and North Gouverneur, while inconsistent with the time frame of 047's known communications with Syracuse and flight over Oswego, were given added weight in the days that followed by additional accounts from North Country residents, and two reports in particular.

Sometime around 4 a.m., apparently during a break in snow squalls, a driver of a fuel truck in the Adirondack town of South Colton reportedly saw a plane's red-and-green running lights drifting over Catamount Mountain.[15] The following day, two woodsmen encamped in the area told state police they saw "lights burning" on the mountainside, presumably a signal from crew who had parachuted. The unidentified woodsmen "attempted to reach the spot but had to turn back," according to the report.[16]

A separate account, just fifty miles to the south, lent credence to the woodsmen's story. The justice of the peace for the town of Denmark, Gerald Clemons, reported an explosion in a wooded area near his farm sometime after 4 a.m. His wife and fourteen-year-old daughter were awakened moments prior to the blast by the sound of a plane passing overhead. Drifting snow prevented investigation, though he immediately notified the sheriff upon learning of the missing plane the next day.[17] Within hours, a detail of state troopers arrived on his property and began staging for a search with snowshoes and survival gear, while other parties organized in South Colton. In coming days the prospect that all or some of the crew parachuted over the Adirondacks and the plane traveled another fifty miles before crashing in the Tug Hill region would guide parties—on the ground and in the air—far into the snowy reaches of both areas.

As events unfolded, local newspapers did what they could to make the story of the missing bomber their own. Some readers feared the plane was lost over water; perhaps more believed it was lost over land; and most seemed to believe it was lost somewhere near where they lived.

Accordingly, accounts in folded newspapers tossed on the snow-covered doorsteps of northern New York in subsequent days varied in story lines and sources. Yet as each day passed and the search continued, it became clear they shared a particular error that cropped up with growing frequency. Perhaps it originated with a legitimate typo by a reporter banging away on the unforgiving keys of a Smith Corona typewriter, or maybe a deliberate slip by an inventive editor or reporter. Either way, *Gateway Gertie* became *Getaway Gertie*—and the name stuck.[18]

The fate of *Getaway Gertie*, while a featured saga for local papers, was a two- or three-paragraph brief buried on inside pages of most other newspapers, if it appeared at all amid the pressing news of the day from Europe and the Pacific. After the first hectic weeks of the search, expectations of the plane being found would gradually dissipate. As generations passed, details and then entire accounts would drift from memory; the surviving body of knowledge regarding the plane's fate, with few exceptions, would amount to imperfectly recounted fragments of tales, worn and burnished like beach glass found around a lakeshore campfire. These fragments—iterations of accounts found in newspaper morgues, stories of people now deceased, and research guarded by a few freelancing parties of war buffs and wreck seekers—reside vaguely and latently in pockets of public consciousness today. In short, the story of the lost bomber and crew is kept by an assortment of workaday people rather than historians, to the extent it is kept at all.

One story holds that Ponder and his crew, searching for landmarks on the featureless snowscape below, spotted train tracks and attempted to follow them to Syracuse or another metropolitan landmark that might set them back on course.[19] When seen by Earnest Spink—the trackwalker— the plane, engines laboring, was headed west over a rail line that approached the lake before veering south. The lost crew might be found if only a thorough enough search were to be mounted along the trajectory over the lake.

That may be a reach, but the theory is not without contextual merit. The use of rail lines as navigational tools (as with bonfires for landing beacons) was a celebrated tactic in the early days of flight when the term "iron compass" became part of aviation nomenclature. Stories abound of heroes following the iron compass in and out of hostile territory during wartime, or of it guiding mail pilots cross-country. In *Gertie*'s case the tale resonates, perhaps, because it conjures the kind of steely nerved ingenuity and skill one would expect from "our boys" of World War II, coupled with potent images of rail and flight: symbols of leaving home and coming home, markers and connectors, peril and safety.

Or maybe it resonates because it's true. The New York Central did in fact connect points where the plane was said to be heard in Philadelphia and Richland, and from there the rails did lead—if indirectly—to bases in Rome and Syracuse. The Liberator was capable of flying as slow as 110 mph, and a skilled pilot could bring it one hundred feet or less from the ground. Snow bands of varying intensity would have come and gone through the night, and a gibbous moon was up, perhaps allowing enough ambient light during periodic lulls in the storm for the crew to make out certain features of the terrain. With no other options, it may have warranted a try.

For years, Ruth Spink, niece of the trackwalker in Richland and a lifelong Oswego County resident, heard the story of the iron compass. And she dismissed it as nonsense. There were few if any lights along railroads, or roads for that matter, passing through these remote stretches of northern New York. Following train tracks in a storm at night, even from a height of one hundred feet, would have been futile if not impossible. She informed a reporter for the *Oswego Palladium-Times* of this on the fiftieth anniversary of the plane's disappearance. She did have her own convictions of what happened, however, and they were not lacking in elements of tragic romance.

She was in her thirties and a resident of Oswego when the plane was lost, and it was obvious—at least in her memory—that the pilot was circling low, searching for a place to land. In that regard her account squares with news reports of the day, with a few exceptions. In Ruth's version, the delay in lighting the CAP airport near Fulton was displaced with the notion that, because of bureaucratic bungling, the airport was never lit at all. It was this failure, and none other, that ultimately cost the airmen their lives. The pilot intentionally flew the plane over the lake, she maintained, to avoid crash landing in a populated area.

"Neighbors were upset because they felt eight men didn't have to die," she told the *Palladium-Times* reporter. Her version of the story ended with something of a moral. Because of the tragedy, she said, "a spare key was made and kept nearby at all times."[20] Presumably, she was talking about a key to the airport, but it was an apt piece of advice in general.

Ruth's recollection was recorded in 1994. At that time, she was in her eighties. And therein lies a confounding element of the broader story: few people are now alive who can recall the events of the day in much detail, and none who actually saw the plane after it took off from Westover. Still, incidental memories, which seem to run particularly deep in the large extended Spink family, surface from time to time, and sometimes they take material form.

Seventy-five years after the plane disappeared, Frederick Spink III, nephew of Ruth Spink and distantly related to Earnest Spink, the track-walker, found a cigar box containing some of his late father's keepsakes. Among a few personal items and papers sat a small brass and stainless steel hydraulic coupling. The hardware, family history holds, came off flotsam the Army recovered from the south shore of the lake, just east of Oswego, sometime after *Gertie* was lost. The elder Frederick Spink was a gregarious presence in the community, according to his grandson. As he searched along the rocky shoreline in the days following reports of the plane's disappearance, he talked his way into a restricted zone through a family friend who was an MP. There, after milling around at a distance, he recovered and pocketed the coupling, which had fallen from a wing panel that salvage crews had dragged ashore with a large crane and loaded onto a flatbed: the wing panel itself eventually become scrap, and the coupling, a treasured piece of history. The elder Spink was said to have cherished the memento and dedicated a cubby in his toolbox for its safekeeping. He may have seen it as a bona fide token of untold sacrifice. But to a man who keeps precious things in his toolbox, it might also be a touchstone to another iconic American value—that which gave rise to the unprecedented technological enterprise responsible for the whole imponderable reach and outcome of the war.

Spink, well into his seventies when he recovered the piece, had been a young man when the Wright brothers made history at Kitty Hawk with the first powered flight on a craft that was little more than an oversized kite with a small engine. Now, a thirty-seven thousand pound, four-engine bomber could span oceans and continents in a matter of hours, effectively making all the world a battle front. As astonishing as the Wright brothers' Flyer was, the Liberator's raw mass and form were mind-boggling by comparison. Yet even more remarkable were the warplane's massed-produced intricacies, like the piece Spink must have occasionally removed from his toolbox and turned admiringly in his fingers. It was the sum of these parts, precisely handled by untold numbers of other fingers working in harmony and speed, advancing down a line on conveyers, becoming parts of bigger parts, assemblies, and then units that collectively and seamlessly became the bomber—the one that ended up in the lake, and umpteen thousand similar military craft around the world, without which his country would be doomed.

The artifact eventually passed to Spink's son with the toolbox. The second-generation Fred Spink, who was said to be present on the beach when his father acquired the treasure, enjoyed recounting his personal connection to the lost bomber to skeptical coworkers at a food-packaging company in Fulton. By then, in the 1950s, the record of the lost bomber's last flight and missing crew had been buried in classified Army files and their story overshadowed by more salient accounts of overseas heroics and casualties that came to define America's World War II legacy. Spink's coworkers seemed no more convinced of his yarn when, unfailingly, he produced the two-inch coupling as proof.

More decades passed before Fred Spink III found the cigar box while sorting through lifetimes of accumulated possessions as he and his wife prepared for a move from Oswego County to South Carolina to be closer to their grown children. The third-generation Spink immediately recognized the keepsake and was happy to find it. By then, details of how many men went down with the plane or even what kind of plane it was had been lost in three generations of forgetting, but the younger Fred vividly recalled his aunt's story of the pilot crashing into the lake to spare lives on land. In her version of events, which he had no reason to doubt, there had been a blackout drill in the city of Oswego, compounding the pilot's confusion and adding to the hazard and heroism of the crew's actions.

Spink, a sinewy man with flowing white hair and powerful hands, discussed these memories on a summer day in 2019, while taking a break from the move. The keepsake that prompted the discussion sat on the kitchen table, which had become a small refuge in a household in the throes of transfer. Over a cup of tea, the conversation turned to war memories in general. Spink served as an Air Force mechanic in Myrtle Beach during the Vietnam War, and now a story came to mind about the time

Figure 5.2. Fred Spink III, a Vietnam War veteran, keeps a coupling thought to be from *Getaway Gertie*, recovered on an Oswego County beach by his grandfather in 1944 and passed down as an heirloom. Photo by Tom Wilber.

he was getting ready to head out on leave with a carful of his buddies. As they threw duffle bags into the trunk, Spink recalled, "the sergeant told us 'Don't stop long at the gas station with your uniforms on. You might get spit on.'"[21] It was a time when the public's transformative view of war, reflected in the daily coverage of riots and protests, was sometimes projected onto the rank and file who fought it. Certain images, perhaps didactic and surely divisive, outlast more mundane memories of military life in the 1970s.[22] And they have become emblematic of how attitudes from the Vietnam War era differed vastly from public sentiment of 1944. And today. Yet one aspect remains universal, Spink offered. "War memories are important. A lot of people who fought in Vietnam pay to go back with guided tours. They're after closure."

After awhile he excused himself to get back to work. He had much to sort though and get rid of, ranging from motorcycles to shop equipment, accumulated from his career as a mechanic. But the small brass coupling was going with him. "The junk man doesn't give things back," he said.

My own understanding of events would begin to crystallize with each story recovered from the past, including one about another father and son who reportedly found traces of the lost plane on the beach in 1944. But that would come later.

I first became aware of the story of *Getaway Gertie* during summers of my youth—in the 1960s—in an ancestral cottage on the east end of Lake Ontario, not far from the Port Ontario Lighthouse. I have no definitive recollection of when it entered my consciousness. Among my Oswego County ancestors and neighbors, the plane's history was likely rooted in the original flurry of news reports in local papers, the essence of which were re-remembered with reasonable and some unreasonable convictions, interpretations, or embellishments. I remember, or re-remember, a story I attribute to my uncle, himself a World War II pilot and somewhat of a raconteur, though it may have come from any number of family members of his generation: Flying at low altitude and peering out windows for identifiable landmarks, the crew—none of them familiar with the area—abruptly found themselves over the vast blackness of the lake. Disoriented and with no visible frame of reference to gauge their height, the pilot began to circle back. The plane banked steeply. A wingtip caught the water. The plane broke apart and sank.

This, I was informed, happened directly in front of our camp—a place not far from where Tim Caza and John McLaughlin's search for the wreck would, in a broad way, later intersect my own. I grew up nurturing the possibility that I crossed the crew's vanishing point, somewhere between hard reality and imperfect memory, whenever I ventured offshore in a small craft or snorkeled in the shallows. The notion that the remains of World War II airmen are entombed in a bomber—long lost and long forgotten—in a lake where I fished, swam, and took in the view while picnicking on a nearby bluff always struck me as unsettling and even a little far-fetched.

On any Memorial Day or Fourth of July, lakeshore communities are awash with visitors drawn by green-on-blue, whitecapped waters against cumulus clouds on the horizon. Amid scenes of jet skis and floaties, Frisbees and Wiffle Ball, lifeguard stations, and the smell of charcoal fires and tanning lotion, the New York State Office of Parks and Recreation proudly invites attention to the state's history. And there is plenty of it. At Sackets Harbor, near the headwaters of the Saint Lawrence River, monuments recounting American defenses in the War of 1812 abound. Fort Ontario in Oswego, once a crucial outpost defending the gateway to inland North America during colonial times, is now a museum chronicling history on the north coast. In addition to the restored Army barracks, it encompasses a well-tended cemetery with the remains of seventy-seven men, women, and children who died, many of them tragically and violently, at the old Army post. Twenty miles to the east, a state park at Mexico Point features the cordoned-off grave of American patriot Silas Towne on a tiny wooded island near a public boat launch. History shows it is here—Spy Island—where Towne's vigilance saved the day after he overheard plans by the British to take Fort Stanwix.

The absence of a plaque, memorial, or any public acknowledgment to suggest closure to the tale of the missing bomber adds to its incongruity. As with others who knew the essence of the story, there was more I didn't know as a youth, including one critical point: I couldn't name a single crew member, much less where they were from. My days of beachcombing were nurtured by the idea that the tale of the lost bomber was a remarkable and isolated event, a ghost ship shrouded in mystery, legend, and hyperbole.

Over time, I learned that what happened to Keith Ponder and crew on February 18, 1944, was nothing out of the ordinary. In fact, it was commonplace.

A Few of Fifteen Thousand

On an autumn day in 2005, amateur mountaineer Michael Nozel was ascending the Mendel Glacier in the Sierra Nevada when something strange caught his eye. At 12,600 feet there was nothing but rock and ice, and his focus was on his next foothold; yet he was periodically distracted by a flicker of motion on the periphery. As he drew closer, he found a tattered shred of material dancing and settling in the glacial wind, anchored to a prone figure protruding from the ice. The figure's head was desiccated and featureless, save for a few tufts of sandy-blond hair. An arm was melted free of the glacier. The discolored fabric that first caught Nozel's attention fluttered from a deteriorated pack strapped to the corpse.[1]

Upon learning of the discovery, rangers at the Kings Canyon National Park searched reports for any reference to a missing paraglider, hiker, or other signs of a recreational adventure gone awry. They found nothing. The corpse's clothing, however, appeared to be military, according to Nozel and his climbing companion Mark Postle, and looked to be from another era.

The Sierra Nevada, with localized and unpredictable weather, treacherous changes in topography, and fierce downdrafts known to pull planes into mountains, has claimed a staggering number of fliers over the years. Park museum archivist Ward Eldredge dug out a map peppered with these crash sites, traced his finger to Mount Mendel, and found a dot below the summit on the northern flank of the mountain. The corresponding index number led Eldredge to a file in the recesses of storage. There, five hundred linear feet of records held a single, thin folder on the matter at hand. Inside, he found a typed label pasted on a four-by-four-inch scrap of aluminum:

U.S. ARMY AT-7 41-21079. Missing 18 November 1942. Found 24 September 1947 in Mendel Glacier (Darwin Canyon). Based at Mather Field. 4 on board. All buried at National Cemetery—San Bruno, California.[2]

The AT-7—short for the Beechcraft AT-7 Navigator—is a twin-engine plane that was used to train navigators during World War II. The reference and the dates provided a line of inquiry to Nozel's discovery, but hardly put the matter to rest. The national cemetery in San Bruno would be the Golden Gate National Cemetery, and if all four airmen were there, who was the person on the glacier, and where was the plane?

In time, public interest in this sliver of history would briefly eclipse all other subjects voluminously cataloged in the park's archives since 1890. "If there is a logic to that," Eldredge later reflected, "it's the force of remembrance. That's what carried the day." The force of remembrance overcoming the inertia of oblivion.

After several days consumed by a weather delay, rangers and a military forensic anthropologist arrived at the site by helicopter. They set about their work, chipping and digging around the corpse with ice tools—allowing a wide berth to capture pieces or items possibly hidden in the snow near or under the body. By nightfall, they had freed the remains encased in a rectangular four-hundred-pound mass of ice. They slipped a body bag around it, loaded it into a helicopter, and flew it to the Fresno County Coroner's Office, where it was placed on a tray and slowly thawed.

The autopsy revealed a Caucasian male twenty to twenty-five years old, with blond or light brown hair, in attire suggesting he was an aviation

Figure 6.1. A team of park rangers and a military archaeologist secure remains of an unidentified AAF flier found entombed in ice on Mount Mendel in 2005. National Park Service, Sequoia and Kings Canyons National Parks.

cadet from World War II. There was uncertainty as to his height, recorded between five-foot-nine and six-foot-two. Multiple fractures showed he died instantly, though he was not burned. The pack was an undeployed parachute made of silk—standard issue in the early 1940s before nylon was completely phased in following embargos against Japanese silk. His pockets held forty-five cents in dimes and pennies, none dated later than 1942, a Sheaffer fountain pen, the unreadable remnants of three leather address books, and a black plastic comb. A name tag was too corroded to read, although some letters were visible. There were no other legible clues for identification.[3]

Circumstances suggested a World War II training death. Yet, as with *Getaway Gertie*, investigators would encounter a record that was fragmented, incomplete, and contradictory. After sixty-three years, any conscious memory of the event was as hopelessly elusive and scattered as the AT-7 itself, pieces of which might be found, with some extensive searching, by anybody with the wherewithal and gumption to climb Mount Mendel. And upon finding this evidence of a lost past, viewers still might not quite grasp what, exactly, they're looking at.

The failure of US Army AT-7 41-21079 to return from a training flight on November 18, 1942, was undoubtedly tragic for the families and personnel involved but, in the grand scheme of things, hardly noteworthy. It was eleven months after Japan's attack on Pearl Harbor triggered the United States' pivotal commitment to the bloodiest war in history. World War II epitomized a concept aptly known in history books as *total war*, and it unfolded on an unprecedented scale. More than four hundred thousand American soldiers, most in the prime of their lives, would meet their end in battle or training for battle. Other countries fared far worse—the Soviet Union alone suffered *ten million* combat deaths. The number of war dead globally fell in the *sixty million* range, more than two-thirds of them civilians claimed by genocide, persecution, and bombings.[4]

Americans—favoring a policy of neutrality following World War I— had initially stood by as Axis forces invaded Europe and the Pacific.[5] But after their own vulnerability to conquering armies was graphically exhibited at Pearl Harbor, every available mineral, agricultural, technological, and human resource the country could muster was redirected to the war effort. The Office of Production Management froze the sale and delivery of new cars so that automobile companies could dedicate factories exclusively to production of airplanes and military vehicles. Other factories large and small adapted their lines from household goods to munitions and supplies: fine china companies produced ceramic land mines; washing machine companies made antiaircraft gun mounts; typewriter manufacturers made rifles.[6] Farmers, after years of dealing with Depression-era surpluses that drove down prices, found the burgeoning US military a voracious consumer of all the dairy, meat, and grain they could produce.

Patriotism ran high, and civilian energy was effectively channeled into any number of paramilitary organizations tasked with protecting the home front, building morale, and supporting military operations. Participation became a point of pride and sometimes status for civilians who could not enlist.[7] Municipal branches, corporations, and a legion of volunteers were marshaled through the Civil Defense Corps as military adjuncts— identifying and reporting aircraft seen overhead, monitoring rationing and reclamation drives, encouraging material sacrifices, educating soldiers, selling war bonds, watching for sabotage, coordinating air raid blackouts, and training for search and rescue, chemical decontamination, first

Figure 6.2. By 1943, Onondaga Pottery, makers of fine china and glassware, was repurposed to design and manufacture land mines that defied metal detectors—one of many examples of how US industry was retooled to supply the war effort. This ad boasting of the company's contribution to the war effort appeared in the September 1944 *American Restaurant* magazine. Courtesy of Stephanie Vincent.

aid, and any number of other paramilitary functions.[8] Moreover, civilians, as well as soldiers, were on the move. More than thirty million Americans—nearly one in four—relocated during the war, many of them from rural areas. Trains and bus stations teeming with young people bidding farewell to their prewar lives provided an enduring symbol of the times. As people moved to aircraft and shipbuilding industries, scientific centers, and military bases, farm populations fell by about 20 percent during the war, while metropolitan areas and suburbs increased by 20 percent and 30 percent respectively, with the largest gains in the South and West.[9]

US government spending grew by a factor of ten during the country's mobilization for World War II, with its influence over the country's citizenry reaching even beyond the lofty ambitions of the New Deal.[10] There was a good chance anybody not counted as a war volunteer or booster was among the sixteen million people—including twelve million soldiers—employed by the US military or tens of millions more employed to supply the war effort. Government partnered with industry to build ships, planes, weapons, camps, barracks, bases, auxiliary fields, bombing and gunnery ranges, warehouses, training areas, and housing for a country of newly mobilized workers, soldiers, and their families.

Some top-secret projects—and there were many—were among the most impactful. By war's end, the Manhattan Project alone would grow to more than 130,000 civilian workers at dozens of sites on hundreds of thousands of acres seized by eminent domain.[11] The Pentagon, perhaps the most enduring representation of our modern military establishment, was completed in 1943, its sprawling cement construction dictated by a steel shortage and the defensive imperative for a low profile.[12]

All these changes were accompanied by no small degree of social upheaval, including racial turmoil fueled by institutionalized discrimination and social injustice. Racism was pervasive, most visibly against Blacks in the Jim Crow South, while US citizens of Japanese descent throughout the country were detained and interred. A backlash of resentment from African Americans subject to the hypocrisy of being called on to serve as "defenders of freedom" in a county that denied them fundamental rights is articulated deftly in the epitaph attributed to a Black draftee: "Here lies a black man killed fighting a yellow man for the glory of a white man."[13]

As dramatic as the changes were to the social and physical American landscape, one of the most noticeable transformations was overhead.

Every day brought an air show of sorts, over big cities and small towns, featuring planes of all shapes and sizes—bombers, fighters, trainers, and cargo planes. Some were fresh off the assembly line, paired with pilots and crews who had camped out on cots while awaiting finishing touches and final inspection of their crafts; others were approaching obsolescence or relegated for training after extensive duty.[14] Mostly piloted by novices tasked with becoming experts within months, they flew cross-country, practiced formations, waged mock battles, and bombed targets. Sometimes on an hourly basis, somewhere in the country, planes fell from the sky, flew into mountains, collided on runways, or simply vanished.

On the day the AT-7 disappeared with its crew of four in the Sierra Nevada, plane crashes at military bases in Georgia, Alabama, Texas, Ohio, and California killed eight other airmen—making November 18, 1942, a very ordinary day for training fatalities. In the three years and nine months of America's World War II engagement, 7,100 fatal crashes of military aircraft stateside—more than five a day—would claim 15,530 lives.[15] "It's interesting to note," researcher Anthony Mireles points out, "that the AAF lost over 4,500 aircraft in actual combat against Japanese army and naval air forces, at the same time losing over 7,100 aircraft in the states while moving airplanes around and teaching people how to fly."[16] The fatalities (and even greater numbers of nonfatal accidents and injuries) would come with mechanical malfunctions, judgment lapses, communication breakdowns, fatigue, inexperience, and frequent weather surprises, compounded by the sheer numbers of planes and fliers in fixed spaces.

The majority of the stateside accidents occurred out of public view and received scant news coverage compared to inspirational and more dramatic battle losses. To this day, downed World War II aircraft of all types are being discovered in unlikely places, including scores of fighter planes littering the bottom of Lake Michigan, somewhere below whatever point on the lake they missed their marks attempting to land on the USS *Wolverine*—a passenger steamship repurposed as an aircraft carrier for training.[17]

Most crashes went largely unnoticed, yet some were public spectacles. Such was the case, for example, on a spring day in 1942 when airplane parts rained over Teaneck, New Jersey, after two P-40F Warhawks collided at twelve thousand feet. One plane sheared off the back of a garage and burst into flames; the other plowed nose-first in the middle of the road in a nearby neighborhood "in full view of wide-eyed residents," according to one newspaper report. Several minutes later, one of the pilots drifted onto the front lawn of a home near the local high school, while the other parachuted safely into a swamp.[18] In May 1943, a Republic P-47 Thunderbolt flew into Barnard Hall at Hofstra College in Hempstead, New York. The pilot was killed. Students, on spring break at the time, were spared.[19] Weeks later, an instructor attempting to land a B-24 at the Chicago airport with spotty radio contact and poor visibility clipped a gasometer—a natural gas storage tank that, back in the day, was elevated like a water tower. This one, the largest of its kind, held twenty million cubic feet of natural gas. The twelve crew members died instantly. The concussion of the explosion and heat from the resulting fire were felt for miles.[20] Several weeks later, another B-24, crippled by engine failure, crashed into a neighborhood near Denver, Colorado. The pilot, trying for an emergency landing at the nearby Lowrey Field, managed to bring the plane down in an undeveloped space between two residential streets as people scattered. The resulting fire killed all seven crew and destroyed several structures as crowds gathered and watched from a distance.[21]

In September 1943, a Navy Grumman F4F Wildcat struck a suspension cable of the San Francisco–Oakland Bay Bridge.[22] The wings and tail sheared off and fell onto the roadway as cars swerved around the wreckage. The pilot, who had been practicing takeoffs and landings at a nearby naval air base, fell to his death into the bay with the rest of the plane. The bridge held. In Sacramento, residents going about their business one day in January 1944 were startled by an explosion overhead. They looked up to see a burning four-engine bomber list to one side and dissolve into fragments. Moments later, a lone parachute opened. The bodies of thirteen other airmen plunged to the ground with burning sections of the plane.[23] That July, a young B-24 pilot flew over his family farm in western New York to salute his hometown on his way from a training base in Kansas to the European theater. He had notified his friends and family, including his pregnant wife, of the flyover, so they were on hand to wave the bomber and crew off to war. The plane took a low pass over the town's four corners in full view of the crowd, passed low over the pilot's house, clipped the top of a tree, then another, plowed through a field, and erupted in flames. Five of the crew burned to death, including the pilot and soon-to-be father.[24]

By miracle or just outstanding luck, people on the ground escaped with their lives with these particular accidents. Others were not as lucky. Days before the crash in western New York, a pilot was guiding his Douglas A-26 Invader—a twin-engine bomber—into Portland, Maine, where his wife, holding their infant daughter, and other family awaited his arrival. One report held that the pilot was given "improper clearance" from the Portland radio range station to land. The plane could be seen briefly emerging from a dense fog over the airport at two hundred feet before disappearing again as the pilot, acting on instructions from the tower, apparently tried to abort the landing. Moments later, bystanders heard an explosion. Flames erupted over a nearby trailer park that housed ship workers and their families. Nineteen people on the ground, including young children, were killed, along with the pilot and flight engineer aboard the plane. Another twenty were injured. It was the worst aviation disaster in Maine's history. That distinction, until then, had been held by a B-17 with a crew of ten, lost and far off course, that had flown into Deer Mountain in the northern part of the state earlier that day.[25]

A year to the day prior to *Getaway Gertie*'s disappearance over upstate New York, a prototype of the B-29 Superfortress caught fire over Seattle. This was the model that would eventually end the war in the Pacific, but not before it encountered a rash of problems getting off the drawing board.[26] On this day, the test pilot could not nurse the failing craft back to the runway, and it smashed through the roof of the Frye Meat Packing Plant. The impact and resulting fire killed twelve crew, twenty workers in the plant, and a Seattle firefighter.[27]

As the war dragged on, the death toll from domestic military accidents mounted. On July 28, 1945, Lieutenant Colonel William F. Smith Jr. piloted his B-25 Mitchell bomber to the approach of the Newark Metropolitan Airport. Becoming disoriented in low-hanging fog, he took a wrong turn and crashed flush into the Empire State Building, which stood as the world's tallest building before the World Trade Center.

"Flaming gasoline and wreckage exploded through the building, smashing down people and severing elevator cables," Mireles writes. Three elevators fell more than a thousand feet, carrying passengers to their deaths. The bomber's crew were killed instantly, along with eleven civilians inside the building. Twenty-six were injured. The explosion blew the fog away from the top of the building, and for thirty minutes debris rained down from the wreckage lodged between the seventy-eighth and eightieth floors.[28]

Thumbing through Mireles's three-volume compilation of fatal stateside AAF crashes between 1941 and 1945, one might find a number of them attributable to overzealous youth making reckless decisions. Yet the vast majority involve pilots—some experienced, many not—trying to overcome breakdowns in the system: mechanical failure, unforeseen weather, faulty communications, and myriad other circumstances beyond their control, often with selfless acts of bravery. When a P-38 Lightning caught fire over a populated section of Burbank, California, the pilot, William Edwin Dyess, refused to bail out. He guided the plummeting fighter into a vacant lot and died in the crash. His decision to go down with the ship, two days before Christmas 1943, saved countless lives.[29]

The list of public tragedies goes on. But a less reported problem involved planes and crew that took off into the blue yonder and were never seen again. One emblematic case involves Gertrude Tompkins, who on October 26, 1944, hopped up on the wing of a P-51D Mustang fresh off the assembly line in Los Angeles and climbed into the cockpit. The plane was one of forty that Tompkins and her fellow Women Airforce Service Pilots were delivering to Newark, New Jersey, for deployment overseas. Tompkins finally took off, well behind the others, after a delay due to problems with the plane's canopy. Apparently there was some confusion whether she had turned back or taken off at all after the glitch, and five days passed before anybody realized she was missing. No trace of Tompkins or the plane has ever been found.[30]

The idiom "no guts, no glory" was popularized by the American military flying ace Frederick Corbin "Boots" Blesse in a fighter pilot training manual published after World War II. Yet it represents a mind-set fixed in the military flying record from the very first flight.[31] On September 17, 1908, Lieutenant Thomas Selfridge was at Fort Myer, Virginia, for trials of a craft built exclusively for the Army by the Wright brothers. He took a perch on the canvas of the lower wing of the Wright Military Flyer, next to Orville Wright and some prodigious levers, grabbed hold of a wing strut, and purchased his feet against the frame. The engine was started, the signal given, and a counterweight released from a tower, boosting the craft's acceleration down the launching rail. Moments later, Wright, with his first-ever passenger aboard, clutched the levers and banked graceful arcs around the fort as the internal combustion of the thirty-horsepower engine—a noise that had been heard with growing frequency across hill and dale—pugnaciously reverberated *above* the countryside. The plane, in contrast to vulnerable and comparatively erratic balloons and zeppelins of the day, would provide speed and agility in delivering messages between units or providing reconnaissance behind enemy lines.

The demonstration was going swimmingly until, in Wright's words, "two big thumps, which gave the machine a terrible shaking, showed that something had broken." It was a propeller. Wright shut off the power in an attempt to regain control and glide to safety, but the plane began a steep dive. Later, Wright recorded Selfridge's final moments: "Up to this time [he] had not uttered a word, though he took a hasty glance behind when the propeller broke and turned once or twice to look into my face, evidently to see what I thought of the situation. But when the machine turned headfirst for the ground, he exclaimed 'Oh! Oh!' in an almost inaudible voice."[32] The plane smashed upon impact with the ground, not far from a crowd of twenty-five thousand assembled to witness history in the making. Selfridge was pitched headfirst into the plane's framework, thus becoming the world's first airplane fatality. Although it's impossible to know what accomplishments he may have achieved had he lived, it is hard to imagine that surviving that flight would have brought the young lieutenant more substantial recognition than he received in his untimely death, "the Army's first sacrifice to the science of aviation," according to a War Department history.[33] He is buried in Arlington National Cemetery (a short distance from the crash site), memorialized by a cenotaph at West Point, and a National Guard base in Detroit is named after him. Orville Wright, hospitalized for three months with multiple bone fractures, survived and returned to Fort Myer the following year for a successful trial of the Military Flier, which the Signal Corps then bought for $30,000.[34]

From the earliest accidents came efforts to improve safety—in the case of the Wright Military Flyer, the use of headgear—though safety innovations invariably lagged behind other developments. An obvious factor was lack of experience. "As is usually the case in advances that are taking place daily in aeronautics," one Army commander observed, "there were no precedents to follow."[35] Moreover, the idea of "safety first" was

Figure 6.3. The first military training flight also resulted in the first airplane fatality. Rescuers tend to pilot Orville Wright or passenger Lieutenant Thomas E. Selfridge after the crash of the Wright Military Flyer at Fort Myer, Virginia, in 1908. National Archives and Records Administration.

often at odds with the culture of risk that ushered in every aeronautical achievement from the Wright Brothers to Lindbergh. Equipping and training an army of novices to fight an air war under urgent deadlines was a task less celebrated but proving to be no less dangerous than preceding milestones—the very embodiment of an axiom, expressed by Winston Churchill, that "there is no less likely way of winning a war than to adhere pedantically to the maxim of 'safety first.'"[36] It is fair to say safety did not come first or even second in building the AAF. In fact, a postwar study by the AAF Office of Flying Safety found that "the design of military aircraft has been predicated on many factors other than safety."[37]

Though the hazards of any given flight were perhaps less in 1942 than those tolerated in the days of the Wright brothers, technological innovations and their application to warfare were advancing rapidly, again with "no precedents to follow."[38] Inexperienced pilots were called on in unprecedented numbers to fly planes designed on "factors other than safety." Radio systems had become a crucial navigational tool, yet their operation became such a common problem that, by 1943, dire warnings to pilots were written into AAF flight manuals:

> There is one man in particular who is supposed to know all there is to know about this equipment. Sometimes he does, but often he doesn't. . . . Too often the lives of pilots and crew are lost because the radio operator has accepted his responsibility indifferently.
>
> Radio is a subject that cannot be learned in a day. It cannot be mastered in 6 weeks, but sufficient knowledge can be imparted to the radio man during his period of training in the United States if he is willing to study. It is imperative that you check your radio operator's ability to handle his job. . . . To do this you may have to check the various departments to find any weakness in the radio operator's training and proficiency and to aid the instructors in overcoming such weaknesses.[39]

The expectation that radio operators were "supposed to know all there is to know" about radio equipment, coupled with the observation that the subject "cannot be mastered" in the six weeks allocated for training, might fairly be considered specious. More accurately, the lives of crews depended on unreliable systems operated by chronically underqualified personnel. Flight officers had been duly warned about the latter.

During the earliest days of flight, every enterprise was a potential catastrophe, and Selfridge or anybody else who took the risks necessary to advance the application of the science in the public interest could rightly be considered at least brave and probably heroic. Yet, by World War II, "brave" and "heroic" were not words commanders generally lavished on the rank-and-file flier learning to fight an air war, recruited en masse from a pool of talent for which standards had been eased to boost numbers. Chuck Yeager, the flying ace who famously rose from an enlisted airplane mechanic in 1941 to a brigadier general in 1969, boasts of the heedlessness that marked his own training during World War II among "hell-raising fighter-jocks with plenty of swagger." At one point, he recounts in his autobiography, he was grounded for damaging a wing on a P-39 after intentionally trimming a farmer's tree with it "as a challenge," though he got around the punishment by flying other types of aircraft. Yeager attributes training fatalities from that era to "a gruesome weeding out process" of incompetent fliers. "When one of them became a grease spot on the tarmac," he writes, "I almost felt relieved; it was better to bury a weak sister in training than in combat."[40]

Yeager is perhaps the most venerated of World War II pilots, and no doubt his swagger portrayed in movies and books plays to appreciative audiences. His better-off-dead rationalization might be passed off as part of the act if not supported, in a more measured tone, at the highest reaches of the establishment. Henry Harley "Hap" Arnold, who trained at the Wright Brothers Aviation School only a few years after the Army acquired its first Military Flyer, became a commanding general of the AAF by the end of World War II. Preparing fliers for combat, Arnold stated, "requires that they be trained in night and bad weather flying, which, of course, raises the accident rate here, but which tremendously reduces the combat losses abroad."[41] His line of thinking is well supported by the numbers. During the first thirty-two months of the war, the AAF lost thirty-three hundred fewer planes in battle than in accidents on the home front. The toll of domestic casualties "was the price that had to be paid to achieve the air power required for victory."[42]

Many of the domestic crashes happened at or near air bases, where broken and burned young bodies were retrieved from wreckage with sad frequency. Accordingly, the number of unrecovered World War II dead stateside is small when considered as a percentage of the total who died here. Yet the raw number appears substantial. Along with *Getaway Gertie*, at least seventy-five aircraft and 250 crew are estimated to be still missing in the Continental US or off its coasts. The whereabouts of others may be obscurely known, as with the AT-7 on Mount Mendel, though their status and history are all but forgotten.[43]

After the Fresno County coroner determined that the body found on the Mendel Glacier in 2005 was a soldier from World War II, the remains were flown to the military forensic lab at Hickam Air Force Base in Hawaii for the tedious process of identification. For their part, rangers, anthropologists, and journalists started piecing together the backstory of the missing AT-7. The label on the aluminum square filed away in the national park's archive was a starting point, and it suggested mountaineer Michael Nozel was not the first to come across the crash site. Subsequent clues emerged with a review of newspaper archives, military records, and reporting by Peter Stekel, a freelance writer who, in 2005, became deeply engrossed in the story and, eventually, a central part of it.

The backstory began in the late summer of 1947, when a party of adventurous UC Berkeley students exploring the Sierra Nevada high country happened upon a piece of aluminum lodged in the scree at the base of the Mendel Glacier. Their curiosity piqued, they made their way as far as they could up the steepening slopes. Here and there they came across more metal pieces, an embedded engine part and, by and by, more disturbing telltales: a torn shoe, a name tag, a back of a watch. One of the students, William Bond, told of something that looked like shreds of flesh, possibly human, though no skeletal remains.

Sometime later, Bond led a small party of Army officials and a ranger to the site. It was late September, and though hindered by a blanket of fresh snow, they were able to recover a serial number from an engine part.[44] This, along with the tag bearing the name of one John M. Mortenson, provided sufficient evidence to identify the wreckage as the AT-7 last seen when it took off on a training flight from Mather Air Force Base, near Sacramento, nearly five years prior.

The record shows the plane carried three cadets: Ernest Glenn Munn, a coal miner's son from Farmington, Ohio, known by some female admirers as the "Blond Bomber" for his strapping physique and wavy pompadour. Leo Arvid Mustonen, a son to Finnish immigrants from Brainerd, Minnesota, was studious, always well-dressed, and, as one relative recalled, never without a comb and coins in his pocket. Less is known about John Mortenson. At twenty-five, he was the oldest of the crew by several years and reportedly was schooled in business at the University of Idaho, near his home in Moscow.[45] It is no coincidence that the cadets' last names all began with *M*, as classes were organized alphabetically and personnel grouped accordingly. They would have sat at chart tables built into the cabin of the AT-7, at work with navigational tools while taking turns directing the pilot to various waypoints along the route.

Contrary to the German practice of routinely keeping the best fliers in combat, a number of promising American pilots were assigned as instructors. Lieutenant William Gamber was one. He had a degree in mechanical engineering from Tri-State College (now Trine University), where he had been MVP of the varsity basketball team. After joining the Army in 1941,

Gamber would have proven himself one of the best in class to achieve his position. Standing six foot four with dark eyes and an easy smile, he was as comely and popular as he was skilled—hardly the intended image of Yeager's "weak sister" metaphor. "He had everything going for him," Gamber's nephew and namesake Bill Ralston told me much later. "One only imagines what he would have accomplished had he lived."[46]

Though the twenty-three-year-old Gamber lacked combat experience, his credentials spoke for themselves; moreover, he was acquainted with the weather and hazards of the mountains. He had learned to fly at Mather and subsequently logged five hundred hours leading his charges on flights from the base.

On November 18, 1942, the cadets would have been tasked with guiding the AT-7, with Gamber at the helm, south to Los Banos, north to Roseville, then farther north to Orland before turning around and heading back south to Mather.[47] Though the accident file suggests Gamber had submitted a crude plan, there is no record of radio communication after takeoff. In these respects, the final flight of the AT-7 differs somewhat from that of *Getaway Gertie*, though both would end in similar fashion. Gamber and his team—possibly trying to maneuver around changeable weather, deviating off course as part of the exercise, or perhaps lost owing to equipment failure, human error, or any combination of those factors—left so few clues, rescue parties would search vainly in the wrong spot for a month before closing the file.

Nearly five years later the college students would find the debris in Mendel Glacier, 150 miles from the southern point of Gamber's intended route. After recovering only the serial number from the engine and Mortenson's name tag in September 1947, the Army would stage a second attempt to find the bodies when the glacier was again accessible, in early autumn 1948.

Helicopters of that era could not effectively drop troops in inaccessible terrain; the party used jeeps and pack animals to get to a base camp below the cirque. Reportedly equipped with pneumatic hammers, ropes, and other gear, they set about what would be hailed as a perilous and ultimately successful mission. An Associated Press account from the day, citing official Army sources, states the bodies were recovered from an ice pack up to fourteen feet thick and "brought down from their icy crypt" in a "triumph over the elements."[48]

Families, however, received a different report. General Garrison Davidson, chief of staff at the Presidio in San Francisco, wrote to survivors concerning, as he circuitously expressed it, "the remains of the crewmen of the plane on which your son lost his life." Individual identification of the bodies was not possible, he explained, "due to the manner in which the crewmen lost their lives. Therefore, a group burial must be made."[49] Whatever individual or collective constituents the recovery party may have extracted from the glacier were laid into a single casket, and on October 15, 1948, that casket was interred at the Golden Gate National Cemetery under a headstone bearing the names of the four men.[50]

"It would be convenient to say that some dissembling went on when it came to informing the families," writes Stekel, in his 2012 book, *Final Flight*. "At worse, not telling the truth was perpetuating a fraud. But I doubt the Army people of 1948 had any other thought than to cause as little pain and distress as possible."[51]

Regardless of motives, military officials "checked the boxes [for body recoveries] in the 1940s much differently than they do today," Megan Lickliter-Mundon, an aviation archaeologist who has worked on projects associated with both the US military and private museums, told me. "What passed then would never pass now."

Short of exhuming the casket, it's impossible for those concerned with the details of such things to know what exactly is in it. One might imagine the shoe, the name tag belonging to John M. Mortenson, and any other personal effects reportedly found on the glacier as fitting surrogates. If frozen tissue or decomposed fabric embedded in the exposed mountainside proved other than a product of the students' imagination or something dropped from the talons of a raptor, the military burial would at least put these to rest with dignity and honor.

Or perhaps, as some suspect, the coffin contained only sandbags. Regardless, neither General Davidson's version of the story nor the saga that appeared in newspaper accounts of the day would square neatly with messy circumstances that would later emerge, quite literally, from the glacier.

After five months at the backlogged military forensic lab in Hawaii, the body recovered on the mountain in 2005 was identified as AT-7 crew member Leo Arvid Mustonen, the fastidious son of Finnish immigrants who was supposedly buried at San Bruno, California. Here was a tale of loss and recovery, forgotten sacrifices newly remembered, and homecoming; it resonated, as they say in the media business, and it was featured in local and national outlets.

Many among the sizable crowd gathered for the lost airman's funeral in Brainerd, Minnesota, had no direct memories or connections to the Mustonen family beyond a sense of gratitude for the man's service and sacrifice, and a compelling desire to witness his homecoming. Yet Brainerd is the kind of place where family ties run deep, and services at the First Lutheran Church featured what memories could be assembled by neighbors and distant relatives, supported by pictures of the uniformed Mustonen. The photos—of Leo squatting to strike a pose with a baby girl (a niece, since deceased); of Leo standing formally with his proud parents—are personal but also archetypical of generations of uniformed sons and daughters off to war. The most vivid image shared on this occasion, however, was not on film—it was a recollection. And it was not of Leo, but of his mother, Anna Mustonen, bearing up after learning her child would not be coming home alive or, apparently, dead. "I can see her so plainly," said a family friend, "sitting across my mother-in-law's kitchen table—my mother-in-law on one end and Mrs. Mustonen on the other—having coffee, and tears running down her face."[52]

Nearly forty years after Mrs. Mustonen passed away, a soldier in dress uniform carried a small box with her son's cremated remains to the family plot at Evergreen Cemetery.[53] There they were laid to rest, next to a mother who carried the uncertainty of her son's fate to the grave, and a father, reportedly a stoic, unable to bring himself to talk much about it. Rifles fired salutes. Taps played. With that, the story of Leo Mustonen was brought to an end, though the broader issue hardly resolved.

The discovery of Mustonen raised anticipation among families of the other missing airmen that a long-lost relative might also be coming home with a military tribute. And for some, the aching expectation that had long ago softened was again renewed.

For Lois Shriver, the youngest sister of Glenn Munn, the news in 2005 that a body had been found on the mountain where her brother's plane crashed sparked a vivid memory from sixty-four years prior: Her parents had not yet told her of her older brother's disappearance, but a man at a gas station, who had read about the missing AT-7 in a local paper, asked if she was related to "the Munn boy." His tone was foreboding, and as she took in the details of the lost plane with her brother on board, she did her best to dismiss the implications. "We naturally thought he was going to be found because at the time they said he was missing," she recalled in a 2005 interview with a Seattle newspaper. For years after, she and her two sisters had observed their absent brother's birthday. "I just missed him terribly," she added. "After that, we had kind of let it go, but we didn't forget. . . . When it wasn't him [found on the mountain], it was a big disappointment."[54]

Any expectation that the Army would send a party to resume the search on Mendel Glacier, however, would be in vain. A congressional directive has allowed approximately $150 million annually for the Defense Department to search for missing soldiers in combat zones, but no specific mandate or allocation for that job at home.[55] The Park Service, for its part, has not pursued a search because "the area is very well known and trafficked," and "it would be very unlikely to find any remains," according to a spokeswoman.[56] As with *Getaway Gertie*, future searches for remains of the AT-7 and crew would be left to others.

After Mustonen's body was found, Stekel, a naturalist who grew up exploring the Sierra Nevada, set out on his own pilgrimage to the mountain. He wanted firsthand knowledge of the setting for a magazine article, he said, and "to clear up inconsistencies and errors in the record." Finding actual wreckage to confirm reports from the 1940s would put to rest speculation that Mustonen's presence on the glacier may have been the result of an unsuccessful parachute attempt, a theory that suggested the plane may have crashed elsewhere. But other factors were also drawing him in.

"A history of a lot of these men is lost," Stekel later reflected. "But even so, there are people named after them, their pictures are on mantels. Some families have found closure. The military might do nothing because it's easier to do nothing, but also because there is no reason to stir up new grief."[57] In the case of the crew of the AT-7, however, the grief had been stirred.

A full day of hiking and a night of camping in the late summer of 2007 brought Stekel and his climbing partner, Michele Hinatsu, to the glacier's final approach. Another day negotiating slopes of rock and ice, provisioned with abundant stores of perseverance, modern GPS equipment, and perhaps an element of luck, found them studying a tangle of metal and gears exposed on the lower slope—remnants of an engine that must have migrated down from steeper terrain. Stekel wiped grease off a plate and found a serial number that matched the AT-7. Here he could touch cold hard evidence of a story that, until then, had been an abstraction of news reports and bureaucratic records.

Relishing the discovery, he began to refocus on footholds as he turned to join Hinatsu, who had resumed her survey below the engine, when he was distracted by what he mistook for a small tree. It took him a moment to consciously process the idea that trees, even the gnarled, stunted alpine variety, do not exist at this elevation. He studied the darkened form, puzzled over sunlight glinting off something on a branch. Moving closer, he realized he was looking at human remains: a figure "hunched over, his left arm curled under his body. On the third finger of his left hand, a gold intaglio signet ring of a Roman soldier."[58] The figure, wrapped in shreds of a wool olive-drab jersey, had blond hair; the bundled fabric of an undeployed parachute nested in a cluster of nearby rocks.

Years later, Stekel, a wiry, convivial figure in his late sixties known to hike with a teddy bear sticking out of his pack, paused to compose himself when relating details of the discovery. "I was fairly confident we would find airplane wreckage," he told me. "There was no way in the world I thought we would find another aviator. The discovery of Mustonen, after all these years, had been serendipitous enough. This blew me away."[59]

Seven months after the discovery, the forensic lab identified the remains as Glenn Munn, and the second of the frozen airmen of the High Sierra, as they were now known, was brought home.

On a mild spring day, Munn's three younger sisters, all well into their eighties, and a contingent of reporters watched at the Delta Airlines cargo terminal at Pittsburgh International Airport as a VFW honor guard transferred a flag-draped coffin from a plane into a hearse for Munn's trip home to Pleasant Grove, Ohio. Before the procession drove off, reporters pressed in, and Shriver, Munn's youngest sister, responded. "It's joyful in a way to think that we're really bringing him back, but it's kind of sad in a way, too," she said. "I remember him as a young boy, a young man. I don't think of him as an old person like us."[60]

Memories of that young person bubbled forth in the days that followed: Glenn Munn, joy-riding an old piece of farm equipment or blasting the radio while practicing his dance moves, delighting his sisters and irritating his father.[61] "Here comes the Blond Bomber," his sisters' friends would call. The older brother of the Munn sisters was fun, attractive, and going places; he took business classes by night and worked at a finance company during the day. When the draft was inevitable, Munn, like many of his peers, thought flying would advance his career after the war, so he joined the AAF without really knowing what he was in for.

After that, his frequent letters home reflected a youth coming of age, resolutely if not passionately embracing his duty, often homesick, and developing an acute awareness of the danger that would kill him. "We ran into a storm and came back," he wrote in his last letter.

> They don't like to fly over those very high mountains when it's stormy, because they are afraid of downdrafts forcing the plane into the side of a mountain. . . . It gives one a funny feeling to be flying in a cloud with hailstones beating against the wings and windshield when you can't see ten feet ahead of you. Not that I was scared, but I was glad when they decided we had better go back.
>
> . . . Gee, I'd like to see some Ohio winters again.[62]

After Glenn Munn's burial in Pleasant Grove, sixty-five years after his death, a headstone was removed at Golden Gate National Cemetery in San Bruno, California, and another set in its place. The updated version bears the names of William R. Gamber and John M. Mortenson. A military cemetery is, among other things, a place of order; and it's reassuring to consider that the memory of the service of those two individuals has a placeholder, at least, among waves of markers rising and falling in impressive geometric unison over the rolling landscape.

Two hundred and fifty miles to the southeast, granite peaks rise like cathedral spires around a cirque below the summit of Mount Mendel—a place of entropy. The extreme pitch, elevation, and northern exposure shelters this recess from heat and light. Yet, at certain times of the year, the sun, cresting high enough to clear the summit, reflects off pieces of aluminum set in receding glacial ice.

7

SEEKERS

It was some years after Glenn Munn's body was reclaimed from the glacier atop Mount Mendel that Tim Caza and John McLaughlin searched for the grave of Keith Ponder and crew at the bottom of Lake Ontario. The pair proceeded with their dive at a point several miles off the southeast shore, guided by a grainy sonar image suggesting a craft with features of a B-24 was mostly buried in sediment, though parts of it remained visible.

After plunging off the swim platform, Caza was quickly out of range of a drop camera suspended over the side, leaving McLaughlin searching vainly for form and movement in a screen of blue-green haze animated with drifting sediment. After a few minutes he gave up and refocused his attention outside the boat. Clusters of bubbles drifted amorphously around the anchorage, suggesting to the practiced eye the dive was progressing smoothly, or at least safely.

McLaughlin is a bear of a man with a broad neck, sloping shoulders, pale blue eyes, and a neatly barbered crown. Prior to retirement, he spent most of his days with the ironworkers local, building or main-taining infrastructure at one of the two nuclear power plants in Os-wego County. Though similar in blue-collar backgrounds and Oswego County upbringing, McLaughlin and Caza had arrived at this point from divergent paths.

Caza, from the time of his youth, was driven by the simple promise of discovery. In an age when oceans had been crossed, continents mapped, mountains climbed, and celestial bodies explored, the retired UPS worker was one of very few souls who, through his own ingenuity and persever-ance, could still go, or at least see, where no living individuals had been. For his part, McLaughlin, the retired volunteer fire chief, had begun div-ing as a young EMT for the Brewerton Fire Department on the Oswego River. For him, diving is less about finding wrecks than, in his words, "looking for people who don't come back . . . doesn't matter if it's a kid at a campground or an airman from World War II."

The wind freshened—a possible precursor to a shift onshore and waves that gather and build across open water from the west, even in fair weather. But after a few minutes the breeze settled back from the southeast, in the direction where, some miles off, the eclectic assortment of camps dotting the shore gradually give way to stretches of vacant beaches and estuaries.

From the locker above the helm, McLaughlin retrieved the crisply folded American flag sealed in plastic. Over the course of a public safety career spanning forty-five years, he had participated in far less pleasant scenes, often played out in front of family members broken by grief, hud-dled in staging areas on riverbanks or lakeshores while divers set about their grim duty with tanks, flippers, and hooks. This day's enterprise was a different drill. The grief was no longer palpable, and the mission lacking in urgency. The survivors were unknown to him, and the recovery of victims not part of the plan. Nobody waited breathlessly on shore for the out-come, but the essence of it, in his mind, was the same. Indeed, McLaughlin half expected this day to bring an end to his diving career of forty-some years. It would mark a terminus, of sorts, but discovery of the lost tomb would undoubtedly raise new questions. After generations of wondering where, the question would be, now what?

Discovery might be close at hand, but experience and temperament also prepared him for another outcome. He was ready to learn that what he and Caza thought was the Twenty-Four was not the Twenty-Four, maybe not even a plane. He would not be entirely surprised if it proved to be some workaday item—a piece of manufacturing machinery, a boiler, a prefabricated building truss—that becomes a diving oddity when separated from its transport. He had been puzzled by more than a few vestiges of Rust Belt enterprise, neither nautical nor aeronautical, littering the lake's bottom. Half buried and disguised by rocks and sunken logs, aligned with other shapes, arrestingly unfamiliar, they become a kind of Rorschach test for expectant minds projecting order onto randomness and seeing a rare artifact, a B-24, the Holy Grail, in an otherwise unimpressive piece of junk.

The sun rose higher and played off the water. McLaughlin looked at his watch. The train of bubbles became stationary and more concentrated before erupting at the diving platform. Caza had been down for twenty-five minutes. He shook his head as he removed his mouthpiece: "Nothing," he said.

"Nothing," echoed McLaughlin, in a note hanging between expectation and resignation. Caza climbed onto the platform and began shedding gear. "Unless the bottom can be counted as something," he said. "Plenty of that." McLaughlin helped Caza with harness and buoyancy belt. Then he returned the flag to the locker above the captain's wheel. He let out a chuckle. . . . There was no end to the wonder.

If the men were discouraged, they didn't much show it as they went about stowing gear. After all, the result of the dive was no different from many less-anticipated but equally puzzling outcomes that make up an outsize aspect of any explorer's career. They had opened a box to find another box, and the discovery prompted a new avenue of conjecture. If they were off the mark, Caza reasoned, they were not far off. Nailing coordinates in ninety feet of water from a drifting boat was not remarkably difficult, given their experience and electronics, but by no means was it a sure thing. Nor was examining the lakebed through the frame of a diving mask, yard by yard with few points of reference, while limited by time and buffeted by current. It was a familiar drill, and they excelled at it; conditions this day were ideal. But they couldn't rule out that Caza had missed it.

The sonar image suggested a thing of material dimension and substance firmly embedded. Caza could have missed it; more likely, whatever it was, it was now entirely buried. On this part of the lake especially, sandbars and silt shape-shift with waves spawned by prevailing westerlies across a 190-mile fetch—sometimes enough to sculpt the soft lakebed, even at ninety feet. It was precisely this sort of gale that had prevented an immediate return to the site after Caza first captured the image on sonar. What the lake might yield at any given time, both divers knew, was up to the whims of nature.

As they considered these possibilities, they had to allow for another: through an error of transposition or notation, they could be in the wrong spot.[1] Caza could go back down for another look, but time would be better spent, they decided, working from the boat. Debris fields can span acres, and if wreckage was buried in one place, it may be exposed in another. Electronics would be deployed. But first, lunch.

Voyager was well equipped and meticulously organized but not especially large, and now deck space became more precious as Caza retrieved a small cooler from the cuddy and set several burgers sizzling on a portable grill on the stern locker, next to a bright yellow torpedo-shaped sonar fish that Caza had made from a piece of PVC pipe fitted with fins and a nose cone. The discussion turned to equipment. Caza's hobby, if it could be called that, already ate voraciously into his budget, but a certain urge had just grown stronger for a sub-bottom profiler—a sonar system that can penetrate sand and silt. It's expensive, with considerable limitations, but he found the mere idea of researching and building one a tonic for morale.

After lunch, with McLaughlin at the wheel, Caza released his sonar fish over the gunwale and took a step back with his hands on his hips. Cable unspooled evenly at the stern as the device parted from the boat and disappeared from the surface. Satisfied that all was running fair, Caza took the helm. With one eye on the monitor, he aligned the boat's course on the chart plotter and adjusted speed to tow the probe at the optimal depth, explaining the process to McLaughlin, who would later share in the piloting. They would overlap the area where the missing target had registered and work their way out from there.

The transducer housed in the fish began transposing sound waves into visuals on the monitor—silent, gliding form conveying more a sense of motion than definitive shape. The effect is eerie, and fascinating—for a time. Inevitably, sonic shadows on an empty lakebed, devoid of color or vitality, become as compelling to an expectant observer as a vacant wall at an art show. Boredom courts distraction, and distraction can be costly; something big could slip under their noses. For this reason, monitors on Caza's boat are large and prominently positioned—one to show the boat progressing along its charted course, others to show the scan.

As the day wore on with no sign of the lost bomber in the lake, it began taking shape in conversation. Caza was the provider of technology that enabled the search, McLaughlin the keeper of the story that compelled it. The tale of *Gertie*, as assimilated by McLaughlin, bears a patina wrought in fact, missing fact, and informed conjecture, burnished by his impressive command of what's known and skepticism over what's not.

Decades before internet search engines put such things at our fingertips, McLaughlin had begun amassing a paper file on the specifics of the Twenty-Four (as he prefers to call it) and its final flight on February 18, 1944. The dossier includes technical renderings, manuals and schematics detailing the craft's architecture and physical properties; accident reports, newspaper accounts, and military records; and well-worn legal pads filled with notes from interviews with lakeshore old-timers and, over the course of decades, their surviving sons and daughters, friends, and neighbors. In this manner, McLaughlin has amassed an unabridged history of the lost plane from a combination of credible sourcing and local legend, not unfit for comparison to his favorite Clive Cussler novel.

The novel, *Vixen 03*, is about a military plane that disappears with a top-secret cargo during the Cold War. *Vixen 03* remains "lost" for a reason, until protagonist Dirk Pitt unsuspectingly comes across salvaged airplane parts in a garage while vacationing at a cottage on a Colorado lake. One clue leads to the next, and a sonar scan by Pitt, whose day job is special projects director for the National Underwater and Marine Agency, reveals a plane in the lake. He makes the dive to investigate and discovers *Vixen 03*. Only somebody has gotten there first.

And the plot thickens from there.

That a B-24 Liberator crashed into a lake in upstate New York during World War II is less surprising to McLaughlin than the presumption that, after all these years, nobody has found it. As cast in local legend, the Twenty-Four has not one story line but many, any one of which might fit a Cussler mystery, as far as McLaughlin is concerned.[2] Some involve

Figure 7.1. John McLaughlin participates in a recovery dive in an icy tributary of Lake Ontario sometime in the early 1970s. It was about this time that he first heard the story of the lost B-24 from his diving colleagues when he was a young EMS technician. Courtesy of John McLaughlin.

the plane's disappearance, others the alleged discovery of crew or craft. McLaughlin knows them all. There's the case of human remains said to have washed ashore at Southwick Beach on the lake's east end in the 1960s; the story of rotted cords and a harness hanging from a tree in an inaccessible section of woods near the south shore; and the fabled report of the outline of a massive aircraft spotted in the murky depths off Oswego, beyond reach of most recreational divers.

As tenuous as these leads might be, McLaughlin, perhaps channeling his inner Dirk Pitt, approaches each with due diligence and an open mind. He knows better than anybody that the lake has claimed countless bodies, some forgotten with time or, sadly, never missed to begin with. On occasion the dead will emerge in various states of decomposition in unexpected places, including at least one instance that explains the report at Southwick Beach some years ago, but none identified by public records as the Twenty-Four's crew.[3]

McLaughlin's shoe-leather inquiries once led him to a lifelong resident of Shore Oaks, ten miles east of Oswego, who earnestly reported seeing the parachute cords—or something that surely looked like parachute cords—hanging from a willow tree in a wooded marsh some distance from his house. He and his friends, as children, used to make pilgrimages to the place. But that was many years ago. Today the exact spot remains elusive, as does permission to access the private property.

The oldest and most persistent tale concerns the submerged aircraft and divers purportedly unwilling to disclose its whereabouts or unable to find it a second time. Recreational divers, McLaughlin knows, can be notorious BSers . . . unless they're not. In which case it's possible they came across the Twenty-Four, or any of several other military aircraft or drones used for training that sometimes ended up in the lake.[4]

Regardless of origin, these and other scraps of oral history have taken root in the silt of conscious memory. Whether conflations, simple misunderstandings, or outright falsehoods, they beckon with the promise of discovery, which in diving circles represents a kind of currency, and McLaughlin gives them their fair due.

One story stands out above all others, however, and it happens to be a matter of record. On February 24, 1944, nearly a week after Ponder's last static-filled radio contact with the tower, a wing section of a large craft, buoyed by empty fuel tanks, was spotted drifting just off the shores of

Oswego County, four miles east of the harbor. The discovery and subsequent salvage of the part, verified by media accounts and Army records, have served as a solitary point of reference for wreck seekers ever since. Because items adrift in Lake Ontario tend to move eastward on prevailing winds and currents, most parties have looked for the lost plane to the west and north of this point.

McLaughlin and Caza are quite familiar with this bit of history, as well as the lake's tendencies. Yet on this day they were combing a grid well to the east. If whatever they had found buried in the sediment turns out to be the Twenty-Four, its resting place defies conventional wisdom and, some would say, the laws of nature.

The day slid by. The men switched turns at the helm and continued on course, east northeast, before coming about yet again on a vector parallel to and slightly overlapping the previous one. Caza was pouring coffee, his favorite beverage though not for want of energy, when McLaughlin nodded to a form scrolling into view on the monitor. Both men stood transfixed for a moment before Caza pointed out the subtly shifting outline of the image. "Baitfish," he said. "They do that."

With each about-face, the sun hung noticeably lower over the water. At dusk, beach fires appeared and grew brighter as distinguishing features of the shoreline faded. Now and then a Roman candle or skyrocket streamed over the water, followed, with a moment's delay, by whistles and pops. Inside the confines of *Voyager* the monochrome rendering of the lakebed floated by like a recurring dream.

Caza often searched through the night when conditions were good, but this evening other business was calling him home. After a final pass, he and McLaughlin retrieved the gear, carefully stowed it, throttled up, and were eventually within sight of the channel lights. The day's effort had produced no new signs of the target. Still, they counted it as time well spent in the service of their quest. The lake had remained workably calm, and they had logged a sizable area, adding incrementally to Caza's survey of the lake bottom. They were sure they would be back.

"You've got to understand things don't happen when or where you want them to happen." McLaughlin will later tell me this as I study Caza's screen shot of the sonar rendering for myself, perhaps seeing in it what I believe is there and expect others to see, like the form of the Blessed Virgin vaguely manifested in a knot of wood or stain of blood, obvious enough

Figure 7.2. Tim Caza (*left*) and John McLaughlin study McLaughlin's files on the lost bomber on a midwinter afternoon in 2018. In their search for *Gertie*, McLaughlin provided the backstory, Caza the technology. Photo by Tom Wilber.

to those with faith. McLaughlin agrees; the image can have that effect. He knows of some divers, he adds, driven to the brink of obsession looking for things they know are there.

Gertie, wherever she was, remained lost in good company.

The kindred forces of entropy and oblivion at work in Lake Ontario are capable of erasing vast stretches of history, only to leave an arcane vestige in some random spot, a tantalizing answer to a question never asked. So it was in 1929 when a jeweler, Augustus Hoffman, excavating the foundation for a boathouse near Sodus Bay, on the south shore, turned up a corroded blade. He thought it might be a piece of junk, but given that it was unquestionably old, oddly shaped, and entombed in hardpan below the water level, he entertained the notion he had found a Native American relic.

As a jeweler, Hoffman had a discerning eye, though historical artifacts fell outside his field. He knew the local banker, however, and the banker knew the newspaper editor, and it was through these connections that Hoffman's find arrived at the Royal Ontario Museum in Toronto. A subsequent analysis by the curator, Dr. Charles T. Currelly, confirmed that the relic was indeed ancient—it had been kicking around for the better part of a millennium, perhaps longer. And it was authentic, though not produced by the natives, who made weapons from stone. This was a spearhead—elegant and lethal—cast from iron, and it had come from Scandinavia.[5]

After spending time in a bank vault in Lyons, New York, the relic was delivered to the Museum of Wayne County History, where today it invites wonder whether Viking ships actually plied inland waters long before the most distant ancestors of Christopher Columbus were born; or whether the corroded specimen was some archaeological outlier, a chance item of trade or a spoil of war that came into the possession of Native Americans who brought it from a Viking settlement on the Atlantic Coast.[6] Or maybe it's something entirely misunderstood—a vehicle on which personal fancies are projected and affirmed.

The lake is a veritable sump of history, and the Norse relic encourages reverie of what other mysteries might emerge. Jim Kennard, the wreck seeker who found the Revolutionary War ship, once came across channels cut into the lakebed, as dramatic and unexpected as canals on Mars. "Hour after hour of seeing nothing, you get pretty bored, even sleepy," Kennard told me. "Then something like that comes on the screen, and the adrenaline starts pumping. You're on high alert."[7] Here was striking evidence, he suspected, of tributaries that flowed through dry land ten thousand years ago toward Lake Ontario's prehistoric and somewhat smaller predecessor, Lake Admiralty. Kennard was rapt with the possibility that the submerged landscape held remnants of paleo-American encampments brought to an Atlantean end with retreating glaciers.[8] "There's no telling what might be found down there," he mused.

The prehistoric topography was a wonder to behold, but Kennard, like Caza, was after more accessible history, evinced by ships that sailed on the lake in its current form. During colonial times until well after America's independence, the freshwater sea was a contested frontier for warring European powers and the Native American forces they allied with or antagonized. With the discovery of the HMS *Ontario*, Kennard has earned exclusive possession and corresponding bragging rights to a remarkable secret. Yet the Revolutionary War ship is but one of many vessels that went down with crew, armaments, and cargo, sometimes at the hands of adversaries, more often victims of nature.

With international boundaries settled in the early nineteenth century, the Age of Sail gave way to steamers and barges and an ever-expanding network of locks and canals brimming with industrial and agricultural enterprise as immigrants and migrants, labor and capital, followed the call of the American Dream westward. Oswego, one of the country's oldest freshwater ports, served as a gateway from these inland routes to the Great Lakes and the American heartland.

The twentieth century left its own unique trail of history. During Prohibition, bootleggers—"rum runners"—ferried contraband from Canada to various drop-offs along the US shore. Much of the cargo, smuggled in fishing boats, made it to speakeasies in New York City and elsewhere. But quantities were sometimes thrown overboard during raids or lost at sea with their carriers. Scattered somewhere over thousands of square miles of submerged sand, rocks, and biota, these cases of vintage whisky lie with cannonballs fired from broadsides in the War of 1812, World War II avionics and weaponry, and eighteenth-, nineteenth-, and twentieth-century merchant vessels. Owing to natural and geographical factors, this archaeological record is especially rich at the lake's eastern end, a place known through legend and scholarship to a number of archaeologists and wreck seekers as the "Bay of Dead Ships." But scarcely is any of it appreciated by the greater public.

It is amid this trove of ruin and lore that Phil Church came across a precious opportunity—one expected to propel the search for *Getaway Gertie* from a local affair to a national endeavor.

As Oswego County administrator, Church oversees a $220 million budget and a workforce of more than eleven hundred people in departments ranging from public works to social services. But a favorite aspect of his job is economic development, especially projects involving lake-related tourism and diving. A well-groomed man of robust build, a wide-set, even gaze, and ministerial temperament, Church has searched for Getaway *Gertie* on and off over a span of decades, mostly to protect her from the consequences of other people finding her first.

Church's career began modestly enough in the early 1990s. Fresh out of college with a degree in archaeology and a budding interest in public administration, he landed a position with the Oswego Maritime Foundation, a nonprofit affiliated with a local museum, to promote the area's seafaring heritage. This was something of a dream job for Church—who might fairly be thought of as a policy wonk with a zeal for adventure—and he set about it with gusto.

For starters, he learned how to dive, and he nearly drowned, according to his instructor, after botching a back roll off the boat and losing his mask and a fin. Years later, Church admits that a few mistakes left him rattled, but he regained his composure as the instructor, Dale Currier—a seasoned commercial diver who would later become director of Oswego County Emergency Management—swam down and recovered the items. "If he had ended the dive," Church recalls, "I probably would have been embarrassed enough to feel I wasn't cut out for diving." Yet Church caught on quickly after that, and it became a passion.[9]

This passion led to an early career milestone, described by a local tourism newsletter as "perhaps the first ever live broadcast of an underwater ribbon cutting." That event came after Church and a team of colleagues working with the maritime foundation surveyed the *David W. Mills*, a steamer that broke apart and sank in twenty feet of water after running aground on Ford Shoals with a load of timber in 1919. Following an assiduous process of archival research, liability assessment, environmental reviews, permit applications, and approvals, the ribbon cutting, in May 2000, marked official designation of the wreck by the State of New York as an "underwater cultural preserve and dive site."

The *Mills*, the first state-sanctioned public diving site of its kind in Lake Ontario, was intended as a single piece of a broad network of underwater attractions—a "diving trail" beckoning tourists along the length of the lake—to be promoted by the foundation with city and county governments. Yet the plan lacked a clear vision—a problem compounded by jurisdictional issues that made it "difficult to get anything done," according to Church. "Everybody had bits and pieces of knowledge," he recalls, "but there was no coordinated effort."

As the plan for a universal attraction highlighting the Bay of Dead Ships languished in red tape, the old steamer attracted novice divers and weekend warriors but proved underwhelming as a tourist draw. Meanwhile, further offshore, a vast frontier of submerged history—uncharted, unsanctioned, and mostly out of sight—beckoned to those familiar with the stories.

Oddly, Church himself was unfamiliar with the local tales of "*Getaway Gertie*" until after he began diving, even though his paternal grandparents lived in the very town where Keith Ponder rattled rafters as he desperately piloted the heavy bomber low over rooftops in search of a place to bring her down after missing the Syracuse airport. In 1944, Church's father, Frank, was a gunner with the Eighth Air Force in England, from where he flew missions over Germany. Though Frank's parents—Phil's grandparents—belonged to a generation of Oswego County residents who would know of *Getaway Gertie*, her story would scarcely endure on the sweeping scale of loss, triumph, and change when the troops finally returned home. And by then, who could blame a public eager to turn its attention away from war? Any distant recollection of *Gertie* held by Church's ancestors and neighbors would grow only dimmer in the following decades, before the evolution of diving technology brought underwater exploration into the mainstream.

Anniversaries have a way of rekindling memories, however, and so it was, fifty years after Keith Ponder vanished with his crew, that a newspaper headline in the Oswego County edition of the *Syracuse Post-Standard* would catch Church's eye: DIVERS IN LAKE ONTARIO CLOSING IN ON LOST BOMBER. This news was accompanied by a photograph of two serious-looking men posing in front of a salvage vessel bearing the name Emark Marine Services.[10] Church read on: "Somewhere in the deep and silent waters of Lake Ontario, eight American airmen still await the end of World War II. Jim Coffed and Mike McGourty expect to see them there, their bones still strapped into the seats of a heavy bomber that went down 50 years ago. And they hope to bring them home at last, to the military burials they deserve."

Jim Coffed, the story reported, was a retired detective and insurance investigator who claimed to have narrowed the location of the wreck to an undisclosed place in Mexico Bay, and Mike McGourty was the manager of a salvage company apparently capable of raising it. They led a group from western New York associated with the National Warplane Museum in Geneseo. "Our intention is twofold," McGourty was quoted. "One is to recover the bodies for the Air Force once the plane is found, and the other is to recover the aircraft for a museum."

Church had to reread that part: "recover the bodies. . . . recover the aircraft."

The task was sensationally ambitious—and destined for failure. Still, it was a heck of a story. And it would pique Church's concerns over non-sanctioned parties, however well intentioned, availing themselves of wrecks.

The story, by *Buffalo News* reporter Mike Vogel, had been picked up by the Associated Press and gained regional coverage that prompted a flush of reconstituted memory circulating at Oswego County diners, marinas, and shoreline campfires. Here, again, was the account of the rail workers who saw the plane flying low over the tracks—a tactic Coffed attributed to the pilot's attempt to "follow the iron compass" back to Syracuse. The newspaper account also held revelations, sourced to Coffed's detective work, including a wakeful woman who saw a brilliant flash over the lake reflected in her bedroom mirror at 2:20 a.m. the night the plane crashed; and a diver, swimming alone in the 1950s, who reported seeing "a huge form emerge out of the murk" that "coalesced into a large bomber with a missing wing." The unnamed diver claimed the wreck "was in pretty good condition."

When the anniversary article ran, a confluence of factors held both the promise of *Gertie*'s discovery and peril of the consequences. Scuba gear had improved enormously since its development in World War II, and natural and regulatory factors were making Lake Ontario's sometimes-murky water reliably clear. Once the domain of specialized salvage and rescue operations, Mexico Bay was becoming a playground for sport divers.[11] At the same time, nostalgia for "the Good War," fought by "the Greatest Generation," waxed strong, and people coveted a piece of it.[12] Certain weapons and avionics that survived the scrap piles and garbage dumps were becoming collectors' items in a global market, with authenticity commanding a premium. "We're well aware of the antique warbird market out there," Jeff Hunston, an official with Yukon's Heritage Resources Department, would later reflect after two men were busted for retrieving part of a B-26 Marauder from a remote Canadian lake. "There's a lot of money to be made and even parts can be hot commodities."[13]

This especially applied to the once-ubiquitous and now-rare B-24. Even if *Gertie* lay in moldering ruin, which would be expected, certain parts, to say nothing of stand-alone accessories, might hold value for an ambitious restoration specialist.[14] A vintage Browning M 50 machine gun, the famed Norden bombsight, or any number of gauges, instruments, or other items might add prestige to the mantels of collectors or command sums on a black market.[15]

Fifty years after the end of the war, *Gertie*'s stock was on the rise. Perhaps all this explains strange sightings off the shores of Mexico Bay in the mid-1990s, and even not-so-strange observations regarded with new suspicion. Among shoreline residents used to seeing boats with anglers and outriggers in front of their camps, speculation circulated when vessels were spotted with nobody aboard, anchored at certain spots east of the Oswego harbor.

Church well knew what a diving boat looked like and could guess what they were after. Yet it was another image from that period that would lodge in his mind in years to come: a silhouetted figure, hands outstretched, balancing at the bow of a vessel. Closer surveillance revealed the person was clutching a divining rod. "I doubt he was looking for water," recalls Church, who observed the scene from a neighboring boat.

A group of mystics, I would learn, was but a subset of an eclectic assortment of devotees pursuing the lost airmen, on and off, for years.[16] Some of these parties valued honor. Others chased riches, or adventure, or the status of being first, or maybe a compelling interest in World War II history. Whatever their motivation, they formed loose alliances or grudging rivalries and shared or guarded information accordingly. They were, as Church later described them, "people with good intentions and people without good intentions."

Apart from John McLaughlin—who knew almost all the players and held his own judgments regarding their motives and qualifications—there was Bruce Miller, an entrepreneur who believed, reasonably, that finding the lost bomber would bring an element of fame to his fledgling marine electronics business, K&S Minicomputer Inc., if only he knew where to look. Miller lived in the Southern Tier of New York, three hours removed from the people and affairs along the lakeshore from which he might gather intelligence. For this local knowledge, he teamed with Neil "Bud" Duell, a fishing guide and Oswego County native.

Duell, a lively, elfin man, was not a diver, though he was an esteemed figure at American Legion Post 1532, where he might have been found offering counsel on steelhead runs up the nearby Salmon River, or maybe relating stories of the German prison camp where he was held captive in 1945 after the B-17 on which he was a gunner was shot down near Leipzig.[17] Few people had a more direct and personal knowledge of vintage aircraft, local history, and every contour and snag in the eastern end of the lake. Amid the vast catalog of experience lodged in Duell's mind was the night of February 18, 1944, when, while home on leave, he heard the familiar thrum of a heavy bomber, obviously lost and laboring in the storm.[18] Fifty years later, as Duell entered his golden years, the story of *Gertie* provided an odd and enduring connection of his war experience with his love of the lake.

Though Miller and Coffed led competing teams, Duell offered counsel to each when they arrived with boats and crew from out of town. Moreover, the old guide and many of his fellow anglers were beginning to routinely use fish finders. Although the devices of the early 1990s were primitive by today's standards, they effectively amplified the old timer's already acute attunement to the lake's features. Duell spread the word: watch monitors for strange profiles. "It might be sitting high and large. If we pass within three-hundred feet of it, we can find it."[19]

Miller, Duell, and Coffed are no longer alive to tell their tales, though their reported intentions were remarkably similar: find *Gertie*, raise her with airbags, and tow her to shore. The military's involvement in this endeavor seemed to be a given, if something of an afterthought. "The Air National Guard," noted one account sourced to Duell and Miller, "would be responsible for the bodies and notifying surviving relatives."[20] For his part, McGourty recalls anticipating outside help "after we located the plane and confirmed the bodies were on it." Looking back, he adds, "I find it kind of odd that the military's effort to find it has been so halfhearted, especially when you see the extraordinary effort to return soldiers lost on foreign soil."[21]

Whatever the dynamics, the prospect of effectively salvaging *Gertie* and recovering the bodies of her crew without a well-funded archaeological team and specialized equipment and know-how was, in hindsight, naïve. Even so, reports of this ambition suggested at the time that *Gertie*'s discovery was imminent if not a fait accompli. A lot of people were now looking. If she were found in accessible depths, Church knew, it would be dangerous though feasible for divers, through ignorance or avarice, to help themselves to anything they might pull free of the fuselage or pluck from the debris field. "Coming up with something from a wreck was the macho badge of diving," Church later reflected. "It was a bad idea, but people did it all the time. Some of the older divers began to realize that wasn't such a good idea when they went back to show people a find and there was only an empty box."

Likewise, Currier, Church's diving mentor, knew that if the wreck were found, word would get out, and if word got out, there would be no keeping people away. Older than Church by nearly twenty years, Currier belongs to a generation inspired by Jacques Cousteau, the famed underwater adventurer and scuba pioneer, and Mel Fisher, the celebrity treasure-seeker. Pillaging was not only accepted during Currier's formative years, but a consummating part of the adventure. "We used to make a contest out of what we could pull up," he remembers.[22] "With something with the status of *Getaway Gertie*, there would be no way to protect it. People would not stay away."

By the mid-1990s, preservation laws were in place, but enforcement remained lax; diving practices were changing, but slowly. It was with the intention of thwarting desecration of the resting place of *Gertie*'s crew, then, that Church assembled a team of volunteers working on behalf of the maritime foundation.

"With sport diving becoming so popular, it's inevitable that someone will find it," Church announced at a press conference in the summer of 1996. "We want to reach it first. . . . We don't want souvenir seekers pilfering it."[23] There was, in truth, no surefire way of preventing that. But, the reasoning went, an exploiting party would have a more difficult time raising or covertly pillaging a wreck in a place known to a network of monitors working in the public interest.

For this mission, Church had recruited engineers employed by various Oswego County businesses. "In our free time, we were divers into finding wrecks," remembers Dennis Gerber, the General Electric engineer who would, much later, join Caza in searches aboard *Voyager*. "Back then, people would try to find stuff by dragging their anchors or using fish finders. . . . It could be done, but it was slow going."[24] Also, destructive. Dragging an anchor to snag a wreck is nails on a chalkboard to archaeologists and preservationists.

As Kennard and Scoville had done in Rochester, this like-minded group of techies, including Gerber, Tim Shippee, and Doug Low, assembled side-scan systems that, when mounted on tow fish, project signals across the bottom from an angle, offering greater range and clarity than a fish finder, which projects signals straight down. While some people unwound after work with bowling leagues, happy hour, or poker night, these guys got together to mount transducers. They called themselves "the Sonar Guys."

For the price of gas for Shippee's boat, the Guys agreed to team with Church and the maritime foundation for a systematic and public search of four square miles northwest of Shore Oaks in depths from 50 to 140 feet. *Gertie* may have gone down in deeper water, or anywhere between or beyond Rochester and the Thousand Islands for that matter, but this was a zone where people were looking based on assumptions of the wing section's drift, calculated from rudimentary meteorological records of 1944.

Narrowing the search to 4 square miles out of 7,320 might be considered a reasonable start. Even so, it presented a sizable and uncertain task. And perhaps this uncertainty added to the excitement when, right off the bat, the Sonar Guys located a target at 135 feet while scanning the furthest leg of the grid, three miles due north of Oswego.

The object was not in the obvious shape of a plane, nor did it look distinctly like a ship, though they couldn't rule out that it might be some part of either. The matter was settled when a drop camera captured images of an encrusted upright form roosting in silt—a vessel with a wooden lapstrake hull and squat pilot house adorned with fishing lures. They had found the *Cormorant*, a tugboat swamped by high seas in 1958 while returning from the Saint Lawrence Seaway, where it had played some role—undoubtedly minor but perhaps emblematic—in the construction of locks and dams that, when completed the following year, opened the Great Lakes for the first time to ocean liners. Excepting that it was not painted primary colors, the *Cormorant* looked as though it originated in a children's storybook of that era, and it had a tale to match: as the little tug foundered nearing the port of Oswego, its crew had escaped death by clinging to a tractor tube.[25]

That Church's diving team had found a wreck tied to a monumental chapter in the Great Lakes' commercial history offered some consolation for their efforts. Yet the season wore on with no sign of *Gertie*. And so did the next. When the third year came to a close, the Guys could say with confidence that the tomb of the lost airmen was not to be found in the vicinity where people had been looking for it. If any doubts remained, they would be settled, at least in Church's mind, in 2000. That was the year the US Navy joined the quest.

The USS *Kingfisher* cut an incongruous image among seasonal pleasure craft as it cruised off Oswego on a fair day in mid-July. As a featured component of the Navy's recruitment tour of the Great Lakes, the *Kingfisher* was meant to impress, and with banners flying and uniformed crew at the ready, it was undeniably good at it. Approximately 190 feet long, the *Kingfisher* was by no means large by Navy standards, nor especially fast. It had neither big guns nor flight decks. But in respect to what it was built to do, which was locate hard-to-detect items in the water, it was peerless. The *Kingfisher* was a coastal minesweeper, loaded bow-to-stern with the most sophisticated and expensive underwater-searching technology available and a crew of thirty-eight men and fourteen women brimming with confidence. The plan was for the *Kingfisher* to expand, by two square miles, the four-mile grid that the Sonar Guys had surveyed over the course of several seasons. For that, the Navy budgeted half a day.

Why this hadn't happened before was anybody's guess, but a well-timed phone call by Church may have planted the seed. Whatever the prompt, the Navy's public affairs office seized on the idea, and the mission, from a public relations standpoint at least, was a success before it even began. Outlets in both Rochester and Oswego ran features on the *Kingfisher*'s pending assignment to "fire up its state-of-the-art equipment" to locate "the long-lost bomber."[26]

The appointed day was calm, the water clear, conditions ideal. "If the plane is there, we will find it," chief operations officer Ed Goubian promised a gaggle of local reporters and dignitaries, including Church and Currier, as they were escorted aboard.[27] Within minutes, the ship was plying a mise-en-scène of blue-and-green elements; its guests, expecting to be part of a national story from Oswego, New York, removed sunglasses as they were ushered below to a windowless room, dimly lit and silent. Here, with headphones and glowing monitors, technicians tracked signals of varying direction, distance, and frequency. The ship's technology revealed the submarine environment so thoroughly, Goubian boasted, they could detect a fish and then watch it get caught by an angler in a distant boat. A hulking airplane wreck should be abundantly obvious.

What that might look like was anybody's guess. But journalist Mike Vogel's original description of *Gertie*'s crew—strapped in their seats awaiting military burial—provides a vivid stand-in. Those who consider such things might also wonder what the lost airmen would have made of this peacetime combat drill aboard the *Kingfisher* characterized by skill, acuity, and material wherewithal. Perhaps it would strike them as ironic, and certainly beyond compare with their own desperate dress rehearsal for war.

Despite the impressive resources at hand on this morning, however, the crew of the lost Twenty-Four would remain wherever they were. The US Navy ship and the AAF aircraft, worlds apart in time and circumstances, appeared to be no closer in physical proximity. They were, however, bound by the same military protocol: schedules must be met, orders kept. The *Kingfisher* was due at the next port. The demonstration was ended after three hours. With that, Church and Currier and the various reporters were ushered to shore. It was all very anticlimactic.

"I wonder if they were telling us everything," Currier recalls thinking as they took leave of their escort. Church, though disappointed, was pretty sure that if the Navy hadn't found the wreck there, it must be someplace else. "I think we know where it isn't," he replied.

The year 2000 ended with gales blowing whitecaps across the Bay of Dead Ships and ice fringing its shores. Nothing of a B-24 Liberator, in toto or in part, had shown up in the National War Plane Museum, though it would be much later before I learned the particulars that brought Jim Coffed and Mike McGourty's quest to an end.

As for Church, his search for the lost bomber had run its course for the time being, as did his broader plan to inventory and sanction wrecks off Oswego as tourist attractions. "With no clear way forward," he explained, "I kind of gave up on the idea." The tale of *Getaway Gertie*, with the exception of details preserved with monkish devotion by John McLaughlin and a handful of other enthusiasts, slid back into oblivion.

Fifteen more years would pass until the story was revived once again. By then, the dynamic of the search would change greatly, and so would the players involved.

The spark of resurrection came on a day in early spring 2015. Church was in his corner office, adjacent to the legislative chambers and overlooking the port of Oswego on the top floor of the sprawling redbrick county government building. Now credentialed with a master's degree in public administration and seasoned by almost twenty years in government work, he was routinely consumed with affairs involving department heads, unions, legislators, bureaucrats, and citizens; and he was thus occupied when his secretary rang. A Mr. Reed Bohne from the National Oceanic and Atmospheric Administration was on the line. Church didn't know Bohne, though he interrupted what he was doing to take the call. Happily, the conversation turned to diving.

NOAA, Church would learn, oversees federal marine sanctuaries—underwater national parks managed and promoted as world-class attractions. These, in essence, are the Yellowstones and Yosemites of the maritime world, and they showcase the kind of iconic conservation priorities and natural settings one might expect in a national preserve: humpback whales breeding off the shores of the Hawaiian Islands; loggerhead sea turtles finning over the coral reefs of the Florida Keys. They also focus on "underwater cultural heritage" or, in less bureaucratic terms, the stories and remains of ships and people lost at sea. A NOAA sanctuary in North Carolina, originally developed around a Civil War ship found off Cape Hatteras, was now expanding to encompass seventy-eight merchant marine ships sunk during World War II dozens of miles offshore, the German U-boats that brought them to their end, and Allied warships that defended them.[28] NOAA manages fourteen parks in all, and the missions of some extend well beyond preserving contemporary history. Archaeology teams at the Channel Islands national sanctuary off the California coast are uncovering traces of some of the earliest inhabitants of North America, ancestors of the Chumash, who migrated in plank canoes along the Pacific Rim thirteen thousand years ago.[29]

Bohne was calling because NOAA was taking nominations for a new sanctuary. Church, perhaps glancing over at a vintage diving helmet punctiliously displayed on a console table in his office, listened intently to what he had to say. As a student of archaeology and history, Church knew that a record from precolonial times through World War II was literally embedded in Lake Ontario's depths and manifest in landmarks along its shores. So he shouldn't have been surprised when Bohne got to the point of the call: eastern Lake Ontario would be a prime candidate for a national diving preserve, the federal administrator said. If Church were interested in being involved in exploring the feasibility of such a project, Bohne offered, they could meet to talk about the application process.

"There *is* a way," Church recalls thinking. "Here was a federal agency reaching out with a program in place and the jurisdiction and know-how to get it off the ground." It was thrilling and, frankly, a bit unsettling, in the way fishing for perch and hooking a king salmon is unsettling, and it took a moment for Church to fathom the ramifications.

The scope of the project was indeed massive, far bigger than anything Church and his colleagues at the maritime foundation originally imagined. When all was said and done, it would encompass seventeen hundred square miles of lake waters and bottomlands bordered by four counties in New York State. Within the area, coordinates were known of twenty-one shipwrecks and one military aircraft—a C-45 transport lost in 1952 after its crew parachuted to safety.

Yet the potential for new discovery was a compelling driver of the project. Apart from *Gertie*, at least forty-eight other planes or ships had disappeared in the Bay of Dead Ships or west of there. These ranged from a C-47 military transport that vanished beneath the waves off Sandy Pond on June 23, 1944, after its hypothermic crew were pulled from the water by recreational boaters, to the *Lady of the Lake*, an American schooner built for the War of 1812 and lost with all hands in a storm in December 1826 while sailing from York to Oswego.[30]

With Oswego at its nexus, the federal designation held the promise of dive shops and boutiques, charters and hotel business, and research and educational programs ranging from underwater imaging and robotics to archaeology and American history. A national sanctuary in Thunder Bay, on Lake Huron—the only other NOAA preserve on the Great Lakes at the time—drew nearly one hundred thousand visitors a year to Alpena, a city of ten thousand, generated an annual economic impact topping $100 million, and has spawned marine curriculums in schools and colleges.[31]

Church would learn these details over time, though he immediately gathered that the project could put Lake Ontario on the national diving map. That was clearly the good news. But it wasn't so simple. The application process would take years, Bohne emphasized; critically, its success depended on "comprehensive community support."

And there came the tricky part. The stakeholders were legion: fishing charters, commercial shippers, recreational boaters, a bevy of state and local entities, environmental and hunting lobbies, property owners, researchers and educators, public safety personnel, hotel and marina proprietors, historic preservation agencies. The list went on. Church had worked with these groups and could anticipate their grievances and petitions. For many of them, wariness of federal involvement in local affairs ran deep; the mere utterance of the words "federal sanctuary" could torpedo the conversation before it began.

As for local divers, they were relatively small in number with an outsize interest, unlikely to fall in with any particular voice. For generations they had explored the depths freely, governed, for the most part, by their own self-enforced codes of honor, ethics, and notions of best practices. Their ghost ships, mysteries, and legends would now be branded, in the parlance of officialdom, "national historic treasures," "submerged cultural resources," and "underwater heritage sites"—all mapped, marked, and served up to the mainstream as an in situ national museum.

Diving-related businesses and their customers had plenty to gain, Church knew, and the plan would no doubt be a boon to local museums and their cohort of preservationists and historians. Kennard and Caza, the sonar explorers who had managed something of a truce as they surveyed different sections of the lake, would likely see the sanctuary as a government boondoggle and heedless claim to the lake's secrets. They had already released public videos, photographs, and 3-D computer models of their hard-won discoveries—everything except for their locations. That, Church would accurately anticipate, was information the wreck seekers would not be eager to share, especially with a federal agency.[32] Rules would have to be established, priorities set, methods of enforcement well thought out. In short, what Bohne was describing would involve a dissonant mix of rogues and rule makers negotiating a web of bureaucratic tape and strongly held opinions, all parsing fine lines between preservation, exploitation, and regulation.

Bohne, as it would turn out, had found a person well suited for the job.[33]

After Church hung up, he let his mind decompress for a moment. Out an office window, sunlight played off the remnants of the ice pack in the harbor as it rode the current to the lake. A new season of enterprise and recreation would soon begin on and under the water. Nearly seventy years had passed since Keith Ponder, the boy from Forkville, Mississippi, piloted the four-engine bomber low over rooftops, circling from land to lake and lake to land, agitating residents and police during his desperate attempt to navigate the storm and save his crew. It was but an instant, really, in the sweep of Oswego's maritime history, cherished by a small number of regional divers and World War II aficionados lacking, so far, the where-withal to find the Twenty-Four.

When NOAA's marine sanctuary came to fruition, there would be no denying *Getaway Gertie*'s place in the spotlight, an unclaimed prize, the very prospect of her discovery beckoning some of the most ambitious and well-equipped divers in the country.

HOPE AND PRAYER

After passing over eastern Lake Ontario in the early morning hours of February 18, 1944, the nor'easter that claimed *Getaway Gertie* tracked along the Saint Lawrence River and pushed into Canada with growing vigor. Before it retreated off the coast, it would find a second victim.

The storm was fierce but unremarkable by the standards of what the North Atlantic could dish out in mid-February. Still, it had developed into what the old-timers might call a ripsnorter, and those in its path, accustomed to dealing with such events, hunkered down. An exception was a crew aboard a B-24 approaching a Royal Canadian Air Force Base in Newfoundland. Unlike their American counterparts, British and Canadian planes were not typically personified with names and artwork; this one was known simply as Liberator 586. The crew of six had departed Iceland under clear skies, though as they approached their destination in Gander, pilot A. A. T. "Al" Imrie called the base for conditions and learned the airfield was closed because of poor visibility and heavy snow. Imrie was advised to proceed to Goose Bay, about 350 miles north, on the mainland.

The circumstances were similar to what Ponder and crew had experienced during the waning hours of the previous day, with a few crucial differences. Imrie, formerly a professional rugby player, was a squadron leader and veteran U-boat patrol pilot; his crew were battle hardened and comfortably familiar with the North Atlantic climate, terrain, and one another. Critically, 586 was guided by an experienced navigator: Lieutenant Garnet "Gar" Harland, one of the best in the business. He had been charting their course since takeoff and knew exactly where they were.[1]

Imrie had banked the aircraft north over the Gulf of Saint Lawrence toward the new destination when 586 passed from the clear arctic air into the saturated and relatively warm mass of the advancing front. Visibility abruptly fell to a half mile. Worse, the plane grew heavy and unresponsive as ice coated its wings and engine cowlings.

The storm had 586 in its grip. Still, the plane held its own for the next hour and a half. Imrie checked in with Harland, who was calculating the rate of descent, distance to landing, and the height of the small mountain range they needed to clear to get there. They would make it, Harland advised: steady as she goes. A slight break in the storm at that moment was reinforcing his optimism. With only twenty miles to go, he began packing his maps for the anticipated landing when a sudden change in the plane's harmonics signaled a new problem. The inboard engine on the starboard wing cut out as ice choked off the carburetors.

Imrie called the navigator to the deck. Harland was crawling through the lower bi-level compartment of his Plexiglas station in the nose when the second starboard engine sputtered and died. By the time he squeezed through to the upper level he found a crew animated by crisis. Imrie and copilot Doug Campbell were locked in a mortal struggle with yokes, rudder pedals, and throttle levers to keep the plane under control. In the station behind them, the flight engineer Johnny Johns had peeled off his mitts to adjust the fuel controls. Gil Gilmour, the radioman, was trying to get a distress message to Goose Bay with equipment rendered nonfunctional by weather interference and an iced antenna.

It was no longer a matter of whether they would make the base, but where in the Canadian wilds they would come down and how well they could control their descent. Hills loomed ahead and to either side; hazy features of the ground gained definition. Directly below and in front of them, a ribbon of white bisecting patches of scrub pine and balsam widened to a frozen lake. It was long enough and wide enough, but Imrie had a bad feeling about it. Labrador ice, often undercut by spring-fed channels and currents, was suspect for the purposes of ditching twenty tons of falling metal. Like Ponder, Imrie was faced with a critical decision. And when the third motor cut out, he had seconds to make it.

He avoided the lake. And even as he shouted directions to the copilot while his crew fumbled with buckles at their crash stations, the plane began shearing off treetops like matchsticks. With the sound of splintering wood and rending metal, the plane came apart.[2]

In days that followed, arctic air swirled in behind the departing storm as search crews took to the air, eyes straining against the snow-swept Labrador bush for a wisp of smoke, shred of debris, or fluttering parachute from the Canadian plane. At the same time, eight hundred miles to the southwest, RCAF planes aided in the search for Army 047—soon to be known as *Getaway Gertie*—along the New York border, allowing for the possibility that the American ship, lost in the early phase of the same storm, had crossed blindly into Canada before running out of gas. On the US side of the border, pilots and spotters searched for signs of 047 in the rugged crags of the Adirondack Mountains and the drifted forest, fields, and whitecapped waters of central and northern New York. Here, the air search proceeded haltingly as lingering snow bands off Lake Ontario menaced bases from which search parties took off and landed.

The American search fell under the authority of Colonel Austin W. Martenstein, commander of the Rome Air Depot, who could do without it.[3] The base, thirty-five miles east of Syracuse, was facing an acute manpower shortage. It was a problem that was hardly unique to Rome as men left en masse to overseas assignments, and to address it, the military, following the example of industry, was turning to women. Martenstein, a Virginian in his early fifties with a magnificent double chin and fiercely penetrating eyes, was heading a recruitment campaign in cities across the state. Sometimes the colonel himself, accompanied by an entourage of officers and aides, seized photo ops at recruiting stations set up in department stores, where he promised women "a variety of interesting jobs bearing directly on the war effort."[4]

The Women's Army Corps was a patently good fit for Rome's noncombat operations—predominantly airplane maintenance and logistics.

Yet despite these overtures from impressive male and female officers in impeccably tailored uniforms, the response was lukewarm. Martenstein and military brass across the country were learning that it was not easy to persuade women to forgo good-paying factory jobs, of which there were plenty, for comparatively low-paying Army positions. Adding greatly to this hurdle was stigma from an effective slander campaign—fostered and encouraged by certain elements of the press, clergy, and various male soldiers and their wives—that disparaged the morals and sexual conduct of women in uniform.[5]

Lack of personnel aside, the emergency of the lost bomber—around which other priorities and deadlines would now have to be shoehorned—was exacerbated by a want of intelligence. Nobody could say when the plane went down, where, or even how much fuel the missing craft had; lacking that information, there was no telling how long it had remained aloft after its last garbled radio contact at 2:07 a.m. There, too, was the problem of the missing crew—eight men ordered to bail out, any number of whom may have come down well apart from the others and wherever the plane ended up. The less that was known, the broader the search would have to be, and the broader the search, the more personnel it would require.

For much of the task, the Army would rely on the US Coast Guard and a network of civilian agencies. State and local police, foresters, game managers, and civilian fliers, all with different training and protocols, would require coordination under a central chain of command.[6] The operation would grow to involve dozens of disparate parties chasing a slew of reports from residents across upstate New York, newly aware that the sound that had interrupted their sleep that night could have been the lost bomber they heard about in the news in the days that followed.

The job of overseeing all this fell to Colonel Martenstein's subordinates, beginning with Lieutenant Colonel Melvin B. Skinner. The youngest of eight children raised on a farm in rural Michigan, Skinner possessed a down-to-earth approachability that served him well as the Army's liaison with the community offices that would provide the backbone for the search. As an aviation engineer educated at Northwestern University, he had a quick, analytical mind, and as a World War I flier he also had ample experience. At this stage of his career, apparently, Skinner also retained a fondness for flying. The fifty-two-year-old senior officer, seizing a brief weather window and perhaps a chance to escape from his desk in the wake of the departing storm, was among the first to take off in search of *Gertie*.[7]

With visibility improved by Friday afternoon, though still less than ideal, fifteen fighters, surveillance planes, and bombers provisioned with air drops of food, gear, and first aid took off from Army bases in Rome and Syracuse.[8] The bombers were uniquely suited for search-and-rescue missions owing to their speed, range, the panoramic view offered from their Plexiglas noses, and cargo space from which to air-drop supplies. But the big planes required multiple crew and lots of gasoline, and Army fliers and planes of any type were in short supply.

In coming days, civilian pilots and spotters, including instructors and students from Civilian Air Patrol bases in Potsdam and Massena, were called on to search the Adirondack Mountains and Saint Lawrence River valley. More planes took off from civilian bases in Fulton, Syracuse, and Utica to cover Lake Ontario and the Tug Hill Plateau, Oneida Lake, and Sand Plains—an area of woods and swamp west of Rome.[9] Qualities that made the smaller, lighter CAP craft—Porterfield Collegiates, Piper Cubs, and others of their class—desirable for learning also made them suitable for "low and slow" surveillance; some called them "flying jeeps" owing to their maneuverability and utility.[10] This came into play especially when doubling back and dropping down for a closer look at terrain obscured by ravines and forests, or open water where debris might be camouflaged by floating ice chunks and whitecaps.

If Ponder and copilot Bickel had been able to finesse ditching *Gertie* in Lake Ontario, the crew could have found means of escape through a hatch above the engineer's station at the rear of the flight deck, where an inflatable life raft in a spring-loaded exterior compartment awaited deployment. At least, that was the drill in the training manual.[11] The bomber would have to be laid on the water at reduced speed, wings level and nose slightly raised. Even under optimal conditions, it would take considerable skill and even more luck to hold it together. At best, the crew would have mere minutes to escape.

If the plane didn't meet the choppy water perfectly, it would break apart. The impact from a wingtip catching a wave would be catastrophic. The inevitable result would be a "debris field" of items spilling and breaking off from the plane—canisters, foam cushions, equipment and personal items, life preservers, and perhaps bodies, alive or dead.

Debris and people that didn't go down with the craft would be pushed by prevailing winds and currents to lee shores, where they might end up somewhere between Oswego, to the south, and the Thousand Islands, at the northeast corner of the lake. In that case, they would likely make landfall along a stretch where there was nobody to discover them. Away from Oswego, with few exceptions, unplowed seasonal roads on the southeastern shoreline led to shuttered summer dwellings or expanses of frozen swamps, estuaries, and pastureland.

The job of organizing a search along these empty stretches fell to Ensign Joseph Hebert, a career coastguardsman and commander of the Oswego station. The Coast Guard, also being deployed to support the impending invasion of Europe, had no more personnel to spare than the other branches, so Hebert would eventually incorporate the search drill as training for reservists called up from Syracuse.[12] For the time being, they were sailors on snowshoes; powerboats were drydocked over the winter for maintenance and repair, and harbors were choked with ice. Transport trucks delivered searchers as close as possible to certain vantage points on the lake, which they then covered on foot.[13]

Viewed from the air, the shoreline, freshly topped with meringue drifts, offered a surreal flourish to gray and brooding waters. Approached from the ground, it lost all its charm. Heaved and compressed at the water's edge, ice banks were sculpted into a procession of formidable ridges, fused by freezing spray and snow, obscuring crevasses and hollows. Picking their way along, ever mindful of their footing, searchers steadied binoculars and sought views that might produce something that overhead spotters had missed. On the morning of day two, Saturday, winds shifted offshore, making the search a little easier but also lessening the chance that flotsam would make landfall. In the days that followed, winds picked up again from the north and west, producing only snow squalls, freezing spray, and more ice piled upon ice.[14] The search over the lake and shoreline pressed on intermittently, with growing conviction that if anything turned up, it would not be survivors.[15]

There was still hope, however, that the crew would be found on land.[16] In fact, there was an overabundance of possibilities. From the lake's east end, the Tug Hill Plateau gradually ascends to the foothills of the Adirondacks and, farther east, the rugged High Peaks region. Between lakeshore and summits, in a span of about one hundred miles, a smattering of small

Figure 8.1. The icebound shoreline of Lake Ontario in mid-February appears much as it would have in 1944. This recent view from the southeast end of the lake looks west toward Nine Mile Point, the headland that forms the western end of Mexico Bay. In the distance, a cooling tower of a nuclear plant sits inland of a former artillery range. Photo by Tom Wilber.

towns and villages dots farmland, woodlots, and wilderness. A sparse web of roads connects more populated areas along the Saint Lawrence River to the north and Mohawk Valley to the south.

This geography was a matter of frequent consideration for Captain Walter Begland, assigned under Lieutenant Colonel Skinner's command as intelligence officer for the search. A studious man of modest height and soft features, he might be found in a briefing room at the Rome base, placing a pin here, tracing a finger there, on a large wall map.[17] Begland was head of military police at the base, though he did not particularly look the part of an enforcer. The only child from a Scottish banking family, the young captain would pursue a law degree and a career in land conservancy in his hometown in Gnadenhutten, Ohio, after the war.[18] Perhaps this budding interest predisposed him to relish this survey of upstate New York's impressive topography, from seaway to mountaintop, that held the key to the puzzle now occupying his waking hours.

On Saturday—day two—the problem was becoming too much rather than too little information. That morning Begland had been urgently summoned to the Rome police station after a resident on the western outskirts of the city reported hearing "what might have been a plane and then an explosion sometime early Friday morning." As a search plane circled overhead, Begland, with ample assistance from an eager deputy police chief, consulted a map of Sand Plains, a stretch of woods and swamps immediately west of the city "where a plane could crash in certain areas . . . and be a distance away from any roads or inhabited sections."[19] A beat cop familiar with this area was called in to help the desk sergeant survey residents in that neck of the woods. The upshot was a morning spent in the field chasing conflicting reports that amounted to nothing.

A flurry of such reports continued to occupy precincts south and southeast of Lake Ontario. At first blush, each lead seemed relevant. Yet it soon became clear that the mere fact that a plane was heard by many near where it was trying to land told nothing of where it later ended up. Air and ground searches concentrated within a fifty-mile radius of Syracuse turned up nothing; and despite reports concentrated in Oswego County, searches over and along Lake Ontario also proved fruitless. Skinner himself reported having covered the Great Lake as far west as Rochester "without sighting a single piece of wreckage, parachute, or any other object."[20]

Now, conferring with Begland over a gallimaufry of points and lines—ostensibly representing *Gertie*'s final hours—that crisscrossed the map in the operations room at the Rome base, Skinner had begun redirecting resources to fortify the search inland, where there was still hope the men might be found alive. To this end, the officers had been puzzling over points where the plane was reportedly heard over the Saint Lawrence River valley, the Tug Hill Plateau, and the Adirondacks between 2 and 4 a.m. Friday.

This sequence began with a report from the lookout of a Coast Guard station on a small island at the head of the Saint Lawrence at 2 a.m. and was followed by encounters later reported by rail workers on New York Central lines east of the lake, including one from a telegraph worker in the town of Philadelphia and, fifteen minutes later, a trackwalker in Richland, forty-five miles to the south.[21] After a lapse of an hour and forty-five minutes, the lights of the plane were reportedly seen by a truck driver low over the mountains in the Adirondack town of South Colton, seventy-five miles northeast of Richland.[22]

The final pin on the map marked a point near the north end of the Tug Hill Plateau, between the mountains and the lake—the Clemons farm. Gerald Clemons and his family reportedly had been stirred awake by the sound of a low-flying plane sometime after 4 a.m.—followed by a heart-stopping explosion. The blast came from a wooded area too remote, with snow too deep, to allow for a proper investigation at daybreak. But upon hearing a report of the lost plane, the farmer had notified the sheriff.

Though some of these times were approximations, the sources seemed reliable enough. Clemons, a justice of the peace, was a known and respected citizen, and the details from the rail workers, Coast Guard sentry, and fuel truck driver were vivid. The entire sequence might be counted on, if not for inconsistencies with timing. The large gap between the track-walker's sighting and much later reports in the Adirondacks and Tug Hill could be explained by the plane passing back over the lake or uninhabited mountain terrain. Yet it was impossible for the plane to be approaching Syracuse from the east between 1:45 and 2 a.m., as logged by the control tower, while at the same time flying over Oswego, and then the Saint Lawrence River valley eighty miles to the north. Moreover, there was the question of fuel. How could the craft be circling far-flung regions of northern New York minutes and then hours after its tanks were nearly empty?

Begland thought he had found answers to both these questions and was awaiting a report from the field to confirm his hunch.

With the air search over central New York and eastern Lake Ontario having produced nothing, Skinner was equally convinced *Gertie* ended up in the hinterlands east of the lake after flying longer and farther afield than initially thought. As spotters intensified their search over the plateau and mountains south of the Saint Lawrence River, ski troops staged at the Rome base were ready to fly to any one of the airfields fringing the plateau and mountains.[23] From there, they would be transported by truck to the most promising point of access.[24]

That, anyway, was the plan. A plane searching the area around the Clemons farm that afternoon had to turn back after lake-effect squalls kicked up before the spotter could get a look at the forested area below. Now, as darkness set in, Begland would find little encouragement in an update from Lieutenant Charles McCann, the state trooper heading up

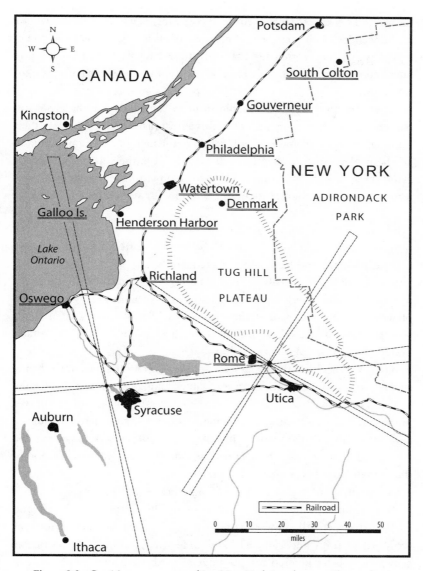

Figure 8.2. *Gertie*'s route over northern New York is unknown. Places where she was thought to be heard between 1:30 and 4:30 a.m. on February 18, 1944, are underlined. Because radio problems prevented crew from reliably picking up tracking beams sent from airfields in Rome and Syracuse, one theory holds they tried to follow the New York Central Railroad (shown as a two-tone line) to a metropolitan area. Map by Mike Bechthold.

the ground search. A party of troopers and rangers had entered the woods in the vicinity of the reported explosion. Breaking trail was slow going, and they had not gotten far before turning back in the face of white-outs and advancing nightfall. They would resume the search at first light tomorrow.[25]

At this point, it was reasonable to hope that if any of the crew had parachuted in the mountains or survived a crash on the plateau, their training, fitness, and youth would get them through one more night in the northern New York backcountry. If nothing else, the war had produced astonishing tales of endurance. But with temperatures expected to drop well below zero again that night, the window for survival was closing.

While those who could joined in the search for *Gertie*, others offered prayers. It was Sunday, the third day after *Gertie* vanished. Smartly dressed townspeople filed into the lacquered pews of the North Scriba Baptist Church with hardly a vacant space. The air, heavy with the scent of damp woolen overgarments, was soon to be lightened by the sound of worship. Outside, a brief snow squall off the lake had coated roads recently plowed and walkways recently shoveled leading to the small, drafty, single-story place of worship.

There was nothing about the scene—the robust attendance or the heavy snow—out of the ordinary for a midwinter Sunday service in this locale, three miles inland from Lake Ontario. Nor was the nature of the prayer unique. Allied troops were advancing to fateful engagements in Europe and the Pacific. Congregations meeting for Sunday services around the world had plenty to pray for as the death, destruction, and persecution of the Second World War inexorably pressed on.

At the front of the church, in a chair beside the pastor, sat Deacon Himes, a poultry breeder of local renown. His neatly parted hair and creased trousers belied the residual aspect of farm labor baked into his scrubbed features and callused hands. He was listening to a particular prayer now being offered for the boys aboard the heavy bomber heard circling low over homes, two nights prior. The congregants would have found the first sketchy details crammed among other war news in Friday and Saturday's local editions of the *Oswego Palladium-Times* and Syracuse dailies, with occasional updates on the WSYR and WFBL radio stations. The plane in question was said to be a Liberator B-24 with a crew of eight on a training flight out of the Westover base, in western Massachusetts. Low on gas and foundering in a whiteout, the pilot had missed a landing at the Syracuse airport. Sometime in the early morning hours, the commanding officer at Westover had ordered the men to bail out. It was unknown whether all or any of the crew were able to carry through, though reports from purported witnesses were pouring in from far and wide throughout central and northern New York.

Search parties hardly knew where to begin. The search area was said to extend one hundred miles from either side of a line extending from Rochester to Albany, an area spanning forty-thousand square miles, roughly half of upstate New York.[26] An Associated Press report in the Sunday morning papers captured the crux of the matter: "It is feared that either they are all dead, or that they are marooned in deep snow in mountain country. Those still alive might be so injured as not to be able to move. Last night's sub-zero temperatures, ranging from 18 to 30 degrees below, would endanger the lives of any survivors unable to reach civilization."[27]

And so, those assembled prayed for the boys' safety, for their loved ones, and for those searching—the auxiliaries and reservists, and for all the men and women fighting oppression and tyranny overseas and doing their part at home.

After the concluding hymn, Deacon Himes—Elwyn—would be found mingling with congregants in the church basement, discussing events of the day over doughnuts and percolated coffee. In the weeks and months ahead, repercussions of the war in Europe would continue being felt closer to home. Thousands of Axis prisoners were being transferred to work camps in upstate New York, including Army bases in Watertown and Rome. In addition to providing labor in canning factories, the POWs—under the keen watch of guards "with business-like tommy-guns ready for instant use as needed"—would soon tend harvests in upstate New York fields.[28]

With a mix of curiosity and pride, an approving public—and probably Himes himself—saw the arrival of prisoners as a harbinger of broader victory, among other good things. The Oswego Farm Bureau, keenly interested in capitalizing on the much-needed source of labor, was formulating inquires as to whether the antiquated Fort Ontario in Oswego, soon to be decommissioned as US soldiers were shifted to other places, might be repurposed as a prison camp for Nazis.[29] As it would turn out, the compound was found ill-suited for that purpose, though before the war was over it would serve a more salient role in the annals of home front history: under orders of President Roosevelt, the old army base that once served as an outpost for colonial conquest of the New World would become "Safe Haven," the first and only refugee camp in the United States for Europeans fleeing Nazi persecution.[30]

All this was yet to come, and Himes would surely have an interest in learning whatever he could about the evolving status of the fort. A man of gregarious and enterprising temperament, he had done well for himself, even during the Depression, despite a formal education that ended in eighth grade. As (at one time or another) scoutmaster, Sunday school superintendent, town dog warden, cemetery sexton, and noted ace on the church's dart ball team, the deacon was in the know regarding goings-on about town. Perhaps even more so was his wife. Marion Himes, future Noble Grand of the local Daughters of Rebekah lodge, was a farmer of sturdy physique given to wearing flannel and denim when not in her church clothes. She would now be among a klatch of women chatting at the Sunday social about events related to various auxiliary groups and church committees, most of them connected with the war effort.

Aside from whose son or daughter was where, practical aspects of rationing, black markets, scrap drives, and blackout drills would typically provide plenty of fodder for conversation. A primary topic on this day, however, would be the lost bomber. Some original accounts of the ordeal would have been seeded and nurtured the previous day by customers at the Perkins General Store. Cora Perkins, a woman of late middle age who owned the store with her husband, Herbert, was a particularly well-positioned source. Quoted in the local newspaper as the Scriba resident being among the first to alert Oswego police of the low-flying craft, she now might elaborate on her fear that the plane would end up in her parlor.

Other reports would surely validate her story. A snowplow driver, heading north on County Route 29, was said to almost have suffered a coronary after the bomber buzzed his truck from behind. Route 29 intersects the North Road, where the Perkinses lived, and the event fit entirely with their experience. In a whiteout, a snowplow with flashing lights on that empty stretch leading toward the lake, in the mind of a desperate pilot, might look like one clearing an airport runway or, at least, a place to be considered for a last-ditch landing attempt.[31]

Figure 8.3. Workers from local businesses and agencies march from
the port of Oswego in a military parade in 1943. The war was front and
center of home front life, with civilian energy effectively channeled into
any number of paramilitary organizations tasked with building morale and
supporting military operations. Participation became a point of pride and
sometimes status for civilians. Library of Congress, Prints and Photographs Division.

In every regard the news seemed tragic. Two days of searching over
and along the lake had found nothing at all. But still, there were grounds
for hope. Notwithstanding a story circulating around town about Grace
Echer, a shoreline resident said to have seen a flash on the horizon reflected
in her bedroom mirror after having been woken by the thrum of a plane
passing overhead, there was still reason to believe the crew had bailed out
or survived a crash landing. There were many places in northern New
York where a heavy bomber, never mind individuals in parachutes, could
disappear without a trace in vast and impassible terrain made even more
impassible when drifted with snow. This, on face value, was not terribly
encouraging, though it might be offered as an explanation for the delay in
positive news, with ample space for hope that, with God's grace, the boys
might still be found alive.

With no shortage of conjecture, the conversation might flit from one
notion to the next before settling on a point of certainty: the parents of the
missing boys. May God be with them. What could be worse? In church

company, the inevitable thought may have been concluded euphemistically, but the summary in the newspaper that morning coldly touched a fear stowed in the heart of any parent. What could be worse than the specter of one of your own lost in a forsaken place, possibly dead, or slowly dying, seeking help nobody can provide?

Between tending to chickens and getting himself ready that morning, Elwyn Himes possibly had not had time to peruse the Sunday newspaper before church. Likewise for Marion, who would have been busy expediting breakfast and overseeing the grooming of their three young children. But at some point, one of them would have surely scanned the latest coverage of the lost plane, note that two days of searching had produced no results, and find a bit of information they could actually act on. It would be in the last paragraph, beginning with "next of kin have been notified."

In coming days, hope for the boys' survival would flicker and wane before vanishing altogether, leaving their loved ones, bereft of answers yet expected to come to terms, to seek what information they could from faraway places. When it became evident more was to be done, Marion and Elwyn Himes would head up the effort.

The Good Lord would be receiving many prayers, including an ample share from Lucy Ponder. Though holy praise and humble petition were as sustaining to her daily life as food, her communion with the Lord would become especially fervent after a Western Union messenger arrived at her doorstep in Jackson, Mississippi, on Friday afternoon, February 18.

Keith's mother now resided in a house on George Street where she had moved sometime after her youngest graduated from high school. The relocation from Forkville may have been prompted by her diabetic husband's need for treatment in his final months and encouraged by her younger children's desire to pursue futures beyond the farm. Regardless, her residence in the center of the city posed a striking contrast to her old life. It was squarely between the Farish Street district, a thriving black business and cultural enclave to the west later to become known as "Mississippi's Harlem," and the sprawling state capital buildings to the east and south. Yet her front door opened to a view across the street that was stunningly serene—acres of lush public green space, shaded by magnolias and cedars, framed by wrought iron and stonework as old as the city itself. Here, an unabridged catalog of once-living southern history had been laid to rest:

governors and generals, soldiers and plantation owners, bankers and mer-
chants, teachers and clerks, servants and maids, and, in unmarked graves,
an unknown number of slaves and paupers.

It was against the backdrop of Jackson's public cemetery that a delivery boy rode up the sidewalk and dismounted his bicycle at the steps of
324 George Street. He would be received by a woman, small and gray yet
sturdy and unfailingly upright, who would surely associate the messenger
with news of one of her children. Three of them were now in the military,
yet so far only Lucy's daughter Sallye, the Navy nurse, was overseas—in
the relative safety of the Hawaiian Islands. This message might be anything: a belated Valentine's greeting, word that someone would be arriving
home on leave, or news of Keith's much anticipated commission overseas.

Upon learning that it was from the War Department, Lucy Ponder's de-
meanor would change. She would accept it warily, perhaps looking for an
error in the address before opening. The communication was brief—two
lines. And they began with the most dreaded words of the war:

I deeply regret to inform you. . . .

And then the rest:

. . . your son, Wendell Keith Ponder, is pilot of an aircraft which is overdue
at its destination and therefore must be considered missing. STOP. Extensive
search is being conducted for the aircraft and you will be furnished further
details as they become available. END.

At some point, she would find space to breathe again.

In the days to come, the message, signed by a Colonel Jones, would
remain close at hand—maybe in the pocket of her housedress or on the
kitchen table, not far from a well-worn Bible, where it would be painfully
revisited. *Overdue* . . . a trying word. Trains could be overdue. So could
pregnancies. *Missing* rang of something more ominous, but the unhelpful
qualification—*considered*—only served to muddy the meaning. And while
the report of an *extensive* search may have meant to convey a margin of
reassurance, she may have felt, with some reflection, this was the telltale
of the true urgency of the situation. How could an aircraft go missing
in Massachusetts and require an *extensive* search? Unless it went missing over the ocean. Or mountains. She believed there were mountains in

Massachusetts. And here, she would be forced again to yield to a certain feeling welling up in her breast, overwhelming and unwelcome, though not completely unfamiliar.

Lucy's husband had been dead for more than two years, and though she routinely visited her oldest daughter, Juanita—now raising a family of her own in Forkville—Lucy's days of child rearing on the ancestral homestead may have seemed like a former lifetime, given all that had transpired since the war. She would wire Sallye, in the Pacific, and Amos, working in a Navy mailroom in New York City, that their brother was reported missing, whatever that might mean. Phone calls would follow with faraway words of reassurance and encouragement. And then she would wait for Juanita to arrive.

As one day slid into the next with no meaningful updates from Colonel Jones, the uncertainty of Keith's well-being would register as a test of faith, to which Lucy would turn to the Bible for answers: "Trust in the Lord with all thine heart; and lean not unto thine own understanding." Lucy would pray for Keith's safety. And if the Good Lord would not grant that, He might allow for some answers.

If given the dreadful choice, a parent might prefer the kind of telegram received by Lucy Ponder over more conclusive news being delivered daily to homes in every state in the nation. From 1941 through 1945, word of sudden and violent death of American youth hemorrhaged from the War Department. Casualties were mostly the inevitable result, it was generally believed, of honorable battles waged against fierce and ruthless enemies in faraway places. It was a noble but incomplete perception. The newsreels that carried images of victory and strife in distant lands gave no mention of the carnage at home.

On the same day Lucy received the telegram about Keith, AAF clerks thumbed through manila files of thirty other stateside fliers, looking for names and addresses of their next of kin, while mortuary and salvage details were dispatched to sites of twisted wreckage and torn bodies spread over woods, field, desert, and tarmacs from sea to shining sea. Consequent telegrams, regretting to inform, would spare details, though AAF accident reports of February 18, 1944, did not.

Sometime after Ponder and crew missed their second landing attempt in Syracuse, and before Imrie and those aboard the RCAF plane disappeared in the Canadian bush, two fliers met their end over Auburn,

California—victims of a sequence of events that began with a faulty fuse that caused a fire in their Curtiss C-46. As they were thrown about the pitching, burning craft, somehow they managed to don parachutes and crawl out the hatch just as the plane began to spiral, only to fall into spinning propellers.[32]

Later that morning, another fire erupted on a B-24 over Daggett, California. The crew of five bailed out. But by the time the last two dropped through the hatch the plane was too low, and they hit the ground before their chutes could open.[33]

Another fire erupted hours later, this one caused by a bearing failure in a Bell P-39 taking off from Selfridge Field, Michigan. The pilot radioed a mayday to the tower and banked the craft in a wide arc back to the airfield. As he approached the runway, the plane lost power and erupted in flames as it hit the ground.[34]

Twenty thousand feet over Maricopa County, Arizona, a B-24 got slightly out of sync with its formation and, with a slight overcorrection, clipped wings with another. Both crafts spun from the sky for several long minutes and exploded when they hit the ground. All of the seventeen airmen aboard the two planes died instantly.[35]

Within minutes of the disasters unfolding at Selfridge and Williams fields, a Women's Airforce Service Pilot was putting her Vultee BT-15 through the paces low over the hills of San Jose. Perhaps executing a textbook maneuver, though more likely showing off, she stalled the plane in the middle of a "snap roll." She came out of it low and fast, and died when she was thrown from the cockpit when the plane hit the ground.[36]

Later that day, in Georgia, a North American AT-6 with an instructor and student took off from Spence Field. As they became airborne, the student mistakenly pulled back on a lever that controlled the fuel mix rather than the throttle. At three hundred feet, there was no time or space for recovery when the plane stalled.[37]

Before that day ended, five more fliers died after a Douglas C-47 towed two gliders aloft—one on a short tether, one on a long, while training for a mission under the cover of darkness from Fort Bragg, North Carolina. The gliders collided after releasing from the tow; one crashed, and the other crash-landed.[38]

While thirty deaths in one day—not including the eight crew aboard *Getaway Gertie* "considered missing"—would rate above average in the obscure annals of noncombat aviation casualties of World War II, it was by no means an outlier.

As Lucy Ponder sought strength in scripture, Keith Ponder was yet to be declared officially "presumed dead." A mother's hope that her son might still be found alive would seem not unreasonable, her faith well placed. Few would argue that the question of who lives and who dies on any given day falls well outside the realm of mortal understanding. Yet it can be fairly said that the pending fate of the RCAF fliers aboard Liberator 586—the plane lost in the Canadian wilds during the storm that claimed *Gertie*—might be taken as evidence of a miracle. Three days after the airmen failed to arrive at the base in Goose Bay, their families had no more information than Lucy Ponder. But that was about to change.

9

DISCOVERY

Trapper Jim Goudie was a person fully acclimated to an environment where little is heard beyond the cry of wolves and the empty rush of alpine winds. After the nor'easter moved off the Labrador coast on February 19, 1944, he set out on snowshoes to tend his trap line in the foothills of the Mealy Mountains. A day later he arrived at his shelter fifteen miles south of Goose Bay. The following morning, Goudie prepared for a trip deeper into the bush. But first he had to backtrack along a streambed to dig out beaver traps.[1]

It was an arduous job made more difficult by freshly drifted snow, and he was singularly focused when interrupted by an odd sound. It seemed to be coming from somewhere upstream, and it took him a moment to quiet his breathing and better position himself to hear it—a kind of knocking, strangely near and strangely far. He waited for it again, and when it came, he recognized it as a familiar sound, so far out of context in the middle of nowhere that he found it disorienting.

Somebody was chopping wood.

Goudie followed the sound upstream, occasionally pausing to distinguish its true direction from the echo. He continued along the contour of a narrow lake and then crested a small rise, where he now caught a whiff of wood smoke. Intimately knowledgeable of this territory, he was bewildered by signs of human habitation where he knew there to be none. He plodded on and eventually stopped, dumbfounded, at the head of an impressive clearing of splintered balsam.

The dismembered elements of a four-engine bomber sat wedged at the base of a tree. The fuselage was broken in two, with the rear section lying almost parallel with the starboard wing. Wires and hydraulic lines spilled from the gap, like tendons of a severed limb. The nose of the plane also had been sheared off. The pilots' seats were empty. Nearby, a man in an aviator suit, engulfed in a nimbus of respiratory vapor, wielded an ax against one of the splintered trees. He paused and looked up. Years later, that man, navigator Lieutenant Garnet Harland, would recall, "About 1:30 Jim Goudie, a trapper working his line, walked into our camp, and with him came an elation and relief that I cannot express. He was the assurance that we would get out. He was the medium through which our families would be notified of our well-being."[2]

Their well-being, all things considered, was positive, as Goudie would presently learn.

The last flight of Liberator 586 had ended at a tree that didn't budge. The impact came on the starboard wing, causing the plane to pivot with such force that the rear section snapped off after whipping against another tree. Remarkably, Harland and the two pilots, Imrie and Campbell, were unscathed. They scrambled from the wreck and wallowed in the snow to fire extinguishers mounted in an external compartment. They found Johns, the engineer, who had been thrown out of the break in the fuselage, buried, on the verge of suffocation, with only his feet exposed. Gilmour, the radio man, was pinned in his station under the collapsed dorsal turret, fighting back panic at the smell of gas and dread of sudden combustion. The snow had snuffed the engine flames, and the pilots and navigator doused remaining hot spots with the extinguishers.

Johns, who had removed his gloves while adjusting fuel controls prior to the crash, suffered frostbitten hands. Gilmour, extracted from under the turret, had a broken collarbone. David Griffin, a public relations officer who was in the rear of the plane with Johns, had gotten caught up in cables as the fuselage parted. He was beyond help.[3] By the time the survivors had taken stock of their situation, the temperature was thirty below zero Fahrenheit and dropping with the fading daylight.

Their exercise of survival had only begun. A long and impossibly bitter night, the first of many, was at hand. The crew dug an encampment in the snow under the starboard wing and lined it with parachutes and sheepskin rugs they had bought as souvenirs in Iceland. To prevent anyone from falling into a hypothermic coma, one man was assigned to stay awake and arouse others every two hours so they could move around.

After the first night, copilot Campbell rummaged some K rations and chocolate bars from the wreck. Though provisions were scarce, they found plenty of matches and a small fire ax that would prove critical. A fire was needed for warmth, to melt snow for water, and to signal search planes; feeding it was a chore that took priority over all other matters. "None of us was a woodsman and maybe it was just as well we didn't know it," Harland recalled. "Our axe, which had a short handle and a light head, was not exactly the kind of axe you would choose to fell much of a tree, but we prized it highly. We knew our very life depended upon the proper use and care of it."[4]

The fire was indeed a lifesaver, though its effectiveness as a signal was hampered by a breeze down the valley that tended to disperse the smoke before it rose above the trees. The clearing, impressive from the ground, would be hardly distinguishable from the terrain's craggy natural features when viewed from the air. At the most obvious place for a signal—the frozen lake—they had anchored a red-and-white parachute that fluttered next to the letters SOS stomped out in the snow.[5] And apparently even that was hard to see.

At one point they heard the drone of engines and caught a glimpse of an approaching DC-3. The men made for a machine gun loaded with tracer bullets and lashed to a stump for this sort of occasion, only to find the breech lock frozen. They fumbled with flair guns, equally useless in the extreme cold.[6] As the drone of the plane faded, there was a moment of despondency, perhaps not helped by somebody's well-intended remark that more would surely follow.

But by day three, with provisions running low, no more planes had come, and the men began planning to hike out while they were still reasonably strong and well nourished. Though they knew the heading and distance to the base, route finding through the broken, hilly terrain would be daunting. Moreover, traveling more than short bursts in untrodden waist-deep snow was difficult and draining. To address this, they succeeded in fashioning a pair of snowshoes from pine boughs and parachute cord.[7] These worked well enough around camp, and they were in the process of making more, though relying on them to cover thirteen miles in heavy snow over unknown terrain would require a vast leap of faith.

That's when Goudie appeared in the woods, bringing "elation and relief" to the survivors, though there was little time for celebration. Within a half hour after his arrival, the trapper—best qualified for the assignment for many reasons—departed the encampment. He would trek through the night and into the next morning. By the time he reached the base at Goose Bay to deliver a note from Imrie detailing the crew's coordinates, provisions, health status, and other essential information, the crew of Liberator 586 had been stranded in the woods for four days with temperatures at night routinely falling below minus forty.[8]

Several more days would pass before rescue came. But things soon got materially better for the stranded crew. About the same time Goudie arrived at the RCAF base with the news of the crew's survival, an American plane aiding in the search happened to fly over the crash site, and a spotter, finally, saw the men's signal fire. After a subsequent pass, billowing chutes drifted from the sky with a cache of K rations, arctic clothing, snowshoes, sleeping bags, tents, and cigarettes. "Stuff showered down like manna from Heaven," said Campbell. "And it was just as welcome."[9]

Later that day, a single-engine RCAF bush plane—a Norseman—carrying more provisions and a medical officer descended toward the lake and landed in an explosion of powder. That craft was followed sometime later by a Piper Cub, flown by Americans. Both planes were outfitted with skis for landing gear, which didn't prevent them from getting stuck. Another day passed before the men were able to free the Piper Cub, and the ailing Gilmore and Johns were loaded aboard and flown, at last, to safety. With conditions on the lake too risky for subsequent landings, the rest of the group, now surviving in what might be described, relative to their previous circumstances, as comfort, would have to endure a few more nights.

On Friday, February 25, a week after they had crashed, the means for rescue arrived with US Army dogsled teams. The evacuation party, now including the doctor and pilot of the Norseman, three mushers, and many energetic canines, blazed the trail back to Goose Bay.[10] Two of the sleds carried provisions, tents, and essential equipment from the bomber. On the other, wrapped in parachute fabric, rested David Griffin's frozen body, followed by the rest of the party on snowshoes. It was well they were not forced to make the trip on their homemade equipment. Well-outfitted and provisioned, with the experienced sled teams breaking trail, it was still an overnight journey to cover the thirteen miles.

Shortly after Imrie's crew began their ordeal in the Canadian outback, trooper Charles McCann, expecting to be among the first to reach *Getaway Gertie*'s crash site in upstate New York, must have wondered, first and foremost, whether he might find survivors. McCann turned up his collar against spindrift streaming off shoulder-high snowbanks as he approached the steps to the Clemons farmhouse. He was received instantly by a man in his late thirties, of solid build and embracing gaze. Gerald Clemons, joined by his wife, Mildred, ushered the trooper into their home.

With few preliminaries, Mr. Clemons recounted how, at around 4 a.m. the previous morning, the household was startled by "a loud crash and explosion like thunder although there was no rumbling sound after it."[11] Mrs. Clemons and their oldest—fourteen-year-old Helen, now joining them—had been woken by the sound of a low-flying plane moments prior to the explosion. They walked into the family room, trailed by Helen's younger siblings, who would be wide-eyed with excitement over the uniformed visitor and others gathering outside.

At a window facing the southwest, Clemons nodded at a landscape of outbuildings eclipsed by snowbanks, to a forested hill standing in the distance against a brooding horizon. The blast came from that direction, he said.[12] News of the missing plane had not reached him until that morning; it was then, realizing the significance of the event, that he notified the Lewis County sheriff. He had set out to explore the area himself and had not gotten far.

There would be little need for elaboration on the rarity of midwinter electrical storms in northern New York. The farmer, moreover, did not strike the trooper as a person given to hyperbole. As justice of the peace of the town of Denmark, Clemons would stand nothing to gain by a false alarm. And as a lifelong resident of the area, he would know thunder when he heard it. In any case, the merit of the whole affair was now a public matter after newspapers in Rome and Syracuse had caught wind of the story, probably from the public affairs office at Rome but possibly the sheriff or maybe a neighbor listening in on a party line. One of the news-papermen, eager for a scoop, had already hazarded the snowy drive from Syracuse to talk to Clemons directly.

Lieutenant McCann, a twenty-year veteran of Troop B stationed in the Adirondacks, had led more than a few searches while working against the elements and the clock, negotiating terrain where a wandering youth or even a seasoned hiker might find themselves suddenly and hopelessly lost after venturing a short distance off trail. Now, unfolding a topographical map, the trooper consulted the farmer on the lay of the land. The area in question—between the northeast slope of the Tug Hill Plateau and a valley to the east bisected by the Black River—was flat compared to the rugged Adirondack country that McCann was familiar with. And it was far more contained—a mere six square miles bordered by town roads. Yet its most formidable feature didn't appear on a map. Whereas most places in the eastern snowbelt tend to get hit by lake effect carried by prevailing winds across the Great Lakes from the west, southwest, or northwest, Denmark, situated squarely off the east end of the easternmost lake, was uniquely exposed to crossfire from multiple angles, making it, with little exaggeration, one of the snowiest places in the country.[13] If they didn't already know this, McCann and his small party of troopers and rangers, staging in the shelter of the barn, would find out.

After packing survival gear and pairing up to share the burden of breaking trail, they set out on snowshoes. Each team would cover ap-proximately a square mile—an area equivalent to about five hundred foot-ball fields, which might require fifteen miles or more of trekking back and forth through terrain where the line of sight was obscured by trees and brush. They were barely under way when, in typical form, a lake-effect band arrived abruptly and unannounced, snuffing out all sensory cues and frame of reference. Roads and trails, shadows and textures, even sounds disappeared in a featureless sweep of white. The suffocating effect was amplified by arctic cold that literally took one's breath away. They didn't get far before turning back.[14]

After overnighting in the nearby substation in the town of Lowville, the team set out again the following morning under clearing skies, this time making better headway on their respective routes. Every so often the

Figure 9.1. Heavy snow obscures a farmhouse in the small town of Denmark, New York, on the remote Tug Hill Plateau. Over the course of a season, lake-effect storms sometimes dump more than twenty feet of snow across the area where civilian and army rescue teams searched for *Gertie*. Photo by Glenn Coin, *Syracuse Post-Standard*, Syracuse.com.

drone of search planes penetrated the muffled silence of the woods. As far as McCann could tell, none lingered.

Weather observations from nearby Army bases showed no indication the farmer had heard anything other than an explosion. But by day three, Monday, anticipatory thrill began yielding to doubt, robustly nourished by tedium and fatigue, and renewed consideration of the possibility of thunder in February. This place, situated squarely between the atmospheric extremes of the Great Lakes seaway and rugged Adirondack peaks, harbored no shortage of localized weather phenomena, the least of which might be an isolated clap of midwinter thunder triggered by a passing front with radical temperature shifts. Deep in the woods, McCann would at some point come to realize that it must have been this kind of meteorological fluke, after all, that brought them here. There would be no other explanation.

Recovering feeling in his fingers at the Clemons farmhouse, the trooper would update Begland, the intelligence officer at the Rome Army base: the party had covered much of the designated area and found not the slightest indication of a plane crash. Air spotters, he would learn, had been no more successful, though they had been recalled because of weather. A warming trend was forecast in days to follow. The break from the cold would be a welcomed relief, but the snow would become like wet cement.

At that point, there may have been some discussion between the veteran police officer and the young Army captain about the merit of a plodding and resource-intensive ground search in the absence of any sign whatsoever of a crash spotted from the air.[15] Or perhaps that disagreement would be taken up by their respective commanders. Regardless, the foot search near the Clemons farm would continue, while the search from the air would broaden over the snow-laden plateau to the southwest.

By late Monday, the remarkable tale of survival that Jim Goudie delivered to Goose Bay would have reached the higher-ups at Rome and Westover, and with it, renewed hope that the American crew might also be found alive.[16] Although Lieutenant Colonel Skinner, the liaison officer directing the search in upstate New York, had not abandoned the idea that *Gertie* may have gone down on the Tug Hill Plateau, new intelligence was shifting focus back to the Adirondacks: two woodsmen reported "red and green lights burning on the side of Catamount Mountain." At first, they thought they were seeing a low-flying plane in the distance, "but later established definitely they [the lights] were on the mountain." The woodsmen "tried to reach the spot but had to turn back."[17] Begland took the call from the state police at 7 p.m. Sunday—two and a half days after a fuel truck driver had reportedly spotted a plane over nearby South Colton the night *Gertie* disappeared. Embracing the possibility that the loggers had spotted marooned fliers signaling with distress flairs, Skinner set about organizing search parties.

Catamount Mountain, with a summit at 1,800 feet, is more of a foothill than a true mountain, closer to the Saint Lawrence River valley to the northeast than the High Peaks to the southwest. Still, it's rugged and remote. At the time, it had a fire tower offering a view of the region where the woodsmen were said to have seen the lights.[18] By Monday evening, reporters learned from a teletype message dispatched from state police in

Potsdam that a trooper had reached the tower and saw nothing, though "sight was limited to only one side of numerous hills in the area."[19] Soon, planes were again circling low over the region while a detail of troopers and rangers geared up for another expedition. "The woods are so thick up that way that it might take four or five days to explore it thoroughly from the ground and the air," an officer at the Rome base cautioned an expectant press.[20]

Each new lead, no matter how tenuous, triggered a spasm of rumor, some of which found its way into local accounts that had little else to offer in the way of advancing the story. On the sixth day of the search, one bulletin turned the public eye again to the Clemons farm: "An imaginative report from undetermined sources that the missing B-24 bomber had been located near Denmark and that several ambulances had been dispatched there early yesterday [Wednesday] was emphatically denied and denounced last night by officials at the Rome air depot." The rumor was blamed on "a badly garbled version of a report earlier in the week from Gerald Clemons."[21]

In search of a scoop, reporters turned to another line of scuttlebutt: the search for the lost B-24 had been abandoned altogether.[22] That assessment—perhaps rising from the fact that search planes were no longer seen abundantly along the lake or over central New York communities after attention shifted to the mountains and plateau—also drew a testy denial from Skinner, who declared the search under way at "every flyable hour."

Still, updates from the public affairs office were growing lackluster and redundant. One summary, reasonably void of spin, put a finer point on matters: "Although theories that the bomber, which vanished with no early confirmed reports of a crash landing, might have plunged into Lake Ontario have not been entirely discounted, army officials expressed belief it probably plowed into dense wilderness in the foothills of the Adirondacks."[23]

And so, the search over the mountains would continue—producing no more success than the search over the plateau. And both were diverting spotters away from where some observers felt certain the bomber actually went down.[24] "Unofficial and semi-official comment persists in the belief that the Liberator may have come to rest in Lake Ontario," one report observed on Tuesday, day five, "but army planes did not return to scrutinize the lake again yesterday."[25]

There was, in truth, no telling where the plane had gone; the officers had little choice but to continue working with the leads they were given, however inconsistent they might be.

Reports that placed *Gertie* simultaneously in multiple places quite distant from one another remained a particular problem, and Skinner and Begland sought answers in the map they continually revised at the small room at the Rome base that served as command center. The most obvious explanation—that another plane was heard to the north and east while Ponder was circling over Syracuse and Oswego—would also be the easiest to dismiss, because airports had been closed by then, and flight controllers posted no record of other aircraft lost in that region.

More likely, Skinner would deem reports of the lost plane's location from observers on the ground, in certain instances at least, more reliable than those given by Ponder and crew from the air. Some discrepancies might be explained, for example, if Ponder had homed in on a radio signal emanating from the Syracuse landing field, or that of nearby Rome, while moving away from the transmitter rather than toward it. In the stress of the moment, their judgment muddled by fatigue, inexperience, and radio interference, it would take a while for the crew to discover that the tone on the radio compass was fading rather than strengthening, and dots and dashes heard on the margin of the beam, if Ponder had deviated from its center, were transposed. If in fact the temperamental receiver was working at all in the extreme conditions.

This, or for that matter any number of other navigational errors and radio problems, might explain *Gertie*'s reported presence low over Oswego about the same time Ponder radioed that he was approaching Syracuse.[26] Visual cues, to the extent they existed at all, would have only compounded the misperception. In a snowstorm, Oswego's lights could easily have been mistaken for those of Syracuse by a crew unfamiliar with either place.

In any event, the radio signal that led Ponder to believe he was approaching Syracuse would be spotty at best, and short-lived. After again losing contact, perhaps well north of her reported position, *Gertie* would circle, perhaps multiple times, before straying across Mexico Bay.[27] Fifteen minutes later the Coast Guard watch at Galloo Island would hear the approaching plane. Trying to avoid torrents of lake-effect snow while also looking for a landing place, the crew would circle blindly around

Watertown—a small city ten miles inland from the northeast end of the lake—perhaps attempting at some point to follow the New York Central train tracks. This would account for reports along the Saint Lawrence River valley and the Tug Hill Plateau between 1 and 3 a.m. (with allowances for a generous margin of error in some cases).

Reports of the plane in the Adirondacks, farther east, well after the plane's fuel presumably would have run out, might be explained, in Skinner's mind at least, by another critical miscalculation by the crew. Planes were typically fully fueled before takeoff, giving B-24s a cruising time of twelve hours. Ponder reported that he was desperately low on fuel at 2 a.m., yet follow-up reports from Westover held that *Gertie*'s gas supply could have held out until 5 a.m. or maybe later. If this were the case, the crew would have had time to execute the order to bail out.

Hunches that the plane ended up in the hinterlands crystallized after the first few days of the search produced no signs of wreckage or crew on the lake or in rural or metropolitan areas of central New York. "We're banking on the probability that the bomber is in the densely wooded area east and northeast of Watertown because most reliable reports of the plane's direction have come from that area," one officer announced after five days of searching.[28]

Despite the optimism, there was no escaping that reports placing *Gertie* east of the lake, though abundant, were mostly circumstantial, and it wasn't precisely clear what made one more reliable than another. Interpretation would boil down to intuition and an attempt at corroboration. At any rate, looking at the points plotted on the map, Begland and Skinner must have seen a pattern develop, with each additional bit of intelligence selectively placing *Gertie* and her crew where the officers expected and, above all, *hoped* to find her—not at the bottom of Lake Ontario, but somewhere in the high country, awaiting rescue.[29]

It would take a discovery by a farmer in Oswego County to set things straight.

By Thursday, the cold snap from earlier in the week had eased, and though the day was not exactly warm, sunlight pierced the clouds as Paul Donahue made his way along a path toward the lake. The farmer had planned this sojourn between afternoon chores and supper and was making good time on a trail likely broken by the Coast Guard the previous week and his own foot traffic since. The sun was still well off the horizon, and in the absence of any breeze, the lake would be calm for a change, promising an unfettered view over and along the water.

Gertie had been missing for nearly a week, and Donahue would have scanned the *Oswego Palladium-Times* that morning for an update. After the initial excitement of her low flight over the city of Oswego and the adjacent town of Scriba—where Donahue lived near the Perkinses and the Himeses—the reports each day had grown shorter and were found, if at all, buried deeper in the inside pages. Speculation that parties were closing in on the crash site, first on the plateau and later in the mountains, had so far amounted to nothing. At Grange Society functions and the Perkins General Store, buzz of the lost plane would give way to other news, including what the local community stood to gain or lose if Fort Ontario became a prison camp, a war hospital, or whatever else the Defense Department might decide with whatever influence local congressional representatives could bring to bear.

Fort Ontario was several miles west of Donahue's path to the lake. But the threat of war had left another imprint on the local landscape to the east, where pastureland and hayfields had been repurposed for coastal artillery and antiaircraft training.[30] The arrangement produced lease income to farmers like Donahue and, at indeterminate intervals, a grand spectacle seen and heard for miles.[31] Such occasions sometimes came at night and invariably began with the sound of approaching aircraft. Searchlights would rake the sky for targets towed on long cables over the water, chased by brilliantly streaming munitions delivered with the sustained crump of "ack-ack" guns.[32]

On this day, however, all was quiet, save the crunch of snow underfoot and Donahue's breathing as he cautiously negotiated the shore ice to survey the expansive view opening before him. The lake's disposition was ever-changing, and at the moment it appeared stunningly serene. Ice banks undercut by waves hung in an attitude of both menace and elegance over water of indeterminable depth. The farmer directed his gaze from shoreline to horizon, his imagination fired by drifting forms—ice mostly—easily mistaken for things they were not. After dismissing several such phantasms, he fixed on an object in the distance directly offshore.

Gauging distance over water was tricky; that this thing appeared to be far away yet plainly visible suggested that, whatever it was, it was

Figure 9.2. A postcard from the 1930s shows farmland on Nine Mile Point converted to an artillery range. Leading up to and during the early years of World War II, antiaircraft batteries sometimes shot at targets towed by planes over the lake.
Collection of Fort Ontario State Historic Site, New York State Office of Parks, Recreation and Historic Preservation.

substantial. It was mostly flat, with a bit of ragged structure jutting obliquely from one end. The other end tapered into the water, its full length coming into view periodically as it moved on the swell. He had seen uprooted trees floating prone like that. Now and then it caught the late afternoon light, and in one such instance he could see, unmistakably now, the gleam of metal and the texture of riveted seams.

Donahue would be well aware of the hubbub raised by the supposed discovery of the lost plane in the town of Denmark, and possibly cognizant of the embarrassment that yet another false alarm might bring. But as he continued to trace the movement of the object, he became sure of what he was seeing. A half hour later, back at his farmhouse, he asked the operator to connect him to the Coast Guard station. The ensuing conversation would be overheard on the party line. Word among the townsfolk spread quickly: "*Getaway Gertie* has been found!"

By nightfall, Coast Guard sentries had set up camp along the shore. More debris was expected to follow. The area was blocked off. And a skiff was launched to investigate.

10

RECOVERY

It wouldn't have provided much in the way of satisfaction, but Ensign Hebert must have felt a touch of vindication that his initial hunch was accurate: the B-24 went down in the lake. The commander of the Oswego
Coast Guard station had held fast to that conviction even after calling
off the foot search along the southern and eastern shore when Lieutenant
Colonel Skinner, at the Rome Army base, redirected air spotters inland.
With no boats and not enough planes to continue a systematic survey of
the lake, a random vigil by foot along the hazardous and largely inaccessible shoreline would be futile "unless some definite word of the missing ship
is received," Hebert was paraphrased in the newspaper.[1] When that word
finally arrived with Donahue's discovery of wreckage off Nine Mile Point,
a reporter felt compelled to note, for the record, that "the Oswego Coast
Guard had insisted right along that the missing bomber was in Lake Ontario."[2] It was an unnecessary detail, one that would hardly engender ca-
maraderie with Hebert's counterparts in the Army, the ensign would find,

if and when somebody got around to noticing it. At the moment, though, all hands were focused on the task before them.

A detail of guardsmen and state troopers, bivouacked at points along the shore, had tracked the object through the night as it drifted around the contour of Nine Mile Point. By dawn the next day—Friday—it had settled into a cove roughly three miles east, on the northeast side of the headland, in front of a cluster of shuttered cottages where Hebert now stood in knee-deep snow surveying the scene. It was already warming up; the air, damp, portending rain. The lake was dead calm, with gray morning light diffused so evenly on the horizon it was hard to tell exactly where water ended and sky began. Search planes droned offshore, their pilots and spotters watching both for flotsam and the threat of approaching weather.

The wreckage could be seen more vividly through binoculars. From the previous night's reconnaissance, Hebert understood he was looking at the portside, inboard wing section of a multiengine craft, presumably the missing B-24, its buoyancy enabled by empty fuel tanks carried within and the absence of two engines once suspended underneath. The sleek riveted surface was almost flush with the water, except for contours of the vacant engine nacelles and a bouquet of shorn metal and dislodged apparatus splayed from the end that once passed through the top of the fuselage. There was no question now—the craft had come to a violent end. If the men had not bailed out (and nearly a week of searching had produced no evidence they had), circumstances suggested more grisly discoveries awaiting on the currents.

Captain Begland, on his way from Rome, was preceded by twenty MPs to keep rubberneckers at a distance, and they were taking up stations at the most obvious access points to the snow-swept shore from plowed routes to the south.[3] They would have their work cut out for them. According to one newspaper account, "during the whole day scores of automobiles virtually blocked the roads leaving from the main highways toward the lake shore. Parking their cars . . . the occupants made their way through fields and underbrush and over fences and also traversed the treacherous icebound shore of the lake in order to see the wreckage and observe the salvaging operations."[4]

Spectators may have gained a vantage point from the southeast end of a section of shoreline after hiking in on an unplowed road. Or some

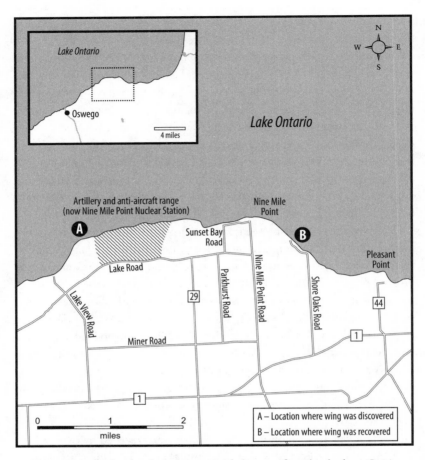

Figure 10.1. A wing panel of a large aircraft, later confirmed to be from *Gertie*, drifted around Nine Mile Point after it was spotted and before it was recovered at Shore Oaks beach. Map by Mike Bechthold.

may have gathered at the northwest end of the same shore after beating footpaths through orchards, woods, and fields from Nine Mile Point. The police, as it turned out, would tolerate these onlookers from a distance. But no photographs were allowed, one reporter observed, because "no doubt there was certain restricted equipment in the wing section."[5]

There would not be much to see, however, until Herbert figured out how to get the piece to shore before the weather changed and the lake reclaimed it. He was separated from that objective by a mere five hundred feet of placid water. Yet the current brought the target no closer, and with no means to secure it, it may as well have been halfway to Canada.

Confidence would not be an issue for Hebert, a trim, neat man who relished the spit and polish of maritime life. At thirty-nine, he had spent the entirety of his adult life in the Coast Guard, and though a junior officer, he was well seasoned compared to many of comparable or higher rank in the Army. With every available resource being deployed overseas, his own moment—on an assault cargo ship transporting troops and supplies to the Pacific—would soon come, and when it did, he would embrace his duties overseeing deck crews and work parties.[6] What Hebert needed just now, however, were boats. The Oswego harbor, ten miles to the west, was iced over, the powerboat fleet drydocked. It might be with tempered satisfaction, then, that he would observe, finally, the approach of a Coast Guard skiff that had put in at an access point between Oswego harbor and where he now stood. It carried a crew of two at the oars and a coxswain at the tiller guiding the craft amid ice floes.[7]

At some point during the morning, the ensign might also have noted, over the ambient drone of aircraft above the lake, the laboring pitch of a diesel engine by land. It grew louder, off and on, signaling the approach of an Oswego County truck, fronted with a Bunyanesque plow, ramming its way through a winter's worth of stratified snow and ice. Progress was incremental; the route to the lake—Shore Oaks—had to be wide enough to accommodate heavy salvage equipment from the Rome base that would allow the operation to begin in earnest.[8]

Back at Westover, Keith Ponder's squadron leader, Captain Paul Lewis Mathison, sat in a hearing room and waited, as it were, to face the music. Though the gravity of the forthcoming interrogation would undoubtedly influence his carriage, his striking Nordic countenance, judging by a transcript of his responses, affected an air of disinterest. Sitting next to Mathison was Major Mitchell Mullholland, Mathison's commanding officer and, apparently, an advocate. In front of them was a formidable table, behind which sat Colonel Sanford Willits and an attentive clerk.[9] Off to the side, a stenographer awaited a break in the silence.

A few minutes earlier, after "reporting as directed" and crisply saluting, Mathison had raised his right hand and taken an oath administered by one of the colonel's assistants and, at the colonel's direction, taken a seat. Now, after dispatching with preliminaries, including the purpose of the hearing—to determine the facts and circumstance leading to the loss of AAF aircraft 41–29047E and crew—Willits consulted some papers before him and got down to business.

"Did you brief this flight?" he asked Mathison.

"Yes, sir. I did," the captain responded.

"What instructions did you give?"

Mathison responded confidently: "Climb through the overcast, fly in local formation, remaining in the local area. . . . Break up before the close of the period and make individual let downs." The planes, the captain added, were expected to pass through two layers of overcast, one on the way to the rendezvous at ten thousand feet. The other as they climbed to twenty-three thousand feet.

Willits held out his hand and received several more papers from the clerk. "What weather briefing did you give?" he asked.

"I don't know whether a weather officer was there or whether the navigator conducted the briefing," Mathison answered.

"Do you know what the weather was?"

"I don't."

Here a moment of silence might have lingered as the colonel again consulted papers. "They were briefed at noon and didn't take off until five?"

"I don't know the actual time of takeoff."

More silence.

"Did they file the flight plan?"

This might have warranted some exposition: Flights plans were not required because Ponder and the five other pilots had been cleared for local high-altitude formation under visual flight rules. Mathison would be acutely aware, however, that commanding officers tend not to like explanations on matters with which they are familiar. Moreover, such an answer would surely invite another question: how the hell did a local flight end up somewhere in northern New York via Pennsylvania? For whatever reason, Mathison proffered an outright falsehood: "Yes, sir," he said. "Individual flight plans were filed."

The colonel, again glancing at the reports before him, turned now to the circumstances that brought 047 to the navigational range in northern Pennsylvania instead of Westover: "Do you think it possible they tuned into the Wilkes-Barre beam?"

"Very definitely," Mathison responded. "Both of them were on [frequency] 272." Here, Major Mullholland, at Mathison's side, interjected flatly: "We told the squadrons not to take out [*sic*] any cross-country flights until six, because we expected it [the weather] to come down at that time."

The scene is not hard to visualize: Willits looking up from his papers, this time allowing enough time for his gaze to take hold. He could be a stickler. As a federal aeronautical inspector between the wars, Willits had once grounded Clarence Chamberlin, the celebrated aviation pioneer, for flying too low over New York Harbor.[10] The colonel's subordinates present in the hearing room would probably have no reason to know that. But they would be keenly tuned in to another dynamic at play before them, and at airfields throughout the world: qualified squadron leaders in 1944 were in high demand, and their transgressions might be weighed on a less discerning scale than those of a civil stunt pilot in 1931. Perhaps this might explain why Mathison's answers, terse and offhand, had so far been delivered without apparent concern for reprimand. Or maybe the captain was responding reflexively, his instincts shaped by an aeronautical tenet rooted deeply in maritime antiquity that held particular sway in the AAF in 1944: it is the senior officer *onboard* the ship, first and foremost, who answers for the well-being of crew and vessel.

Yet when the colonel's questions turned from the preflight briefing to the protocol and involvement of control towers and ground crew guiding the flight, Mathison's disinterest, rather suddenly, seemed to vaporize. "The man could have actually made a landing," Mathison asserted at this point. "It all rests with the pilot anyway. I don't think the [control] tower should take any rub along those lines. . . . I think an experienced man would have gotten through."

Those in the tower, and on the ground, and in the briefing room, would all, eventually, share accountability with Wendell Keith Ponder for the loss of aircraft 41–29047E and crew. But not as far as this inquiry was concerned. Willits had no more questions. There were flights to log and a war to fight. The meeting was concluded in less than fifteen minutes.

A report was due to the Office of Flying Safety, and it was signed by Willits and Mulholland on March 6, seventeen days after Ponder was last heard from and eleven days after the wing piece was discovered drifting off Nine Mile Point. The assessment assigned responsibility for 047's loss and the death of its crew to "100 percent pilot error due to poor technique, inability to decide what to do, and poor judgment in not having the crew bail out. . . . The pilot should have stayed close to Westover Field. . . . Homing in on Wilkes-Barre range was carelessness. At Syracuse the pilot should either have landed immediately or had the crew bail out. The 'milling around' for three to four hours was evidence of mental confusion under pressure."[11] The report acknowledged "bad weather conditions at night and bad snow static which was prevalent throughout the night" as "circumstances directly affecting the accident" but stopped short of listing them as causal factors.

The day before the report was filed, as it happened, Chuck Yeager, on his first combat mission, had been taken prisoner after being shot down over France. At the time it was an unrelated and unremarkable loss; Yeager was still years away from the achievements that would make him an American icon. Yet the AAF ethic that blithely resigned certain fatalities to the laws of natural selection, as Yeager would later express with his "weak sister" metaphor, was already at work in the assessment signed by Willits. In assigning blame, the colonel and his subordinates had also provided cover for the living at the expense of the dead. In this instance, that decision spared Willits from having to implicate Mathison and others under his watch involved in briefing and directing the final flight of 047, much less systemic institutional factors. Yet the colonel would not be able to entirely wash his hands of the matter.

A review by the Office of Flying Safety, appended to the accident report three days later, found Willits's findings "not concurred"—for several reasons. Because Ponder was assigned to fly "above an existing and forecast overcast," instrument clearance was necessary, the review found, along with a requisite flight plan that would have included "the latest and expected trend of weather." Based on Mathison's statement, "it is reasonable to assume that Flight Officer Ponder received little if any weather information." Lack of proper briefing is an especially critical omission in instances where "[poor] radio reception often prevents pilots from receiving route instructions and weather from radio ranges and control towers."[12]

Which pretty much sums up the fate of 047. Still, Ponder himself would receive little in the way of absolution. The final determination held "supervisory personnel" 25 percent responsible "for sending the pilot on an IFR [instrument] flight without a proper clearance and weather briefing," with the rest of the blame attributed to "pilot error for reasons noted" in Willits's report.

The findings by the Aircraft Accident Committee, data points for future analysis by the statistics division, were appended to the accident report with a recommendation "that all pilots and supervisory personnel study AAF Regulations . . . for strict compliance." While confirming that no flight plan had been filed, the assessment did nothing to address Mathison's assertion to the contrary and, regardless, would have little bearing on the rush to war. Mathison was soon on his way to England, where he would lead bombing raids over Germany.

It might be tempting to reach for a timeless moral among these events, yet there is little to be found. Mathison would die seven months after the hearing, at the age of twenty-four, along with seven other crew when his B-24 was shot down over Osnabruck, Germany. Eventually, his body would be recovered and buried in the Netherlands American Cemetery, plot P, row 2, grave 13, amid waves of uniform white crosses marking graves of 8,288 young American soldiers called to drive the German army from the region.[13]

Back in Oswego County, at midmorning on Friday, February 25, the first day of the salvage under Ensign Hebert's command, the Coast Guard skiff had reached the wing piece drifting off Shore Oaks. At the inboard end, among the splay of sheered struts and connecting infrastructure, the pliable acrylic walls of fuel tanks—properties that enabled the structures to self-seal when penetrated by bullets—bulged through ruptured seems. It took some time to secure the ensemble with a network of chains and cable. Then, to the call of the coxswain, the crew began heaving against its bulk.

Progress was marginal, and by and by it became apparent the wreckage was towing the skiff down the lake more than the craft was propelling the wreckage landward. At this rate, the entire operation would have to be moved down the beach, where space was even scarcer. Crews and equipment were presently staged near the northwest end of the cove, on a narrow lane running parallel to shore, which, a quarter mile to the southeast, met the junction branching away from the lake. Beyond that, waterfront access continued only for several hundred more yards, on softer terrain, before petering out in a snow-swept marsh at Otter Creek.

Figure 10.2. The wing section discovered by Paul Donahue afloat at Shore Oaks. The contour of one of the cowlings (*far right in the photo*) under which a missing engine was suspended can be seen on the leading edge of the structure. Empty fuel tanks bulge from the end torn from the fuselage. Courtesy of H. Lee White Marine Museum.

The situation prompted another conference among officers, now joined by the snowplow operator. Surveying the shoreline, they took stock of points where a cable might be payed out amid a low spot among the ice banks. Distances and angles were gauged and discussed. At length, the plow operator returned to the idling vehicle, climbed into the cab, and began maneuvering into position.

The ensuing logistics made for lively copy in the next day's newspapers:

> Hauling the wreckage inshore, a distance of about 500 feet, and pulling it out of the water onto the ice barrier proved to be no easy job. The wreckage, believed to weigh approximately four tons, was dragged along the rockbound bottom of the lakeshore where the water was of insufficient depth to float it. In raising it onto the barrier, a half-inch steel cable parted and heavy ropes snapped.

The job could not have been done except for the power afforded by a huge snowplow truck of the Oswego County Highway Department, which had been sent to clear the trail leading from the main highway into Shore Oaks.[14]

As for the plow operator, she or he was not identified.[15]

As the day wore on, sleet turned to rain, which grew heavier by nightfall. At 7 p.m. operations were suspended, with the wing perched on the ice bank, secured to the plow's winch. The operation had so far provided plenty of color for reporters to fold into their dispatches, yet the Big Story—answers to the questions on everybody's mind—remained conspicuously absent: where was the rest of the plane, and what happened to its crew?

Begland's answer—that there were no new developments—would have provoked palpable disappointment and certain suspicion. Just that morning the *Syracuse Post-Standard* had reported that a party had spotted the fuselage underwater, a mile west from where Donahue saw the wing:

Searching the area in a small boat [Thursday night], aided by state and county police and an FBI representative, the coastguardsmen saw what appeared to be the outline of a large plane beneath the surface of the lake. They could just make out its form with the aid of strong searchlights, but lacked equipment for reaching it.

An attempt to reach the wreckage will probably be made today [Friday] although it was said that necessary equipment is lacking at Oswego. . . . Because of ice and the danger of winter storms on the lake, it probably will be necessary to get a larger craft before any attempt can be made to raise the plane. It is not known whether the bodies of the eight crew members are still in it.[16]

The purported discovery came two thousand feet offshore, about ten miles east of Oswego.[17]

A second report Friday, in the *Watertown Daily Times*, an afternoon paper, took things a step further, claiming coastguardsmen from the Oswego station "mobilized forces this morning in an attempt to raise the wreckage . . . spotted on the bottom of Lake Ontario." Both stories hypothesized that the wing appeared suddenly, after breaking off from the submerged aircraft, thus eluding previous searches from the air. The *Daily Times* added that "an Army insignia . . . identified the debris as part of the missing Liberator."[18] Radio reports from the night before had been even more explicit, promising that bodies of the crew were in the fuselage and would be recovered in the impending salvage operation.[19]

The details were vivid, the explanations lucid. And the report would lead certain wreck seekers to that very spot fifty years later. Yet the anticipated offshore salvage operation—whatever that might have looked like—never materialized. Reporters, pressing for an update, were learning that it was all a mistake. The sighting, sourced in the *Post-Standard* to one Stanley Feldman, evidently a shore patrolman, and unsourced in the *Daily Times*, was flatly denied by Army officials, who, according to a follow-up report in the next day's *Post-Standard*, "clamped down a rigid censorship for security reasons."[20] When pressed about where the fuselage might be, one officer muttered only, "somewhere in Lake Ontario."[21]

The press would find a more approachable source in Ensign Hebert, who was something of a talker, though he had nothing to offer—or at least nothing on the record—about the apparently specious sighting of the submerged fuselage or the source of the rumor. Still, for the benefit of those who had only seen it from a distance, he did provide a generous description of the wing, along with an explanation of the buoyancy of the empty fuel tanks.

Given all the other news to cover and the remoteness of the location, the media scrum would be modest, with reporters from the Mexico weekly, and dailies in Oswego, Rome, Syracuse, Fulton, and Watertown intermittently at the scene or, more often, basing accounts on press releases and reports circulating over the news wire. Those who were there, lacking direct access, would watch from the perimeters, perhaps the more enterprising surreptitiously chatting up rank-and-file soldiers and police as opportunities arose, and finding they knew little more than anybody else.[22] At the end of the day, accounts would rely heavily on what could be gleaned from Skinner, Begland, and Hebert, and updates in the form of news bulletins from the public affairs office at the Rome base.

By and large, the official reports were cautious and generic. The wing still had to be identified. . . . They would continue the search. . . . There was still hope the men had bailed out. Hebert, at least, would offer one tidbit that passed for news in the absence of the Big Story: "There is no doubt that the wing came off the missing B-24 bomber." He would add, as reporters scribbled in their notebooks, an observation that would become something of a refrain in weeks ahead: a thorough search for the rest of the plane couldn't happen before powerboats were made available to drag sections of the lake.[23]

As the day drew to a close, reporters would hustle back to their provincial newsrooms or call stories in from phone booths in downtown Oswego while Coast Guard and Army grunts took shelter in tents pitched back from the shoreline. The exception was those who stood watch by the wing, awash in the glare of spotlights against the enveloping darkness.

The lake remained unusually calm through the next morning. The rain continued, however, grounding planes and leaving Coast Guard parties to search for debris and bodies with binoculars and skiffs.[24] Amid high expectations, a few more counterfeit discoveries appeared, each less dramatic than the previous. Hebert's charges rowed out three times to check individual reports of an object drifting at various locations along the shore, and each time it proved to be "the same big chunk of ice."[25]

It was late morning when a derrick arrived on a flatbed with a small caravan of crews and equipment, which Begland and his subordinates were soon directing to points within the confines of a cramped maze of snowbanks and clearings plowed among the cottages.[26] As the day wore on, the groan of heavy machinery carried up and down the beach, punctuated by the periodic shriek of chains on metal, metal on rock, and alternating shouts of frustration and encouragement. Cables slipped. Parties regrouped. Hours passed. By late afternoon the wing piece, measuring thirty feet by ten feet, had been dragged up the bank and lowered onto a flatbed, covered with tarps, and secured.

It was ultimately heading for the scrapyard. But first, its components would be inspected at the Rome base for serial numbers to confirm what had so far been taken for granted.[27]

Shortly after salvage crews decamped with the wing, Elwyn Himes, the chicken farmer and deacon at North Scriba Baptist Church, negotiated his old Chevy coupe down the deeply rutted road to Shore Oaks. In the seat beside him, Elwyn's eight-year-old son, Charles, peered out the window as the vehicle bounced and crabbed through the muddy troughs. "We'll make it," his father assured. As they approached the place where the road meets the lake they were stopped by a guard, and it may have impressed young Charles that the conspicuously armed and helmeted MP would address his father as "sir." Yet the soldier's clipped sign of respect for the elder civilian would only go so far. The area was restricted, the guard told them. Elwyn explained that he owned a cottage up the road and just wanted to check on things. The guard took stock of the farmer's vehicle and its occupants. He warned Himes that he might get stuck. With that, the young man let them pass.

The ground was indeed getting soft; earth not still covered with snow was prone to something of a quagmire. A little further on, father and son exited the vehicle and slogged up the lane running northwest along the shoreline. They came to their cottage—a tiny three-room affair with a large front porch overlooking a sloping lot to the water. Here, on sultry summer days, the Himeses hosted family reunions and church picnics under a canopy of oaks rustled by cool lake breezes. Himes would take note, with some relief, that the small structure, nestled in retreating drifts, appeared undisturbed.[28]

A bit further on they came to the point, very near the dead end, where an elongated crater marked the wing's ascent up the bank. A large stone hearth—the centerpiece of communal cookouts—had been obliterated, victim of an errant cable, crane, or truck. All around, the thawing earth held the colossal imprints of heavy machinery, and young Charlie found them duly impressive. Yet none of it seemed to concern the elder Himes, who stood surveying the shoreline where a chop whipped up by a mounting north wind lapped against eroding ice banks.

From his exchange with the guard, Elwyn had gathered that a patrol was keeping watch for debris and bodies expected to wash ashore somewhere along this section of beach; it was now deemed just a matter of time. The deacon could well anticipate, perhaps with an unsettled mix of hope and dread, what fundamental evidence of the disaster might at any time drift into public view: a mildewed hat; a sodden duffle bag; the corporeal remains of somebody's loved one, broken, bloated, animated by waves. As sexton of the church cemetery—a custodian of order and dignity at the junction of life and afterlife—he would be particularly wishful for the recovery of the bodies for dignified burial and consummation of this final step of the ordeal, now being carried out nearly at his family's front door. Yet on this day there was nothing to see beyond an unbroken stretch of water and sky, and a few gulls banking over whitecaps. Himes stood there for a while, even as his son found the excitement of the outing giving way to boredom and cold, and a bevy of questions: Where was the plane? Will they find bodies? Can they go home now?

When they finally turned to leave, minding their steps over the torn snowscape, they came to the point where the wing had been loaded onto the flatbed. Elwyn stooped to retrieve an item. It was a piece of hardware, one of several embedded in the thawing snow and mud: a coupling . . . a bracket . . . a tube . . . none of them much larger than a man's finger, unnoticed or simply ignored by salvage crews. Yet here, at least from Elwyn Himes's perspective, were elements of a requiem. And they were in want of composition. He pulled a handkerchief from his trousers and carefully gathered up the fragments.

Back at their farmhouse, Charles found that the pieces cleaned right up with a little kerosene. Moreover, they affected an air of dignity and importance when mounted on a square of plywood covered smartly with blue felt. Newspaper clips, placed judiciously at certain points, would favor the impression. It would be an inspiring display, Himes felt, at church functions or other gatherings for congregants and neighbors who wanted to reflect on the loss and remember the boys' sacrifice. It would be good to have photos of the men, though.[29]

To this end, Mrs. Himes, bent over a large rolltop desk cluttered with an assortment of farm and domestic business, worked on a composition of her own. With a pencil welt wearing on a knuckle of her writing hand, she periodically consulted an address book with eight new entries gleaned from post office directories in Alabama, Wisconsin, Massachusetts, Rhode Island, Oklahoma, California, and Mississippi.

She knew what she wanted to say to the mothers and fathers of the lost boys, and the letters would not differ materially from one to the next. The result, in each case, might include an expression of sympathy and reference to God's blessings and infinite grace. This would be followed by an explanation of sorts: She and her husband, Elwyn, lived in the town of Scriba, where a piece of an aircraft was recovered from Lake Ontario shortly after their son's plane was lost. If wanted, they could forward news of events, some of it firsthand. Meantime, they would be honored to receive pictures and information about the boys to share with congregations and community members as they kept them in their prayers.

She read over each note before sealing and addressing the envelopes. There would not be much second-guessing in the process; she was nothing if not straightforward, and this was the kind of letter she would want to receive if it were one of her boys.

Her instincts proved sound. Responses came quickly, including one from Mrs. Lucy Ponder, of George Street, Jackson, Mississippi. When Marion opened it, a studio print spilled from the folded contents of the envelope—a uniformed young man with an understated smile and bright, equable eyes. The picture was indeed pleasant to look at, capturing something deeply personal and broadly iconic, the sum of its details bearing the story of youth, strength, beauty, and loss written in millions of similar portraits of the day. The accompanying note was signed by Mrs. Ponder, who had gratefully received Mrs. Himes's letter. Wendell, who preferred to be called Keith, Mrs. Ponder might explain, was one of three of her children serving. Keith was expecting his commission to fly the B-24 in Europe on February 25. She thanked the Himeses and people of Oswego for their prayers; she awaited any and all news they could provide, particularly about the status of the search.[30]

As it happened, Lucy Ponder had recently learned that her son was officially dead. The news was conveyed in a letter dated March 1—four days after the wing was recovered—signed by Colonel Jones: "When history is written," the colonel noted, "the name of your son will be recorded among those who have paid the highest price for the salvation of freedom and justice." A day later, a less inspired message of condolence would follow from Colonel Banks, who urged Mrs. Ponder to "please try to understand that his loss was not entirely in vain for other men like Wendell benefit by knowing how he died and are inspired to achieve greater heights in their training."

Whether faced with a death that was heroic or "not entirely in vain," a mother would not let go of her son so easily. In coming days, newspaper clips would begin arriving from Marion Himes; in them, Lucy Ponder would find many details absent in official notifications from the Army or a news brief that had run in the *Jackson Clarion-Ledger* with Keith's picture, notifying readers that a local pilot was among crew on a missing plane in upstate New York.[31]

Figure 10.3. Lucy Ponder provided a photo of her son in uniform, likely identical to the one here, for the Himeses to display at church and community functions to honor the crew. Courtesy of Eddie Evans and descendants of Lucy Ponder.

She learned from the accounts sent by Marion Himes that Keith's plane was lost in a snowstorm and low on gas; the crew was ordered to bail out but radio contact was poor; residents heard the plane circling low over Oswego and Lake Ontario; a local justice of the peace heard an explosion in the woods in the middle of the night; sightings by loggers and a railroad man steered the search into mountains and backcountry; the Coast Guard and Army recovered a wing section in the lake. And then came the heart-stopping report that the plane wreck had been spotted submerged just off-shore, possibly with bodies aboard. But that part ended up not being true.

It was a lot to follow, with much inconsistency, reference to unfamiliar geography, and more speculation than answers. The upshot was, after all the searching, no bodies or personal effects had been found. A week after the plane disappeared, however, an incidental subhead over an article about the wing recovery would likely strike Lucy as relevant beyond anything else: "Army Officials Cling to Hope That Eight in Crew Fell Safely in 'Chutes."

The question of whether *Gertie*'s crew bailed out had been raised in previous reports, always with unsatisfactory and conflicting responses, little elaboration, and no attribution. It was a question that needed to be asked and couldn't be answered; and this article, like the others, provided no specifics.[32] Yet for Lucy, it offered a cornucopia of possibility hidden in the sprawling northern New York countryside. Since the boys had not been found dead, they could be—may well be, in fact—alive somewhere.

It was a feeling that would set in and persist like a fever for all the families of *Gertie*'s crew, waiting for news and praying that it would be good, even when it wasn't. Nearly three weeks after the wing was found, the mother of Kenneth Jonen—the gunner fresh out of high school stationed in the plane's waist with James Cozier—wrote to the parents of Joseph Zebo, the radio operator:

> I heard from the Colonel this week that the wing has been identified as be-longing to their plane and that undoubtedly the crew went down with the ship. But I just can't believe it. . . .
> We will have to keep up the courage and pray that our boys are still alive and will be returned to us soon.[33]

"Our boys" was an archetype, of course. Mrs. Jonen had no way of knowing but might suspect that, with final preparations for the Allied invasion of France under way, a great number would not be returning soon, or anytime at all. It could be said that humanity's most timeless support group is composed of those who lose a family member at war. Concerning relatives of *Gertie*'s crew, Mrs. Jonen's letter showed special empathy for a twenty-year-old woman, also working through denial, as she struggled with the loss of her newlywed husband: "The copilot was a married man and his wife writes me they are expecting a baby, so it's double hard for her. She feels like we do, that the boys just have to be found alive, and it's very hard to believe otherwise."

Mrs. Jonen was speaking of Marion Hardeis Bickel, who had married *Gertie*'s copilot, Ray Bickel, just a few months earlier. Marion may not have even known she was pregnant when the plane disappeared. Yet, in coming months, as the baby became more of a physical presence, her husband would become less of one. Raymond Bickel would miss his own funeral. Eight months later, with the arrival of his newborn son—a thriving amplitude of need—the dashing young officer with whom Marion had planned to spend her life might be no more than a phantom in her oft-interrupted sleep and a conspicuous void in her waking hours. At some point young Ray would begin developing features that would instantly bring to mind her missing husband. When the boy began asking about his father, what memories would she provide for him?

While some sought a record of the past in the depths of the lake, it was this sort of question that compelled me to set off on a search of my own.

11

Misplaced Memory

Charles Himes was eight years old when he accompanied his father to the site where the wing washed up and the bodies didn't. He was eighty-something when I asked him to recall specifics. After being warned by the guard that they might get stuck, he remembers most vividly holding his breath as their '35 Chevy coupe forded an ice-fringed mud-hole: "I thought it would swallow us up," he said, sitting on the front porch of his cottage on a summer afternoon. The rustic character of the seasonal access along the beach at Shore Oaks has not changed appreciably since 1944, nor has the tiny camp, which remains a gathering place for successive generations of the Himes family.

Charles recounted the smashed hearth, the pieces of hardware from the plane his father found, and the care he took displaying them on the blue velvet board at church functions and community events. He can still envision photographs of *Gertie*'s crew, sent to his mother by family members, lined up on the buffet table at a community dinner at the church, like honored guests.

My visit to the Himes cottage was compelled by a desire to see where the forgotten speck of World War II history had come ashore. But I was even more interested in finding correspondence and photos from the crew's families. Reference to these in newspaper accounts from 1944 had hinted at what the families had endured—or in one instance failed to endure—as the grand hope of their boys being found alive succumbed to the modest expectation that their bodies would be recovered. Four months after the wing was hauled ashore and taken away on an Army truck, Elwyn and Marion Himes "received word," according to a single-paragraph brief in the Oswego daily, that the father of *Gertie*'s radio operator, Joseph Zebo, died suddenly "due to the strain and grief he suffered following the loss of the bomber and its crew."[1]

Might any of these letters, or the felt-covered plywood display that Elwyn Himes made, still be among the Himeses' possessions? Charles cast a look at Louise, his wife of sixty years who joined us on the porch. She

Figure 11.1. Marion and Elwyn Himes, shown here in an undated photograph, corresponded with families of *Gertie*'s lost crew in 1944 about the search for the plane and the recovery of a wing section near the Himes family cottage at Shore Oaks. Courtesy of Charles and Louise Himes.

appeared doubtful. "Now I really wish I had them," Charles said. But too many events over the course of too many years had conspired against it. His parents had died long ago; their house in North Scriba had been abandoned and eventually burned down. There would be no looking through attics or old trunks. A later visit paid to Charles's older brother, Leo, would also produce memories, many vague, a few vivid, but no hard record.[2] Unlike the cherished coupling Fred Spink III found in his father's cigar box, any material vestige of *Getaway Gertie*, in this instance, was gone.

It's difficult to conjure events that have drifted to the fringes of conscious memory or pay homage to a tomb that can't be found. Yet it's safe to say that in 1944 the memory of *Gertie*'s crew was painfully fresh and diligently tended by mothers and fathers, sisters and brothers, their grief anchored to a uniquely human compulsion to know how and where things came to an end, and lay to rest the bodies of their loved ones. It was necessary closure, and it seemed imminent after the inboard section of a wing from a B-24 Liberator was recovered at Shore Oaks on February 26, 1944. Yet it didn't pan out that way.

While circumstances suggested the wreckage must have come from *Gertie*, due diligence was required. There was no mention of it in the coverage of the missing plane at the time, but Army officials would have been aware of a Royal Canadian Air Force Avro Anson that had disappeared two years earlier on a training flight from Quebec to Toronto. In the spring of 1942, a resident had found metal debris washed ashore in a bay on the American side of the lake's northeast end. The pieces were believed to be from the Avro Anson, but the plane and crew of four were still unaccounted for.[3]

It's certain that experienced eyes would not mistake a wing from the Avro, a much smaller, two-engine craft, from that of a Liberator, even one badly mangled and incomplete. Still, there were a lot of planes flying along both sides of the US border with Canada, and B-24s and other large aircraft from all over the country frequently flew in and out of nearby airfields in Rome and Syracuse. Another week would pass before crash experts from the Westover base tracked serial numbers found on the wreckage recovered at Shore Oaks to manufacturing records and announced, finally and officially, that the wing belonged to *Gertie*.[4]

Still, nobody had found any signs of bodies, personal items, or more debris, or at least there is no confirmed record of it.[5] At the same time, planes and personnel were urgently needed elsewhere. Boats were scarce and lake conditions hazardous. On March 3, one week after the Oswego County Highway Department towed the wing ashore and two weeks after the plane went missing, the Army called off the search.[6] A Coast Guard detail of four men reportedly continued periodic checks from certain vantage points along a ten-mile length of beach adjoining Shore Oaks. There is no record of any shore patrol farther east, where icebound estuaries, inlets, and marshland would be mostly inaccessible for at least another month.[7]

Nearly eighty years later, the story of *Gertie* waits to be made whole. Lake Ontario is big but getting smaller as practical limits to explore and catalog its depths fall away with technology and gumption. By the spring of 2022, Phil Church, the Oswego County administrator, offering prospects of economic growth and national recognition for towns along the lake's southern and eastern shores, had successfully ushered the exhaustive administrative process for NOAA's Lake Ontario Marine Sanctuary through a series of public hearings. It had taken more than five years, but the proposal, facilitated by well-planned stakeholder meetings (helped further by a potential annual budget of up to $1 million for NOAA to staff sanctuary operations) had met the high bar of community support needed to justify it.[8] The sanctuary designation, expected to be enacted in 2023 after the resolution of certain matters of policy, would, according to the final assessment from NOAA, "provide a national stage for promoting heritage tourism and recreation" and "ensure future generations can learn about and explore these underwater treasures."[9]

From the Himeses' cottage porch, not far from where the only tangible remains of *Gertie* had been recovered, I watched the afternoon light playing off the water to the horizon and thought about what rested below. "Future generations" seemed pretty broad; but I wondered how descendants of Lucy Ponder, Marion Hardeis, or other of the crew's families might, after all these years, feel about current developments in the search for *Getaway Gertie*.

There was only one direct-line descendant of the lost airmen: the son of copilot Ray Bickel, born to his newlywed bride Marion after *Gertie* vanished. Ray junior was in his mid-seventies when I dialed his number from the porch of my own ancestral cottage, about six miles east of the

Himes place. It shares the same encompassing view to the horizon, interrupted on this placid fall day by a few fishing boats pursuing migrating salmon.

I turned my attention to my notes, derived from marriage records, birth records, newspaper files, and information passed along on a genealogy forum from a distant family member of the lost copilot. Understanding one's natural reluctance to answer an unknown out-of-state number, I was expecting to leave a voicemail, and was happily surprised when a man with a Texas accent answered. I introduced myself and, after confirming I was speaking with the son of Ray Bickel, worked toward the point of my call, summarizing the search for his father's plane, plans for a national marine sanctuary encompassing an area in Lake Ontario where it's thought to be lost, and my interest in talking to family members of the crew.

This was met by silence, and I imagined him sizing up my intentions. It might be a bit galling, this rush of information from a total stranger with a probing interest in his family history. For a moment I feared he would dismiss me as a scammer or solicitor. Had I used the phrase "underwater cultural resource"?—probably not the best term. When he finally spoke, he told me I must have the wrong person. It's true that his father was a USAAF pilot in World War II, but he had died in an air battle over Germany.

I double-checked my notes. Tactfully, I tried to reconcile the confusion: I was referring to the Raymond A. Bickel born October 7, 1916, married to Marion F. Hardeis on November 8, 1943, lost over upstate New York on February 18, 1944. The names and dates brought more silence. "Well," he said at last. "That may be. But I never thought of him as my father. . . . That's about all I can tell you." I inquired about his mother. Yes, she was still alive, I learned, but not well enough to talk on the phone. The sadness in his voice gave me pause. I thanked him and told him I hoped we could keep in touch.

Before he hung up, he offered another bit of information: His daughter had always been close to his mother, he said. His daughter, maybe, knew more.[10]

A defining memory of *Gertie*'s lost copilot almost slipped away before Amber Rhea Simmons retrieved a forgotten photo from her grandmother's possessions before she died. It's now displayed on the mantel of Amber's suburban home near Springfield, Illinois, where I reached her by phone, a while after I spoke with her father.

Tracing Amber's connection to the missing bomber gets confusing, but it crystalizes with this picture: two young men in AAF service uniforms flash easy smiles under shiny brims of medallioned caps pushed back on their foreheads. One casually leans a forearm on a shoulder of the other. They are buddies. And, as their attire suggests, they are girding for the largest and most destructive war in history. If they have any regrets or apprehension, it's not apparent the moment the picture was snapped—one of a countless collection of moments shaped by total war in the early 1940s.

One of the men in the photograph—Edward Buckley—would soon be flying fighter planes over Europe with the 358th Fighter Group, escorting bombers to their targets and engaging the Luftwaffe in mortal combat. He would come close to death when his P-47 was shot down over France, and then live to tell of his ordeal in a German prison camp. The other man in the picture, Ray Bickel—the one whose shoulder Buckley leans on—will climb into the cockpit of *Getaway Gertie* with Keith Ponder and six other crew on a training flight over western Massachusetts and disappear in a snowstorm over upstate New York. With time, so will his story.

Figure 11.2. Ray Bickel (*right*) with Ed Buckley at an unknown base stateside during World War II training. Courtesy of Amber Rhea Simmons and the descendants of Ray Bickel, Marion Hardeis, and Ed Buckley.

At different points on the arc of their lives, each man will marry the same woman—Marion Hardeis. Amber—Marion's granddaughter—knows one of the men in the picture well: it's Grandpa Ed, Grandma Marion's second husband, a career Air Force man and later airline pilot. She remembers him as lively and loving. He wasn't one to dwell on action he saw in the war, but when his grandchildren asked, he regaled them with an effective summary: "When he woke up after the crash, he thought he was in his barracks," Amber said. "He heard people talking, and it wasn't in English. Then, he *knew* he was in trouble."

From time to time, Amber wonders about the other man in the photograph, technically a blood relative but not really considered kin. "Ray Bickel was Ed's friend, but we never really thought of him as our grandfather," she told me. Still, she is moved by the man's resemblance to photographs of her father as a young man—the round pleasant face and dimpled chin. "We were never told much," she continued. "My parents didn't talk about him. But I was a little more removed from it all. And I tend to be curious. So, I asked questions."

Amber, two generations removed from the story, had to reach well back into her own memory to retrieve its origins. She was growing up in Abilene, Texas, where she was a frequent visitor to her nearby grandparents' home. "My grandmother was all of five-foot zero, feisty, and willing to speak her mind," Amber recalls. Yet there was one thing rooted deeply in her past that she simply didn't talk about. Nobody did.

Amber happened upon the door to her grandmother's past, quite literally, in the late 1980s when she was in high school. She was exploring the contents of a closet in her grandparents' guest room, intrigued by the styles of her aunt's and grandmother's generation, and looking to expand some wardrobe possibilities of her own. The details are mostly forgotten, but one image remains vivid: voluminous folds of satin cascading from a sturdy hanger: It wasn't what she was looking for. But it was wonderful—a wedding gown with a cathedral train that covered half the floor, puffy sleeves, hook-and-eye buttons, and form-fitting torso. It spoke of love in its most elemental and generous form—an opulent telltale of romance and commitment reaching across generations.

Amber, who shares her grandmother's petite physique, wasted no time trying it on and decided, right then, she would be married in that dress. Where did it come from? She didn't remember seeing such luxurious attire in photographs of her grandparents' wedding.

The dress was from her first wedding, her grandmother explained. She had been not much older than Amber and had been married twelve weeks when her husband disappeared on a training flight. "I was told it was somewhere over the Great Lakes," Amber recalls. "She really didn't want to talk about it." Amber learned, however, that the groom's name was Ray Bickel. Her father, she realized, had been named after this person. And, it dawned on her, so had she—Amber Rhea. That her grandmother kept the gown after all these years was a testament to this past, but it represented a place she wished not to revisit. "She told me I could not be married in that dress," Amber recalls. "And that was that."[11]

It would be much later before Amber would fully understand the circumstances behind her grandmother's reaction. As it turned out, the shock Marion suffered in 1944 from losing her groom, and the aftershock of learning she was pregnant, were followed by another blow: there would be a falling out with Marion's in-laws, possibly sparked over her husband's life insurance benefit. Before enlisting in the AAF and marrying Marion Hardeis, census records show, Ray had lived in Chicago with his widowed mother—a grocery store clerk—and his elderly grandmother, whom he likely helped support. Ray's mother, said to have had "a very strong personality," apparently was not keen on her son's marriage. Though underlying details remain inscrutable, it's evident that, after Ray was lost, financial matters exacerbated the issue, and Ray's family severed whatever tenuous ties they had with his pregnant bride.[12]

After the falling out with her in-laws, Marion moved back with her family in Chicago and apparently picked up work at the Budlong Pickle factory—one of many food processors trying to overcome a shortage of labor to, literally, feed armies. Marion, raised in an era when mothers stayed home to manage domestic matters, would join the growing ranks now compelled to balance work and child rearing.

Her circumstances changed dramatically after the war. Suddenly, there was a flood of young soldiers seeking love and courtship, sometimes marrying the wives and sweethearts of their fallen comrades, and sometimes raising their families. Ed Buckley, Ray Bickel's old friend, also from Chicago, called on Marion when he returned from France. A year later they were married.

It might be said Marion was the personification of a nation eager to move on. Finally settled, established, and once again in love, there was no looking back. Marion's son, Ray Bickel Jr.—Amber's father—became Ray Buckley after his stepfather adopted him. Young Ray would eventually have questions, and his adoptive father would tell him that he had trained and fought with his biological father, who had died a hero when his fighter plane was shot down over Germany. It was an apocryphal tale, surely related in good faith; the essential outcome was valid, after all, and served as an honorable stand-in for the inglorious reality. Moreover, young Ray was extremely fond of his adoptive father, himself a war hero who had filled a gaping parental void.

Yet Marion's feeling of abandonment by her first husband's family would be passed to the next generation. "They reacted the way their parents reacted and with what they were told," said Jean Vanasek, who is married to Ray Vanasek—the son of the sister of *Gertie*'s copilot. Jean, a family genealogist, learned the story through her mother-in-law, and she views it as an ancestral canker. "The problem lay with the parents and grandparents, not the children," she told me.[13]

Though Ray Vanasek and Ray Buckley are cousins and named after the same person, they have never spoken to each other. As far as I could tell, they harbor no ill will. But if *Gertie* is found, neither would be inclined to see it as a moment of reaffirming lost family connections, let alone collectively advocate for an archaeological survey necessary to identify and recover remains.[14] "Let him rest in peace," said Ray Vanasek. "This person was my uncle, but we never knew him, and my mother never talked about him. He's been no more than a phantom of the past all these years."[15]

Amber Rhea, speaking on behalf of the other side of the family, agrees that her grandfather's remains should be undisturbed. "We can remember him and honor him where he is," she said. "With his crew."

The vehicles of remembrance I was most interested in—stories and letters—have been lost over the many years, along with family connections. But Jean Vanasek keeps the family history. And Amber has the wedding dress. "I didn't get married in it," Amber said. "But I keep it packed away in a suitcase. Knowing it's there is enough."

Another story awaited me in Keith Ponder's hometown.

The rutted dirt road to Forkville, Mississippi, from the larger town of Morton to the south has been paved, but traffic is still sparse. I passed

Bethlehem Baptist Church, the most defining feature of the landscape, and bore left at the eponymous fork. A few blinks of an eye beyond that, I found Fairground Road. I pulled my rental car over and looked for the former pride of Scott County, trying to imagine thronging crowds, shouting barkers, braying animals, and a biplane taking off with a young Wendell Keith Ponder, devotee of Lucky Lindy, harboring thoughts of adventure and heroism in the Wild Blue Yonder. Today the view holds nothing more than a thicket of loblolly pines and under-growth. After the war, people flocked to suburbia to pursue the post-Depression American Dream, and Forkville was one of the places they fled. Fewer people live in this nook of rural Mississippi now than when Keith Ponder hunted with his dogs in the surrounding fields and woods; the post office, barber shop, and general store are gone. Yet family roots run deep.

I had come to Scott County seeking records of a personal history that, for me, was an analog to the B-24 at the bottom of the lake. I pulled into the gravel drive leading to a small, meticulously kept home where de-scendants of Juanita Ponder Hardy—Keith Ponder's sister—were gath-ering for a birthday celebration. The guest of honor, ninety-year-old Frank Evans, was a lifelong Scott County resident. I was hopeful but disappointed to learn that, because he had married into the family after the war, he had no direct memories of the lost pilot. The others were too young to know Wendell Keith Ponder, though Robert Keith Hardy, named after his great-uncle and a keeper of family history, had penned recollections of Keith's boyhood that had been passed down orally from Robert's late father and also Robert's great-uncle Amos—Keith Ponder's older brother. "We were never sure, exactly, of the story of how or where Uncle Keith died," said Hardy, a mild-mannered man of lanky build and a distinctive goatee, known to friends and family as Buddy. "We knew it was on a training flight near Canada. I thought it was in the mountains."

The record was served on this occasion by items that Buddy's cousin, Terri Coleman, had found in a chest of drawers once belonging to her great-grandma Lucy Ponder. Here, carefully glued to pages of bound card stock, were memories, or ghosts of memories, of people and events Terri didn't immediately recognize. She had given the albums to another cousin,

Eddie Evans (Frank's son), who also had an interest in family history, and Eddie had brought them to the reunion.

One of the books held black-and-white photographs of young people bearing styles from Depression-era America. They were cryptically captioned, but with Buddy and Eddie's help, I was able to identify highlights of Keith's teenage years—football, dances, and larking about with friends and dates on outings to the park.

The second book was filled with news clippings, beginning with a short item from the *Jackson Clarion-Ledger*: "Local Flight Officer Missing with Plane." Subsequent pages, mostly from upstate New York newspapers, told what was known of the loss of Lucy Ponder's son: orders given for the crew to bail out in a blinding snowstorm; reports from residents that guided rescue parties from the lake into the mountains; the search at the Clemons farm after the family was woken by an explosion in the woods; trained ski troops standing by; and, a week later, the discovery of wreckage floating off the south shore of Lake Ontario.

More articles documented the recovery of the wing section, including one with a photograph of the mangled component buoyed by its empty fuel tanks. Another summarized accounts, apparently false, that the searchers, using spotlights, had found the rest of the plane in the water. Sprinkled throughout two weeks of coverage was vague speculation on whether the boys had bailed out. A column—"Mississippians at War"—appearing March 2 in the *Clarion-Ledger* with Keith's picture gave a final update on the matter: "No trace of the Flight Officer Wendell K. Ponder . . . who was aboard the wrecked Liberator Bomber *Gateway Gertie* [sic], once believed discovered by coastguardsmen and FBI men in Lake Ontario, has been found. The search has been abandoned by his home base, Westover Field, Mass., and he may be considered deceased as of February 18, his relatives have been advised." The reporter or editor, likely having spoken with Lucy Ponder, felt compelled to end the coverage on a sustaining note of optimism: "There is still that thread of hope he may be alive."[16]

I had already accessed the newspaper accounts through digital archival searches, and they held no surprises. But, flipping through the brittle pages, I was seeing another story that had escaped me. It wasn't in the contents of the clips, but the obvious care taken in their preservation and arrangement. The scrapbook also held letters of condolence to Lucy from two colonels and a general; a short column in the Morton weekly, remembering Keith as "one of our 'buddies,' in all that term implies"; and a clipping from the Oswego paper, sent by Marion Himes, of a Memorial Day tribute by residents, scout troops, and clergy, who laid a large floral cross, and a bouquet for each crew member, on the water where the wing piece was recovered.

Lucy Ponder's scrapbook was filled, essentially, with words that must have repulsed and comforted her, information both unwelcome and essential, but never enough. While some looked in Lake Ontario, I had found in Mississippi the ending to a story with no ending: in the absence of a body returning home in a flag-draped coffin, the scrapbook would be a vehicle for the incalculable grief of Keith's mother. It was all she had to say goodbye.

As I studied the clip about the Memorial Day tribute near the end of the scrapbook, the headline of an adjacent article caught my eye: OIL SLICK OUT FROM RAMONA BEACH MAY BE CLUE TO MISSING B-24.[17]

Figure 11.3. In the absence of a body, a scrapbook of press clippings helped Lucy Ponder come to terms with Keith's death. Photo by Tom Wilber.

The clip told the story of Earl Wood, a local fisherman who, four months after the plane disappeared, had snagged a net on a submerged wreck and caused the slick "75 yards in diameter." An official from the AAF in Rome promised that divers would check the site, in ninety feet of water on the lake's east end. I was quite familiar with the story: the fisherman's discovery was near the place where—seventy-plus years later—Tim Caza and John McLaughlin, guided by a grainy sonar image, would unsuccessfully search for the plane. I had been struck by the absence of any follow-up report on the investigation promised in 1944. For editors at the time, it was likely just another news item. For Caza and McLaughlin, a potential discovery. But seeing the incomplete story so carefully preserved in Lucy's scrapbook cast things in an acutely personal light.

Two more months would pass before Keith Ponder's mother would formally say goodbye to her youngest son, without knowing where he was, at a memorial service at the Bethlehem Baptist Church. It was held on August 5, 1944—nearly six months after his last radio call to the Syracuse tower was cut off by static and *Getaway Gertie* vanished with her crew. A one-sentence blurb in the *Clarion-Ledger* noted the ceremony, "in honor of Flight Officer Wendell Keith Ponder, reported missing February 18, following a plane crash near the Canadian border above New York."

Over time, Lucy Ponder's hope that her youngest son was alive would be displaced by faith that he was in heaven. But on any given morning, a waking thought might trouble her on the heels of a certain, restless dream: Could this be the day she received word that Keith had been found?

While I was in Forkville, Keith's distant relatives—interested, mystified, and unfailingly gracious—invited me to accompany them to the cemetery behind the Bethlehem Baptist Church, where multiple generations of Keith Ponder's relatives lie with Forkville's other deceased. A small granite block marks Keith's empty grave near his siblings and parents.

It was midafternoon, and the Mississippi summer heat was relentless. The only other person around was the cemetery steward, a wizened elder known to my party as George, pacing slowly and deliberately at the older corner of the grounds. Suspended in his fingertips were two metal rods,

Figure 11.4. Nearly seventy-five years after Keith Ponder disappeared, the pilot's great-nephew Robert Keith Hardy pieces together family history at the Bethlehem Baptist Church cemetery. The granite stone in the foreground marks Keith's empty grave. Photo by Tom Wilber.

no bigger than knitting needles. He was checking for unmarked graves, he explained. It was an old cemetery, with some plots predating records or outlasting markers. He demonstrated, with a compelling air of confidence, how the sticks turned down in tandem as they passed over a grave. He wanted to make sure they didn't disturb someone while putting someone else to rest.

I stood in the humidity and heat, shirt soaking through, considering what rested below my feet. A disconcerting shuffling of history at the hands of oblivion and entropy: bodies where they weren't expected. Others, missing entirely.

RECOGNITION

It's easy to visualize a certain ending to the quest for the forgotten soldier: bodies of the lost airmen returning to leafy cemeteries in their hometowns with relatives and neighbors there to receive and honor them. That, at least, was the vision that had inspired Jim Coffed, the detective and insurance investigator who teamed in the 1980s and '90s with World War II combat veteran and Oswego County fishing guide Bud Duell to find and salvage *Getaway Gertie*.

When I resolved to learn the story behind the myth of my childhood summers along the lakeshore, my search of newspaper archives first led me to Jim. Before his death in 2020, I visited him on multiple occasions at his home in Lancaster, New York, south of Buffalo, where he and his wife Carol had lived for most of their married lives of sixty-plus years. Jim was well into his eighties by then, and he clung to the old-school way of doing things. Because he eschewed cell phones and computers, and therefore access to texts, emails, and social media, we corresponded by snail mail for some time before he invited me to his house. During my first visit, in the summer of 2017, we sat in the kitchen and he treated me to his favorite snack—creamy peanut butter on toast with whole milk—and a discussion about detective work. After a while he warmed to me. "I'll be straight with you," he said. "I'm interested in finding the airplane and the crew and bringing them to shore. You're interested in finding their stories. We complement one another."

With that, he ushered me to a small office nook off the den, with walls, shelves, and cubbies punctiliously and fully adorned with World War II models, memorabilia, commemorative plates, artifacts, flags, and assorted kitsch. In the center was a massive rolltop desk flanked by two large wooden filing cabinets. He offered me a seat in a wooden swivel chair at the center of it all. We delved in.

The filing cabinets were chockablock with thirty-plus years of the shoe-leather-and-index-card investigative methods of his time. Color-coded binders, neatly labeled and indexed, held accidents reports, notes from interviews, extensive (and outdated) source lists, logs, journals, maps, correspondence with other war buffs, more maps, manuals on the construction, specifications, and history of the B-24, volumes of copied microfiche of Army records, more volumes on the search and restoration of lost planes, and a twenty-page analysis from a meteorologist he had recruited to determine weather patterns, wind speeds, and currents near Nine Mile Point from February 17–21, 1944. One notebook was devoted to his queries to the Finger Lakes Dowsers club, and their detailed responses, along with graphs and charts summarizing their collective divinations.[1]

Jim, needless to say, was an enthusiast—perhaps the only person who had invested more time than John McLaughlin in researching the story of *Getaway Gertie* (which Jim preferred to call Army 047, as it was listed in accident reports). Jim first caught wind of stories about a bomber lost in Lake Ontario in the mid-1980s from fellow warplane aficionados in western New York, including Austin Wadsworth, a founder of the National War Plane Museum in Geneseo. At first, Jim told me, it was rumored the lost plane was a B-17. That was well before the days of Google, and Jim began assembling his dossier with eight-hour round trips to newspaper morgues in Oswego County, where he met Bud Duell and, eventually, John McLaughlin (to whom Jim would later refer me). Jim's motivation, growing more intense as the years passed, was summed up in a letter to a fellow enthusiast: "It amazes me that there are eight American airmen still aboard that aircraft and there is no governmental agency that will do the search."

Although an accident expert, Coffed possessed neither the expertise nor the wherewithal for diving. Moreover, a nagging fear of outside parties exploiting his research for their personal interests had complicated his search for people with the know-how and equipment to do what he couldn't. Coffed eventually teamed with Mike McGourty of Emark Marine Services, as chronicled in Mike Vogel's 1994 *Buffalo News* feature— the report that had inspired a brief renaissance in the search for *Gertie* in Oswego County.

Jim had decided to focus on the area upwind of where the wing drifted in—the point of the discounted sighting of the submerged fuselage by the FBI and Coast Guard the night Paul Donahue spotted the drifting wing piece. Mike and Jim's actual time on the water was short-lived, however. After a few outings with no success, Jim fell off a roof and fractured his skull. He would recover, though his quest for 047—of admirable yet outsize ambition from the start—was now interrupted by injury and age.

The thing I was after—the stories of the crew and their families—had for the most part also eluded Coffed, but not for lack of diligence.[2] He knew their names, their ages, their hometowns, and their lack of experience. He could tell you how many flight hours Ponder had logged and how few the number was compared to today's training. His collection of World War II memorabilia—extending into his basement, attic, and garage—included the same kind of radio issued to the B-24 that Zebo desperately tried to operate in the final hours of 047's flight. He understood the handicap Zebo faced trying to communicate through snow static. And he could vividly see a young aviator confused, frustrated, and necessarily stoic as the crisis deepened.

Reconstructing accidents was what Coffed did for a living before retirement, and he was clearly drawn to that aspect of the case of the missing bomber. Yet his quest was motivated primarily by an ideal. Jim served as an enlisted man with the US Air Force during the Korean War, although he would feel necessary to point out in our conversations that he was stationed stateside and not a pilot. As I got to know him, I came to understand that some aspects of his quest were easier to explain than others, but a telltale clue in this regard was his frequent and fond mention of his older brother, Dale. Dale Coffed was an important figure to Jim the way older brothers often are to younger siblings, but the first thing Jim was likely to tell you about Dale was that he piloted thirteen bombing missions over Germany in a B-24 with the Eighth Army Air Force. Dale, in other words, was the archetypal hero of the Second World War. Jim's insatiable appetite for period detail, however, was not much helped by his brother's reluctance to indulge it. "Dale never said a word about World War II," Jim told me. "It was typical."

When I met Jim, he was in failing health though still committed to his quest for Army 047, impassioned by the belief that its crew are not only lost but forgotten, and the government has failed to give them and fifteen thousand other airmen their due. In the Second World War, people died too often and in ways too numerous to count. If not but for circumstances, Dale may have ended up like them, or any one of them may have ended up like Dale. The mythos of the conflict, abundantly represented in the collection adorning Jim's study, offers a far simpler narrative than current world affairs; back then, it was good guys versus bad guys, with Americans wholly united to fight the bad guys. While not blind to his country's shortcomings and ethical transgressions, Coffed was a keeper of the faith in what was won. For him, the heroism of the rank-and-file soldiers—undecorated and unrecognized—rang pure and true, and was too quickly forgotten.

"This happens to be about eight guys nobody has taken care of," he told me the last time we spoke. "It was a big deal when that plane disappeared. Here we are, years down the road, and nobody cares. . . . On Jeopardy, nobody knows the answers on World War II."

When Coffed was laid to rest, it was in his hometown cemetery with a military funeral—a sendoff fitting and proper for a veteran, the kind of honor he had wished for the crew of Army 047.

Jim Coffed had envisioned an ending with honor and dignity. Yet his expectation to raise the plane and recover the bodies was as ingenuous as it was noble. Today, this kind of enterprise, well-intended or otherwise, is essentially forbidden. The Sunken Military Craft Law, passed in 2004, codifies the sovereign status of sunken US military vessels and aircraft as property of the federal government and "protects vessels and aircraft and the remains of their crews from unauthorized disturbance."

That means wrecks like *Gertie* are to be left alone, pending any extraordinary exception. It's a policy that raises the question: Is a grave sixty or six-hundred-feet deep inherently less honorable than one six feet deep?

It was the kind of question that came up in my conversation with Cheryl Allen, a cousin of Tommy Roberts, *Gertie*'s flight engineer. I had found Cheryl, or she found me, through Wayne Lusardi, a marine archaeologist at NOAA's marine sanctuary in Michigan, who told me—during a call related to other issues—that, by the way, a family member of one of *Gertie*'s crew looking for information about the lost plane had contacted him. Eagerly following up with this lead, I was soon on a conference call with that person, Karen Mickler, and her mother, Cheryl.

They were rapt with the story of the lost crew, though they had little to offer in the way of surviving records or memorabilia, aside from a photo of Tommy, smiling broadly in combat attire with flight goggles propped on his forehead and a machine gun resting on his right shoulder (figure 3.4). My exchange with Cheryl, in short, was similar to my conversations with the relatives of other crew: she remembered hearing about "Uncle Bill's son in Massachusetts" and understood that he was an aviator in the AAF. "Other than that, I knew next to nothing," she said. "My Uncle Bill talked very little about him." Cheryl and Karen listened intently as I shared what I knew about the plane's final flight, those aboard, and the ensuing searches by various parties. Then we talked about NOAA's pending designation of eastern Lake Ontario as a federal marine sanctuary and diving park, and related prospects of the men finally being found after all these years. What would happen then?

Cheryl's feelings were in tune with what families of other crew members told me: "I personally don't see the necessity of trying to recover remains," she said. "The important thing is to recognize their efforts."[3]

Few, if any, would argue against the case for recognition. How this might best be done is another matter.

John McLaughlin, the retired ironworker and recovery diver, had bought an American flag to place on the "Twenty-Four" in 2016 when he explored the compelling sonar image with Tim Caza, the retired UPS-worker-turned-wreck-seeker. Though that mission was fruitless, Caza still keeps the flag stowed in a locker over the pilot's wheel of *Voyager*. "I want it handy for when the day comes," he said as he showed me the flag one late summer afternoon after inviting me aboard. Caza was about to embark on an excursion on the northeast part of the lake with a new diving bot, and he offered to demonstrate how, when *Gertie* is found, he will use the vehicle to document the discovery and take pictures to share with the world.

The target this day was the *City of New York*, a 136-foot steamer, last seen November 25, 1921, when it left the Oswego harbor en route to Trenton, Ontario. That story was tragic in its own right: bodies of five crew, including the captain's wife—likely victims of hypothermia— were recovered the next day in a drifting lifeboat. The body of the captain, Harry Randal, his two young sons, and another crew member were thought to have washed from a second lifeboat, found empty.[4]

Caza and Dennis Gerber had discovered the ship in deep water with their sonar unit earlier in the season, and now I watched the story of its demise through Caza's interpretation of high-definition video relayed from the ROV, piloted by Gerber—the retired electronics engineer and Tim's diving partner. The men sat in *Voyager*'s cramped cuddy, shielded from the midday sun, focused on the monitor as the bot hovered over the deck of the sunken vessel, relaying a stunning view one hundred years into the past: a windlass, a capstan, a cargo hold. Caza issued directions to Dennis, who guided the drone with a joystick, both men mindful of keeping clear of snags on the tether that could damage the wreck or strand the ROV. As Dennis steered the bot around the hull, the *City of New York*'s massive rudder came into view in the blue-green haze. It was off axis, Caza noted, and jammed firmly into the prop. At the other end of the hull, both anchors were deployed, their chains stretched to windward. "They lost steerage in the storm," Caza noted. "The captain tried to hold it to the waves." Caza's sense of wonder was contagious. Knowing these circumstances, it was easy to envision building seas cresting over the bow of the disabled ship in its final moments. The *City of New York* would begin taking on more water than it could pump, while the captain ordered the most able crew into one lifeboat with his wife. Then he and his two young sons, perhaps unwilling to leave their father's side, would attempt to board a second lifeboat with another crew member, too late.

Finding a 136-foot steamer last seen a century ago and completing its story is the type of discovery that Caza lives for. He and Gerber have adapted software to display 3-D animation of this and other wreck sites.[5]

In this way they can share their discoveries with the rest of the world on-line, while keeping their locations secret.

"When I finally find *Gertie*," Caza said, as he dropped me ashore, "the first thing I'm going to do is stop by John's house, knowing what nobody else knows, and say, 'Hey, John, let's go for a boat ride—I have something to show you.'"

John McLaughlin, who hung up his fins some time ago, would welcome the invitation, though the story occupying his mind's eye for the past fifty years is unlikely to be surpassed by whatever remains Caza's growing arsenal of sonar and robotic technology might reveal on the lakebed, no matter how vivid. "There's more to it than anybody knows," John has remarked on multiple occasions as we shared documents and compared notes on the dining room table of his small ranch house over coffee and his wife Donna's homemade spice cake. During these sessions, and similar meetings with Kennard and Caza, I came to appreciate that wrecks exist in their purest form as unseen and untouched possibility. When a mystery ceases to be mysterious, the promise of discovery is lost.

As more advanced technology combs the lakebed, and one season and then another draws to a close with the mystery of her final resting place preserved, *Gertie*'s patina grows richer. That Gerald Clemons—the justice of the peace in the snowy town of Denmark east of the lake—heard something other than thunder the night the bomber was lost; that the wing panel recovered on the beach at Shore Oaks a week later may not have been from *Gertie*; that the federal government knows the whereabouts of the aircraft; that the contents of its payload are unknown: these postulates, rising from an element apart from historicity, bear plausible kinship to speculation about the fate of Amelia Earhart, the aviation pioneer who disappeared suddenly and completely with her navigator, Fred J. Noonan, while attempting to circumnavigate the globe in 1937; or Dirk Pitt's fictional quest for the essential truth behind *Vixen 03*.[6] McLaughlin invites and savors such comparison, though he's not one to proselytize. "Draw your own conclusions," he offers. "Regardless of the crew's mission, they took it on for their country, and they died doing it. We owe it to them and the rest of the world to remember their story."

Caza, for his part, is working with far better equipment than in 2016, when his sonar picked up the image of something resembling the canopy of a B-24, which he unsuccessfully explored with McLaughlin. He and

Gerber have since found dozens of shipwrecks in Lake Ontario and the Finger Lakes. In the process, Caza has come to appreciate that the east end of Lake Ontario is especially dynamic. With churning waves driven by storms that build from the west across the length of the lake, it lives up to its reputation as the Bay of Dead Ships. "It's tough with the sand moving," Caza told me. "An awful lot of things are covered and uncovered on that end of the lake. One year we see them on sonar, then they're gone."

Caza's growing success has caught the attention of archaeologists who regularly seek his pro bono help to locate submerged artifacts in the Erie Canal system and adjoining waters that tell of migratory trends and lifestyles in nineteenth- and twentieth-century New York State. Pulled in multiple directions, with seasons limited by weather, and a finite number of them left in his career, Caza is disinclined to spend much time on sections of Lake Ontario he has already covered. For now.

The only other person with a comparable track record in Lake Ontario is Jim Kennard, the retired engineer and Explorers Club fellow from Rochester. Since his discovery in 2008 of HMS *Ontario*, the ship from the Revolutionary War, Kennard and his team have found and documented the *Washington*, a fifty-three-foot merchant vessel built in the late eighteenth century that sank off Oswego with all hands in 1806, and a US Air Force C-45 lost in 1952 when its crew parachuted to safety after engine failure.[7]

Despite the growing list of discoveries, *Gertie* somehow continues to elude seekers. That could change, however, with burgeoning public interest in the lake and its contents spawned by plans for the federal diving sanctuary. And not everybody is happy about it. Kennard and Caza, the dons of wreck-seeking in Lake Ontario, remain wary of expectation among officials that the wreck seekers will share their secrets to advance the plan. "We are already doing, basically, what they want to do," Caza said. "And we are making it available [through video and internet] to people who want to see it and to learn about it. . . . NOAA wants us to hand over forty years of work without giving us credit."

Due credit is part of the issue. But it's also about access. Well-known recreational diving wrecks are one thing. Virgin wrecks of historical significance, some of them grave sites, are a different matter. These are especially attractive to trophy-seekers and also vulnerable to damage and degradation from well-meaning divers. Typically, they are hidden, well preserved, in cold, deep water—once the exclusive domain of elite divers willing to commit significant parts of their lives looking for them, and out of reach for people lacking the time, resources, and know-how.

The idea of the marine sanctuary, in contrast, is to make "national historic treasures" accessible to all. "The term 'sanctuary' tends to make people think that things are off limits," NOAA's Great Lakes regional coordinator Ellen Brody told me. "That's not the case with these marine sanctuaries. The philosophy is to make them available to use and enjoy." Nevertheless, she added, each site is distinct, "and you have to recognize best practices and be aware of sensitivities."[8]

In addition to NOAA's plan to map and mark sites with buoys, the goal is generously helped, for good or for ill, by twenty-first-century technology and mores. Like GPS units and once-rare sonar equipment now readily found in fish finders, ROVs, which require considerable budgets and special skills to operate, are becoming more available, user friendly, and cheaper. Social media platforms sharing adventure vlogs, images, stories, and technical information with the multitudes are also opening doors to the deep.

"A World War II bomber with eight American airmen in Lake Ontario? There will be no keeping people away," one veteran diver told me. "Everybody has cameras, GPS units, and social media accounts. When one person knows where she is, everybody knows where she is."

Finding *Gertie* might be a fundamental part of recognizing her story. Yet should the airmen's lost tomb be discovered in accessible depths, in an age where more people have better equipment to remotely plumb the deep, featuring it as an attraction raises practical issues of keeping the grave undisturbed.

Despite new laws protecting sunken military craft, Phil Church's worry of "people without good intentions" is no less of a concern today than it was in the 1990s. Church, the Oswego County administrator who facilitated the community support to enable the national designation, acknowledges that the balance of access and protection must be worked out. "It wasn't long ago when Mount Everest was accessible for only a few elite mountain climbers," he told me. "Now, at certain times there's a wall-to-wall line of people to get to the top." As barriers to entry fall, issues of safety and degradation rise. "I'm not sure of the answer, but it has to be addressed," Church said. "NOAA has a lot of experience with this."[9]

At NOAA sanctuaries elsewhere, decisions on if and how to facilitate access for certain vulnerable sites are made on a "case-by-case basis" by NOAA and state officials managing the sanctuary, said Lusardi, the marine archaeologist with NOAA's Thunder Bay sanctuary. There's been no need for restriction on the type of attractions in Thunder Bay, he said, but visitors to the USS *Monitor*, the famous Civil War ship in 230 feet of water off Cape Hatteras, North Carolina, need to be approved through a research application process. Similarly, policy for Lake Ontario would be made based on the nature and vulnerability of the attractions.

Yet it's this kind of uncertainty, coupled with untold emotional capital accrued through a lifetime of devotion to their pursuits, that make Kennard and Caza uncomfortable entrusting their discoveries to NOAA officials. "I won't ever go back to the HMS *Ontario*," said Kennard, who fears being tracked by others. He added, "We know what's there and have documented it with ninety minutes of video. Every time you go back, you are potentially exposing the site."[10]

NOAA has its own wreck-finding resources, including autonomous vehicles outfitted with sensors and sonar that can survey the lake underwater, on the surface, and from the air. Such equipment can make relatively short work of searches that may have taken Caza and Kennard years.[11]

As agency staff and volunteers begin to inventory historical treasures in eastern Lake Ontario and develop policy to showcase and protect them "case-by-case," Caza and Kennard, like mountain climbers drawn to unscaled peaks or pioneers drawn to new frontiers, are drawn to deeper waters. The deepest section of Lake Ontario, which not coincidentally holds the greatest promise of undiscovered wrecks, lies in an elongated basin below four thousand square miles of water running west from Oswego to well past Rochester, beginning with a drop-off several miles off the south shore. With average depths well beyond five hundred feet and the deepest sounding more than eight hundred feet, it has remained out of reach for amateurs, but that will soon change. Caza and Gerber are now teaming with Kennard to develop tow fish that can drag their homemade sonar adaptations deeper.

Here, someday, a haunting image of a noble vessel may glide into view on their monitor, and they will be the first to lay eyes on it since it took off from the Westover USAAF base on February 17, 1944. At some point, after they gather themselves, there will be a moment of silence at the tomb of eight young men, "our boys," who spent their last weeks and hours preparing to aid the liberation of France from the Nazi regime.

Or maybe *Getaway Gertie*, despite the ever-growing arsenal of technology employed to find her, will eternally elude her seekers.

The lake, vast and deep, remains at once ever-changing and timeless. There is plenty to be found and more that will never be found settled in its deepest reaches and cast along its shores. On Nine Mile Point, a cooling tower for a nuclear reactor rises monolithically where World War II antiaircraft guns once took aim at targets towed by small aircraft over the lake. Nine miles to the east, the lighthouse at Port Ontario, which according to local lore remained unlit the night *Gertie* was lost for fear of directing the B-24 into the keeper's living room, presides over a stretch of beach mostly unchanged from when Ponder circled desperately overhead, looking for a place to land. Here, prevailing winds and currents feed sandbars occasionally shaped and reshaped by twenty-foot breakers, and miles of estuaries, marshes, and drifting dunes that offer ample cover for remnants of history they receive from the lake.

NOTE TO READERS

Vanishing Point is, of course, a story of a B-24 Liberator bomber and crew lost over upstate New York in 1944. Moreover, it's a story about remembering.

What I call "the tomb of the forgotten soldier" is indeed a war grave. But to me, its most compelling quality is derived from metaphor. My quest, which spanned more than five years, was not so much about the lost plane's precise location as the stories behind it. Over those years, I found the support of many. John McLaughlin and the late Jim Coffed generously opened their files and guided me through their contents; Tim Caza and Jim Kennard schooled me in matters of past and current underwater exploration; Phil Church found time amid his duties of running Oswego County government to recount his long-held vision of a diving park in eastern Lake Ontario and provide updates on the creation of NOAA's marine sanctuary.

Others, many with less visible contributions, informed decisions that went into developing themes and story lines: author Michael Sledge offered essential perspective on values and traditions concerning recovery and tribute for our military dead; author Peter Stekel shared his knowledge, personal experience, and contacts concerning the AAF crew lost in the Sierra Nevada; author Aaron Hiltner provided review and counsel on home front history and other matters. I also found Anthony J. Mireles's three-volume catalog of fatal airplane crashes on the home front during the war and AAF historian Marlyn R. Pierce's work on the subject to be especially noteworthy resources.

While the work of these and others—referenced throughout the chapters—was indispensable, the bulk of my research entailed combing through primary sources, sometimes looking for material that no longer exists, with occasional payoffs and surprises, and much gathering, sifting, and ordering of elements and background. Here (as throughout my journalistic career) I extend a hearty shout out to clerks, patrons, and curators entrusted with the keeping and access of public memory. For this project, the clerical teams at the Air Force Historical Research Agency, the US Army Center of Military History, and the National Archives at Saint Louis provided timely and fruitful responses to my formal, informal, and sometimes complicated queries and follow-up requests. Other essential records and/or perspective came from Ward Eldredge, curator at Sequoia and Kings Canyon National Parks; Paul Lear, historic site manager of Fort Ontario State Historic Site; Mercedes Niess and Michael Pittavino of the H. Lee White Maritime Museum; and Austin Wadsworth, president of the National Warplane Museum.

I'm especially appreciative of the work of Oswego County native Marie Strong, the town of New Haven historian, who produced a cache of records widening local perspective on the event, supplemented by her own childhood memory. I also had the remarkably good fortune of sitting with lifelong Oswego County resident Laurence "Sparky" Rector. Sparky was fighting with the 157th Infantry in Europe the night *Gertie* disappeared, but he shared hometown memories from the period, including occasionally seeing, from his nearby residence, searchlights raking the night sky during antiaircraft drills east of Nine Mile Point. Horace Backus, another Oswego County elder, provided additional local context of the Oswego County war years, including blackout drills, airplane spotting, rationing, and the goings-on of town and county governmental affairs. I'm also indebted to the late Clayton

"Jack" Weiss (another World War II combat veteran) and Charles, Louise, and Leo Himes for their Oswego County memories and generous hospitality while sharing them.

Archaeologists Wendy Coble and Megan Lickliter-Mundon, who have worked with the Defense POW/MIA Accounting Agency, helped me understand the evolution of governmental policy and practice regarding sunken military craft. Wayne Lusardi, archaeologist at NOAA's Thunder Bay sanctuary, also shared his considerable knowledge and keen interest in the subject; and Ellen Brody, NOAA's Great Lakes regional coordinator, kept me abreast on plans for Lake Ontario.

The book would have been tragically incomplete without the help and interest of family members of *Gertie*'s crew. I remain profoundly grateful to Robert Keith Hardy, Eddie Evans, Terri Coleman, the late Frank Evans, and the late Mary Opel Hardy; Jean and Ray Vanasek; Ray Buckley and Amber Rhea Simmons; and Karen Mickler and Cheryl Allen for sharing their family stories and what they could find in the way of photographs and memorabilia of the crew. To those family members I am yet to find, I invite you to contact me. The story continues, and so will coverage on my blog, *Beyond the Blue Yonder* (beyondtheblueyonder.blogspot.com).

Drawing on these sources and many others, I arrive at the finished product—a mosaic of hard reality and imperfect memory. Imperfect because, even with all this help, I had to bridge narrative gaps in the absence of direct witnesses and surviving records. Certain scenes—the church gathering in chapter 7, for example—are derived from known events and contextual elements of the day, coupled with what I gleaned from family histories, recollections of old-timers, census and ancestry records, local newspaper accounts (which at the time tended to be rich in social minutiae), and reasonable measures of logic and deduction.

The work of writing goes unseen, as do the people who contribute to the process. The book would be no more than a worthy but unfulfilled idea without the publishing team that helped bring it to fruition, led by Three Hills editorial director Michael McGandy and including assistant managing editor Karen Laun, assistant editor Clare Jones, copy editor Glenn Novak, and indexer Enid Zafran.

In addition to this professional help, I owe thanks to qualified reviewers who generously volunteered many hours to vet and proofread the manuscript. They include Valerie van Heest, author and diver; Susan P.

Gateley, author and Lake Ontario scholar; Mark Wood, former Navy pilot; Tracy Wood, writing coach and former Marine logistics specialist; and Julie Boyd, my wife, who has tolerated the lifestyle of a writer for more than thirty years while providing unending emotional support and a sharp eye for errant copy.

NOTES

Preface

1. Anthony J. Mireles, *Fatal Army Air Force Aviation Accidents in the United States, 1941–1945*, 3 vols. (Jefferson, NC: McFarland, 2006). Mireles and other authorities on the subject cite data and records compiled from the *US Army Air Forces Statistical Digest*. The numbers do not include accidents in other branches of the armed forces and the Civil Air Patrol.

2. This story is from Frank Woodmancy, a lifelong resident of Oswego County, interviewed in Mexico, New York, October 13, 2019. The promontory is just east of Nine Mile Point.

3. The story of Frederick Spink III and his family's connection with the lost bomber is recounted more fully in chapter 5.

1. Deep Dive

1. Debate persists about the effectiveness of the Allies' strategic bombing campaigns over Europe. It is generally recognized they hindered the enemies' manufacturing, disrupted supplies, diverted resources, and, critically, outpaced and ultimately contributed to the defeat of Germany's Luftwaffe, factors that greatly helped Allied ground forces advance. But bombing tended to be inaccurate, wantonly destructive, lethal to countless civilians, and by no means ensured victory. The same generally holds true in the Pacific, though the atomic bombing of Japan is another discussion.

2. Stephen E. Ambrose, *The Wild Blue: The Men and Boys Who Flew the B-24s over Germany* (New York: Simon & Schuster, 2002), 23.

3. As far as American-built bombers go, the B-24's place in popular culture is often over-shadowed by the sleeker and more conventional B-17 Flying Fortress. The B-29 Superfortress had a greater range and payload then either the B-24 or B-17, though a more limited deployment. Introduced in mid-1944, the B-29 played a significant role in the Pacific during the final eighteen months of the war.

4. For a complete list of surviving B-24s see www.airplanes-online.com/b24-liberator-surviving-aircraft.htm.

5. Details of McLaughlin and Caza's search for the plane portrayed here and in subsequent chapters are from the author's interviews with McLaughlin and Caza, individually and together, from May 2017 through May 2022. These include multiple meetings at their respective homes in Oswego County; at the author's cottage, also in Oswego County; during an outing on Caza's boat; and follow-up phone calls, text messages, and email correspondence.

6. See also "Oil Slick out from Ramona Beach May Be Clue to Missing B-24," *Syracuse (NY) Post-Standard*, June 17, 1944.

7. Tim Caza, interview with author at Caza's Oswego County home, November 20, 2019. Also Randy Wells, "Sunken Treasure, Unmasking a Sight Not Seen in Centuries," *IUP Magazine*, Fall/Winter 2017, www.iup.edu/magazine/archive/.

8. Information regarding Jim Kennard here and in subsequent chapters is from the author's interview with Kennard on October 25, 2018, in Binghamton, New York, and multiple phone interviews and email correspondence from May 2017 through April 2022. Kennard's diving career is also documented in *Shipwrecks of Lake Ontario: A Journey of Discovery* (Toledo, OH: National Museum of the Great Lakes, 2019), which Kennard authored with Roland Stevens and Roger Pawlowski.

9. Kennard credits Guy Morin with assisting in research of the HMS *Ontario* from reports that were documented in the Haldimand papers from the National Archives of Canada, located in Ottawa.

10. Kennard interview; also, William Kates, "Explorers Find 1780 British Warship in Lake Ontario," Associated Press, June 13, 2008.

11. The "archaeological miracle" quote is attributed in the Associated Press report to Arthur Britton Smith, who had previously chronicled the history of the HMS *Ontario* in a 1997 book, *The Legend of the Lake*. See www.cbsnews.com/news/1780-british-warship-found-in-lake-ontario/.

12. The wholesale abandonment of the Avro Arrow program coincided with development of intercontinental ballistic missile systems and related air defenses expected to limit the jet's marketability and economic viability. For a complete history see Palmiro Campagna, *The Avro Arrow: For the Record* (Toronto: Dundurn, 2019); Greig Stewart, *Shutting Down the National Dream: A. V. Roe and the Tragedy of the Avro Arrow* (Whitby, ON: McGraw-Hill Ryerson, 1988); Richard Organ et al., *Avro Arrow: The Story of the Avro Arrow from Its Evolution to Its Extinction* (Boston: Mills, 2004).

13. "Sunken Avro Arrow Model Recovered from Lake Ontario," *CBC News*, August 22, 2018, www.cbc.ca/news/canada/ottawa/avro-arrow-recovered-lake-ontario-1.4793463.

14. Michael Sledge, in *Soldier Dead: How We Recover, Identify, Bury, and Honor Our Military Fallen* (New York: Columbia University Press, 2005), traces the phrase to the Civil War, when a list of soldier dead was posted at train stations to inform family and loved ones.

Sledge's exhaustive treatment uniquely considers nearly all aspects of identifying, burying, and honoring fallen soldiers.

15. Defense POW/MIA Accounting Agency, www.dpaa.mil/Our-Missing/Past-Conflicts/#:~:text=As%20this%20map%20shows%2C%20at,the%20Gulf%20Wars%2Fother%20.

2. A Boy's Dream

1. A column in the *Jackson (MS) Clarion-Ledger* on June 9, 1926, characterizes Morton as a "railroad town." Though Forkville is eight miles away, "being on the interior does not keep that section from being wide awake and aggressive as known by those who have had the pleasure to visit."

2. Background compiled from interviews with distant relatives, genealogical records, newspaper clips, and headstones at Bethlehem Baptist Church.

3. Descriptions of the setting of Keith's youth are from interviews with family members of multiple generations, contextual research at the Mississippi Agricultural & Forestry Museum and other sources, and a visit to the homestead in July 2018.

4. The origins of the Curtiss JN can be found with the Curtiss Aeroplane Company of Hammondsport, New York, which in 1916 became the Curtiss Aeroplane and Motor Company headquartered in Buffalo. Nearly seven thousand planes were built, with surpluses making it the "backbone of American postwar aviation." See Gilles Auliard, "Maiden of the Skies," *Air Classics*, April 2009.

5. Thirty-four airmail pilots died in crashes from 1918 through 1927. "Airmail, a Brief History," United States Postal Service, March 2018, https://about.usps.com/who-we-are/postal-history/airmail.pdf.

6. "Airmail's Odyssey: Inauguration to Golden Anniversary," *Postal Life*, May–June 1968, https://babel.hathitrust.org/cgi/pt?id=uiug.30112106587246&view=1up&seq=3.

7. "Practical Hints on Flying," *Air Service Journal*, January 10, 1918, https://babel.hathitrust.org/cgi/pt?id=njp.32101048919383&view=1up&seq=7.

8. "Great Crowds Gather to Pay Tribute to Trans-Atlantic Flyer," *Jackson Clarion-Ledger*, October 8, 1927.

9. "Scott County Fair Is to Open on Tuesday: Speeches, Races, Baseball and Barbecue among the Events at Forkville," *Jackson Clarion-Ledger*, August 9, 1929.

10. B.C. lost a limb to the disease in 1934. "Fast Recovery Wish of Friends," *Jackson Clarion-Ledger*, May 9, 1934; interviews with family.

11. In a few short years, the number of manufacturing and railroading jobs dropped from fifty-two thousand to twenty-eight thousand, while payrolls dropped from $42 million to $14 million. Martha H. Swain, "Great Depression," Mississippi Encyclopedia, Center for Study of Southern Culture, 2018, https://mississippiencyclopedia.org/entries/great-depression/.

12. Recounting of oral history by Keith Ponder's great-nephew Robert Keith Hardy, in correspondence with the author on March 31, 2017.

13. FDR's message clearly resonated with Mississippians, though many votes cast for FDR may have actually been votes against the unpopular Herbert Hoover and the party of Lincoln.

14. While the reference here is to a legislative proposal, it is a matter of record that the Baptist Church condoned racist policies in Ponder's time. The Southern Baptist Convention passed a resolution in 1995 noting that "racism has led to discrimination, oppression,

injustice, and violence . . . throughout the history of our nation," and "Southern Baptists failed, in many cases, to support, and in some cases opposed, legitimate initiatives to secure the civil rights of African-Americans." See "Resolution on Racial Reconciliation on the 150th Anniversary of the Southern Baptist Convention," https://www.sbc.net/resource-library/resolutions/resolution-on-racial-reconciliation-on-the-150th-anniversary-of-the-southern-baptist-convention/.

15. About 1.3 million Germans were unemployed in 1929, compared to more than six million by early 1932—an increase from 4.5 percent to 24 percent of the workforce. Nicholas H. Dimsdale, Nicholas Horsewood, and Arthur van Riel, "Unemployment in Interwar Germany: An Analysis of the Labor Market, 1927–1936," *Journal of Economic History* 66, no. 3 (September 2006), https://www.jstor.org/stable/3874859.

16. One argument holds that the country's military buildup caused the shortage of resources. Yasukichi Yasuba, "Did Japan Ever Suffer from a Shortage of Natural Resources before World War II?," *Journal of Economic History* 56, no. 3 (1996): 543–60, http://www.jstor.org/stable/2123713.

3. Readying for War

1. *US Army Air Forces Statistical Digest, World War II* (Washington, DC: Office of Statistical Control, December 1945), table 79, 127, https://apps.dtic.mil/dtic/tr/fulltext/u2/a542518.pdf.

2. Ponder had logged thirty-four hours and ten minutes on "this type" of aircraft, presumably a heavy bomber, and seven hours, thirty-four minutes on "this model," presumably a B-24E. *Aircraft Accidents and Incident Reports 1940 thru 1948*, Accident No. 44-2-18-72, Form 14, General Services Administration, National Archives and Records Services, World War II Records Division.

3. Pilots and crews sometimes slept on cots at aircraft factories while waiting for their planes to roll off the line. Graham M. Simons, *Consolidated B-24 Liberator* (Barnsley, South Yorkshire: Penn & Sword Aviation, 2012), 64, 65.

4. While the B-24 boasted superior range, it lacked the armament and handling of the B-17. Major General James Doolittle, the renowned aviation pioneer and, at the time, Eighth Air Force commander, thought the B-24 was patently unsafe. On February 14, 1944, days prior to events depicted here, Doolittle had written to Lieutenant General Carl Spaatz, commander of strategic forces in Europe, urging "substantial changes in design" to make the B-24 safer. Spaatz responded, "The German Airforce Must be Liquidated if OVERLORD [the Normandy Invasion] is to be successful, and I cannot liquidate it with planes resting in modification centers." With Overlord just months away, Doolittle's plea, forwarded to General Henry Harley Arnold, was denied, though many of the B-24s underwent some degree of modification throughout the war. In short, the B-24 design, the product of hasty wartime deadlines, remained a work in progress, with lessons hard won in battle and training. For a tidy summary of these events see Simons, *Consolidated B-24*, 139–43.

5. For takeoff sequence and other aspects of flying the Liberator see *B-24 Pilot Training Manual*, W. M. B. Burford Printing, 1945, posted by the 461st Bombardment Group, www.461st.org/B-24_Manual/B-24_Manual.html; also, "Flying the Consolidate B-24 Liberator," Consolidated Aircraft Corp., 1943, video archived with Military Arts Pictures, https://www.youtube.com/watch?time_continue=4&v=JO0iSx-ZCAQ&feature=emb_title.

6. The risks are examined more thoroughly in chapter 6.

7. Allied air forces flew some six thousand sorties during Big Week; more than two thousand Allied airmen were killed or captured, and 385 planes lost. Silvano Wueschner, "Operation

Argument: The Beginning of the End of the German Luftwaffe," Air University History Office, Maxwell Air Force Base, 2019, www.maxwell.af.mil/News/Display/Article/1754049/. For more on Big Week see Richard G. Davis, *Bombing the European Axis Powers: A Historical Digest of the Combined Bomber Offensive, 1939–1945* (Maxwell Air Force Base, AL: Air University Press, 2005), 279–90, https://media.defense.gov/2010/Oct/27/2001330220/-1/-1/0/davis_bombing_european.pdf.

8. Congress amended the Selective Training and Service Act on November 13, 1942, to call registered eighteen- and nineteen-year-olds into service. The AAF dropped the college requirement for pilots in January 1942.

9. "Cadet Classification," First Motion Picture Unit, Army Air Forces, 1943, archived by Military Arts Pictures, https://www.youtube.com/watch?v=qhLUAc63--k. The narrator, Ronald Reagan, served in the AAF's Motion Picture Unit—a prolific home front PR function. He would later become the fortieth president of the United States.

10. For more thorough descriptions of training see Eugene Fletcher, *Mister: The Training of an Aviation Cadet in World War II* (Seattle: University of Washington Press, 1992); Ambrose, *Wild Blue*, 49–105; Wesley Frank Craven, *The Army Air Forces in World War II*, vol. 6, *Men and Planes* (Chicago: University of Chicago Press, 1955), 557–68, https://archive.org/details/Vol6MenAndPlanes-nsia/page/n71/mode/2up; Rebecca Hancock Cameron, *Training to Fly: Military Flight Training 1907–1945* (Airforce History and Museums Program, 1999), 383–415, https://media.defense.gov/2010/Dec/02/2001329902/-1/-1/0/training_to_fly-2.pdf.

11. Keith had moved to Jackson with his mother sometime after he graduated from high school and before he signed up with the AAF. Yet family history holds that Keith's mother also resided with relatives on the Forkville homestead and worshipped at the Bethlehem Church throughout her life. Additionally, a clip from the Morton weekly in Lucy Ponder's scrapbook references Keith "visiting homefolks in the community" after earning his wings, so it's evident Keith spent his homecoming at the homestead. See "We Mourn," *Morton (MS) Progress Herald*, March 9, 1944.

12. For summary of overcast and visibility at various altitudes before and after 047's takeoff see *Aircraft Accidents and Incident Reports 1940 thru 1948*, testimony of Captain Paul L. Mathison, also covered in chapter 10.

13. *B-24 Pilot Training Manual*, 137–38.

14. Some 313 cases of anoxia—47 of them fatal—were documented among seasoned fliers serving in the Eighth Air Force (a heavy bomber unit in Europe) between 1942 and 1945. Primary causes included oxygen system failure, the freezing of delivery hoses, personnel failure, regulator failure, and freezing of the A-14 mask. Rates reached nearly two cases of anoxia for every one hundred missions flown in 1943. The number of cases on the home front, or for other bomber units overseas, is undocumented, though the conditions that caused anoxia for the Eight Air Force would not be expected to differ significantly from those of other high-altitude missions of the time. For more on this and other maladies fliers faced see James J. Carroll, "Physiological Problems of Bomber Crews in the Eight Air Force during WW II," Air Command and Staff College, March 1997, https://apps.dtic.mil/dtic/tr/fulltext/u2/a398044.

15. Carroll, in "Physiological Problems of Bomber Crews," writes, "The electrically heated F-1 suit . . . had an inherent weakness—it failed to keep the crews warm. . . . The frequency of failure . . . was so great that most men chose either not to use them or, if they did, to wear heavy clothing over the electric suit."

16. The move of the 471st to Westover freed up room at the Pueblo base for the development of the B-29 Superfortress prototype—the bomber that would eventually finish the war

with an extended campaign in the Pacific culminating with the nuclear devastation of two cities on the Japanese mainland.

17. Charles Lindbergh, *Wartime Journals of Charles Lindbergh* (New York: Harcourt Brace Jovanovich, 1970), quoted in Wil S. Hylton. *Vanished, The Sixty-Year Search for the Missing Men of World War II* (New York: Riverhead Books, 2013), 45, 46. Any mention of Lindbergh's legacy is incomplete without noting claims by critics that the flying ace's public advocacy for neutrality leading up to the war was rooted in Nazi sympathies and antisemitism. See Lynne Olson, *Those Angry Days: Roosevelt, Lindbergh, and America's Fight over World War II, 1939–1941* (New York: Random House, 2013).

18. See Simons, *Consolidated B-24*, 213–30, for a quantitative comparison of the B-24 with the B-17 and other period aircraft.

19. *471st Bomb Group Unit History, March 1 to April 10, 1944*, First Air Force, USAAF, 1944, Major Trevor E. Hodges, Group Executive Officer, status report May 4, citing conditions in the early part of the year.

20. *471st Bomb Group Unit History, March 1 to April 10, 1944*, status report May 4, citing conditions in the early part of the year; Captain Paul C. Baganz, Group Schools Officer, status report March 14.

21. *471st Bomb Group Unit History, January 14 to February 29, 1944*, First Air Force, USAAF, 1944, 17. The shortage of planes was not limited to Westover. On February 10, a Lieutenant Walter Baskin wrote home, "When we are scheduled to fly, we have trouble getting planes that will fly. There are plenty of planes here, but they are old, and over half of them are always on the ramp being repaired." Baskin was stationed at an airbase in Blythe, California. Ambrose, *Wild Blue*, 91.

22. *471st Bomb Group . . . March 1 to April 10*. Full quote: "We hope to be relieved of many of our clunkers in the near future"—John C. Hunt Jr., acting group engineering officer, status report, May 9.

23. *471st Bomb Group . . . March 1 to April 10*, Captain David W. Victor, group supply officer, status report, May 11. Compatibility problems plagued the B-24 throughout the war. Parts from different factories in the production pool often varied in detail, leading to an "interchangeability nightmare," Simons, *Consolidated B-24*, 109.

24. Captain Paul C. Baganz, group schools officer, status report, March 14.

25. *471st Bomb Group . . . January 14 to February 29, 1944*, 14.

26. *471st Bomb Group . . . March 1 to April 10, 1944*, "Abortive Mission Data."

27. *471st Bomb Group . . . March 1 to April 10, 1944*, Lieutenant Augustine J. Gironda, group communications officer, status report, May 10, 1944.

28. *471st Bomb Group . . . March 1 to April 10, 1944*, 14; also, appendix, item 17.

29. *471st Bomb Group . . . March 1 to April 10, 1944*, Lieutenant Colonel Elwood P. Donahue, group operations officer, status report, May 5, 1944.

30. Names and genders of the individuals working in the control tower are not part of the record. It's quite possible that some may have been enlisted with the Women's Army Corps (WACs), commonly assigned to noncombat operations.

31. All quoted communication between Westover and controllers in this section is verbatim from *Aircraft Accident and Incident Reports . . .*, "Transcript of Records on Army 047, a B24, on Local Contact Flight Rules flight [*sic*] out of Westover Field, Mass.," Boston Airway Traffic Control Center, February 17–18, 1944, 1–3.

32. *Aircraft Accidents and Incident Reports 1940 thru 1948*, Form 14. Ponder's situation was not unusual. In addition to requiring mastery of larger, more sophisticated combat aircraft, "transitional training" also involved learning specialized flying skills, battle tactics, and leadership. See Craven, *Army Air Forces in World War II*, 6:557–68, https://archive.org/details/Vol6MenAndPlanes-nsia/page/n575/mode/2up.

33. *B-24 Pilot Training Manual*, 13.

4. Into Thin Air

1. Ponder's plane had crossed from airspace tracked by controllers in Boston into a sector directed from a control room at La Guardia Field in New York City.

2. Now Syracuse Hancock International Airport, the Army base sat just north of the city and east of the municipal Amboy field, which was acquired after the war by Allied Chemical and turned into waste beds.

3. There were not enough heated flying suits for all; accordingly, fliers stationed in other parts of the plane had priority over those on the flight deck. See *471st Bomb Group . . . March 1 to April 10,* 34.

4. *B-24 Pilot Training Manual,* 14.

5. *Aircraft Accident and Incident Reports,* "Transcript of Records," 1–6.

6. "Fifty-Five University Students Take Up Aviation," *Stevens Point (WI) Daily Journal,* November 8, 1939.

7. "Capt. Mathison, on Anti-sub Patrol, Wins Air Metal," *Wisconsin State Journal,* April 20, 1943.

8. *Berkshire Evening Eagle* (Pittsfield, MA), "Ancient Monastery Blasted by Bomb and Shell," February 15, 1944.

9. Jason Dawsey, "Over the Cauldron of Ploesti: The American Air War in Romania," National World War II Museum, August 12, 2019, https://www.nationalww2museum.org/war/articles/over-cauldron-ploesti-american-air-war-romania.

10. Of 291 bombers that departed on the mission, sixty were shot down, with six hundred airmen lost over enemy territory. Seventeen other bombers, many carrying dead or wounded crew, crash-landed on their return to England. "Black Thursday: Schweinfurt, October 14, 1943," National Museum of the United States Air Force, https://www.nationalmuseum.af.mil/Visit/Museum-Exhibits/Fact-Sheets/Display/Article/1519661/.

11. Allied bombing missions would prove more effective in 1944 with long-range fighter escorts to weaken and eventually eliminate the Luftwaffe.

12. My tally of accidents from December 12 to December 28, 1943, as cataloged in Mireles, *Fatal Army Air Forces Aviation Accidents in the United States, 1941–1945,* 2:613–30.

13. *Aircraft Accident and Incident Reports,* "Transcript of Records," 14–22. This record of real-time communication shows how traffic-control radio and interphone protocol of 1944, still in early development, were extraordinarily undisciplined by today's standards. Even so, an AAF investigation noted "very sloppy operation. . . . If all such unnecessary contacts were removed from interphone and radio circuits, the communication problem would have been less acute."

5. The People's Story

1. "Lost Bomber Search Turned to North," *Syracuse (NY) Post-Standard,* February 19, 1944; "Many Planes on Hunt for Lost Bomber," *Syracuse (NY) Herald-Journal,* February 19, 1944; "Lost Bomber Search Is on Again Today," *Syracuse (NY) Herald American,* February 20, 1944; "Two Areas Searched for Missing Bomber," *Watertown (NY) Daily Times,* February 21, 1944.

2. "Coast Guard Here Joins Search for Lost Bomber," *Oswego (NY) Palladium-Times,* February 19, 1944.

3. For a comprehensive study of frequently overlooked impacts that soldiers mobilizing for the war had on community life see Aaron Hiltner, *Taking Leave, Taking Liberties: American Troops on the World War II Home Front* (Chicago: University of Chicago Press, 2020).

4. "Coast Guard Here Joins Search for Lost Bomber."

5. "Coast Guard Here Joins Search for Lost Bomber." The *Oswego Palladium-Times* sourced a summary of the plane circling, offered the following day, to Ensign Joseph Hebert, commanding officer of the Coast Guard station in Oswego (who would also become a primary source of events to come), although the newspaper didn't specify who was on watch at the time. The *Syracuse Post-Standard* identified "CO Bauscher" as the coastguardsman at Oswego who reported to police that he heard the plane heading northwest over the lake. There are no records of Bauscher's first name. See "Lost Bomber Search Turned North by Oswego Report," February 18, 1944.

6. "Coast Guard Here Joins Search for Lost Bomber."

7. Teletype machines, used by police and reporters to relate bulletins and news flashes from trusted institutional sources and one another, were the standard. Hand-held radios had not been sufficiently developed for patrols; telephone call boxes were the norm.

8. Conflicts were unfailingly exacerbated by women, alcohol, the perceived entitlement of uniform, and a general lack of respect for the police. See Hiltner, *Taking Leave, Taking Liberties.*

9. "Coast Guard Here Joins Search for Lost Bomber." The conversation between O'Toole and Brown is referred to in the newspaper account, although no references to Brown or Fort Ontario appear in the AAF accident files of 047.

10. Landing lights, navigational aids, communications, and regulations, while gaining in sophistication by 1944, were still primitive by today's standards. Accordingly, Brown's suggestion for a signal fire harked back to a recent past when improvisational landings were not out of the ordinary.

11. The threat of sabotage by German nationals or sympathizers was constant and pressing. In June 1942, German U-boats successfully landed in Florida and on Long Island, New York. Their crews, equipped with explosives to blow up hydroelectric and manufacturing targets, were later discovered before they could execute the plan. Michael Dobbs, *Saboteurs: The Nazi Raid on America* (New York: Knopf, 2005).

12. The lighthouse story with quote is sourced to the late Joseph Heckle as reported in a column by Bob Peel, "Fate Got in Bomber's Way," *Syracuse Herald American*, July 16, 1989.

13. "Opening Airport Ceremony Magnet for Large Crowds," *Oswego Palladium-Times*, October 25, 1943; "CP Forces Handle Traffic Well," *Oswego Palladium-Times*, October 27, 1943; "Airport Bond Sales Total over $90,000," *Fulton (NY) Patriot*, October 28, 1943.

14. "Airport Lighted to Assist Flier," *Oswego Palladium-Times*, February 18, 1944.

15. "CAP Planes Join Search for Bomber," *Syracuse Herald-Journal*, February 22, 1944.

16. "Searchers Scour Mountain for Lost Bomber," *Rome (NY) Daily Sentinel*, February 21, 1944.

17. Wilbur B. Evans, "Cold and Snow Bar Search of Wooded Section," *Syracuse Herald-Journal*, February 24, 1944; "Cold and Snow Bar Search of Wooded Section: Explosion Heard Friday Morning, Troopers Learn," *Syracuse Herald-Journal*, February 20, 1944; "Two Areas Searched for Missing Bomber," *Watertown Daily Times*, February 21, 1944.

18. The plane is referenced as *Gateway Gertie* in an Army notification of next of kin and in some of the early newspaper accounts. A majority of newspaper accounts have it as *Getaway Gertie.*

19. The train-track theory appeared in various newspaper accounts over the years. See Joe Wilensky, *Oswego Palladium-Times*, "Scriba Man Has Piece of Famed Missing Bomber,"

September 3, 1994; Mike Vogel, *Buffalo News*, "Divers in Lake Ontario Closing in on Lost B-24," August 18, 1994.

20. Wilensky, "Scriba Man Has Piece of Famed Missing Bomber."

21. Fred Spink III, interview with author, June 20, 2019.

22. Some historians argue popular culture has exaggerated or contrived the degree of Vietnam protesters' ill will directed explicitly at soldiers, including incidences of spitting. Regardless, Spink's sergeant would be mindful of inflammatory reports and allegations circulating at the time. See Jerry Lembcke, *The Spitting Image: Myth, Memory and the Legacy of Vietnam* (New York: NYU Press, 2000).

6. A Few of Fifteen Thousand

1. Craig Gima, "Mystery in Ice: Isle Experts Mobilize after the Remains of a World War II Airman Are Found on Top of a Mountain," *Honolulu Star Bulletin*, October 22, 2005, http://archives.starbulletin.com/2005/10/22/news/story02.html; Peter Stekel, *Final Flight: The Mystery of a WW II Plane Crash and the Frozen Airmen in the High Sierra* (Birmingham, AL: Wilderness, 2010), 2.

2. Ward Eldredge, phone interview with the author, August 11, 2020; Stekel, *Final Flight*, 14–15.

3. For summaries of autopsy findings at the coroner's office and, later, at the Joint POW/MIA Accounting Command lab see "Remains of Missing WW II–Era Airman Are Examined," US Air Force website, November 30, 2005, https://www.af.mil/News/Article-Display/Article/132609/; Suzanne Herel, "Frozen Body Believed to Be WW II Airman," SFGate (*San Francisco Chronicle*), October 20, 2005, https://www.sfgate.com/news/article/Frozen-body-in-Sierra-believed-to-be-WWII-airman-2601006.php; Herel, "Authorities Try to ID Frozen WW II Airman," SFGate, October 21, 2005, https://www.sfgate.com/bayarea/article/FRESNO-Authorities-try-to-ID-frozen-WWII-airman-2601090.php; Audrey Mcavoy, "Experts Try to ID Body of WW II Airman," Associated Press / *Wilmington (NC) Star-News*, November 21, 2005, https://www.starnewsonline.com/news/20051121/experts-try-to-id-body-of-wwii-airman-found-in-ice; also, Stekel, *Final Flight*, 22–23, 69–70.

4. World War II casualties remain the subject of interpretation, study, and revision. For summaries see "Research Starters: Worldwide Deaths in World War II," National World War II Museum, https://www.nationalww2museum.org/students-teachers/student-resources/research-starters/research-starters-worldwide-deaths-world-war; Nese F. DeBruyne, "American War and Military Operations Casualties," Congressional Research Service, April 27, 2017, https://www.census.gov/history/pdf/wwi-casualties112018.pdf.

5. Conventional wisdom that US policy favored isolationism after World War I is a point of debate. See Brooke L. Blower, "From Isolationism to Neutrality: A New Framework for Understanding American Political Culture, 1919–1941," *Diplomatic History* 38, no. 2 (April 2014): 345–76, https://doi.org/10.1093/dh/dht091.

6. For a case study of a pottery company's conversion to war production see Stephanie Vincent, "Social Memory Assets as a Defense Mechanism: The Onondaga Pottery in World War II," Kent State University, 2018, https://doi.org/10.1080/17449359.2018.152540.

7. The Office of Civilian Defense conferred a "V Home Award" as "a badge of honor for those families which have made themselves into a fighting unit on the home front" by activities such as buying war bonds and conserving or salvaging needed materials: Richard Polenberg, *War and Society: The United States, 1941–1945* (Philadelphia: J. P. Lippincott, 1972), 133.

8. By early 1942 more than 5.5 million people and some seven thousand local councils, organized through the Office of Civilian Defense, took part in air raid drills, salvage drives,

coastal surveillance for Axis ships, and implementing curfews. Marilyn M. Harper, *World War II and the American Home Front*, National Park Service, 2007, 31, https://irma.nps.gov/DataStore/downloadfile/465955.

9. Harper, *World War II and the American Home Front*, 41, 42.

10. For more on the war's pervasive influence on ideology, culture, and economics see James T. Sparrow, *Warfare State: World War II Americans and the Age of Big Government* (Oxford: Oxford University Press, 2011).

11. In acquiring half a million acres necessary for the program, the Army "required absolute secrecy and unheard of speed" and was met with "a far-reaching tide of local opposition." Competition for the workforce necessary to sustain the program was intense. Vincent C. Jones, *Manhattan: The Army and the Atomic Bomb* (Washington, DC: US Army Center of Military History, 1985), 319, 344, https://history.army.mil/html/books/011/11-10/CMH_Pub_11-10.pdf

12. Alfred Goldberg, *The Pentagon: The First Fifty Years* (Washington, DC: Office of the Secretary of Defense, 1992).

13. Harper, *World War II and the American Home Front*, 155.

14. Ford Motor Company's Willow Run factory had thirteen hundred cots to accommodate pilots and crew waiting for planes. "Willow Run," Detroit Historical Society, https://detroithistorical.org/learn/encyclopedia-of-detroit/willow-run.

15. Mireles, *Fatal Army Air Forces Aviation Accidents*, 1:xi. A tally by the Army shortly after the war puts total noncombat air fatalities at 14,793 in the US and 12,835 overseas. See "Army Battle Casualties and Non-battle Deaths in World War II," Statistical and Accounting Branch, US Army, 1946, 102, 103, https://apps.dtic.mil/dtic/tr/fulltext/u2/a438106.pdf. Mireles's number, the product of exhaustive documentation and ample hindsight, is used as a benchmark for the work of AAF historian Marlyn R. Pierce, who writes that "the actions of the Army Air Forces staff leave the impression that they were deliberately trying to obfuscate the number of training fatalities." See Marlyn R. Pierce, "Earning Their Wings: Accidents and Fatalities in the United States Army Air Forces during Flight Training in World War Two," Kansas State University, 2013, xv, https://krex.k-state.edu/dspace/bitstream/handle/2097/16879/MarlynPierce2013.pdf?sequence=1.

16. Mireles, *Fatal Army Air Forces Aviation Accidents*, 1:xi.

17. Eight pilots (not AAF fliers and therefore not counted in Mireles's work) are known to have died, with an unknown number of fatalities to ground crew learning their jobs under crowded conditions and tight deadlines on the relatively small, converted deck of the former cruise vessel the *Seeandbee*. The ground crew were especially vulnerable to fires, snapped cables, crashes, and spinning propellers. As of 2016, 40 of about 120 planes that crashed into the lake had reportedly been recovered by a team of private collectors sanctioned by the military. See John Davies, prod., dir., *Heroes on Deck: World War II on Lake Michigan*, video/DVD (Chicago: Chicago Marine Heritage Society, 2016), previewed at https://www.heroesondeck.com/.

18. Associated Press, "Falling Planes Scare Residents: But None Hurt, Even Pilots 'Chuting to Safety," *Spokane (WA) Spokesman-Review*, May 25, 1942.

19. Associated Press, "College Building Set Afire by Crash of Army Airplane," *Roanoke (VA) World-News*, March 23, 1943; also, Mireles, *Fatal Army Air Forces Aviation Accidents*, 1:313.

20. Mireles, *Fatal Army Air Forces Aviation Accidents*, 1:377.

21. Mireles, 2:528.

22. Associated Press, "Navy Plane Hits Bay Bridge Cable," *San Bernardino (CA) Daily Sun*, September 13, 1943.

23. Associated Press, "Bomber Bursts in Air, 13 Dead," *Spokane Spokesman-Review*, January 3, 1944. Also, Mireles, *Fatal Army Air Forces Aviation Accidents*, 2:633.

24. Paul Densmore, "Plane Mishap Involving Lt. Nelson Is Not Forgotten," *Jamestown (NY) Post-Journal*, May 26, 2019, https://www.post-journal.com/news/page-one/2019/05/plane-mishap-involving-lt-nelson-is-not-forgotten/; also, Mireles, *Fatal Army Air Forces Aviation Accidents*, 2:856.

25. Edward D. Murphy, "Maine's Deadliest Aviation Disaster Remains Unexplained, 75 Years Later," *Portland Press Herald*, July 11, 2019, https://www.pressherald.com/2019/07/11/75th-anniversary-of-states-deadliest-plane-crash-thursday/; also, Mireles, *Fatal Army Air Forces Aviation Accidents*, 2:851–52.

26. The B-29, the largest and most difficult bomber to fly, was fraught with mechanical problems throughout its rapid development. Accordingly, pilots viewed it with skepticism and reluctance when it was finally rolled out near the end of the war. To demonstrate its safety, training commander Lieutenant Colonel Paul W. Tibbets selected Women Airforce Service Pilots (WASPs) to fly it on a tour of bases. The plan succeeded before it was terminated for fear of showing up the men. See Laurel Ladevich, "Women Fly the B-29," Fly Girls, American Experience, PBS, https://www.pbs.org/wgbh/americanexperience/features/flygirls-wasp-and-b-29/.

27. Paul Dorpat, "1943 Superfortress Crash Shocked Seattle," *Seattle Times*, March 6, 2010, https://www.seattletimes.com/pacific-nw-magazine/1943-superfortress-crash-shocked-seattle/#:~:text=While%20the%20Boeing%20B%2D29,18%2C%201943; also, Mireles, *Fatal Army Air Forces Aviation Accidents*, 1:277.

28. Mireles, *Fatal Army Air Forces Aviation Accidents*, 3:1143.

29. Lieutenant Colonel Dyess was a famed war hero for his service in the Pacific and escape from a Japanese prison camp. See *The Greatest Story of the War in the Pacific: Lt. Col. William Edwin Dyess*, video, narrated by Dale Dye (TMW Media Group, World War II Foundation, 2018); for his death see Mireles, *Fatal Army Air Forces Aviation Accidents*, 2:623.

30. Kaitlyn Kanzler, "The Seventy-Five Year Search for a Missing WWII Pilot from NJ Continues," North Jersey Media Group, updated October 2, 2019, https://www.northjersey.com/story/news/new-jersey/2019/09/30/75-year-search-missing-wwii-pilot-jersey-city-nj-continues/2352004001/; also, Mireles, *Fatal Army Air Forces Aviation Accidents*, 3:946. Tompkins's Mustang accounted for one of thirty-eight fatal aircraft accidents known to involve WASPs, who collectively had a safety record equal to or better than their male counterparts. Because they were not considered active military, WASPs were paid less and did not receive military benefits.

31. Blesse's manual *No Guts No Glory!* (Nellis Air Force Base, 1955) is billed as "a presentation of a way of flying and pattern of thought essential to a fighter pilot," http://www.simhq.com/_air/PDF/NGNG.pdf.

32. Letter from Orville to his brother, Wilbur, as reported by Noah Adams, *The Flyers: In Search of Wilbur and Orville Wright* (New York: Crown, 2003), www.npr.org/templates/story/story.php?storyId=1457681.

33. "The First Army Officer to Fly Solo," US War Department, *Air Corps Newsletter* 21, no. 2 (January 15, 1938): 10. This account also credits Selfridge with being the first US Army officer to fly solo. Weeks prior to his death, he had piloted an experimental craft (not owned by the Army) to seventy-five feet in a flight lasting a minute and a half in Hammondsport, New York, https://web.archive.org/web/20150903213218/http://newpreview.afnews.af.mil/shared/media/document/AFD-110421-039.pdf.

34. Katie Lang, "One Hundred and Ten Years Ago, the US Military Got Its First Airplane," US Department of Defense, August 1, 2019, https://www.defense.gov/Explore/Features/story/Article/1919399/.

35. AAF Commanding General Henry Harley Arnold quoted in DeWitt S. Copp, *A Few Great Captains: The Men and Events That Shaped the Development of US Air Power* (McLean, VA: EPM, 1989), 30. For this and more on the views of Arnold, Yeager, and "cultural dissonance" within the AAF regarding flying safety see Pierce, "Earning Their Wings," chap. 2.

36. Churchill's Review of the War before the House of Commons on April 9, 1941. The full text of this speech is available at Ibiblio.org, www.ibiblio.org/pha/policy/1941/410 409a.html.

37. The AAF counted on a process of trial and error to make up for a lack of experience. See USAAF Office of Flying Safety, "Safety as a Factor in the Future of Aviation," US Chamber of Commerce, 1946, 30, quoted in Pierce, "Earning Their Wings," 1.

38. The accident rate during the war was equal to or lower than the prewar rate, when flight technology and safety protocol were still in their infancy. But given an increase in the number of fliers by many orders of magnitude, the scale of death went far beyond what the Air Corps ever had to endure. Pierce, "Earning Their Wings," table 4, 231.

39. Pilot Training Manual for Flying Fortress B-17, AAF Office of Flying Safety, https://airpages.ru/eng/mn/b17_00.shtml.

40. Chuck Yeager with Leo Janos, *Yeager: An Autobiography* (New York: Bantam Books, 1985), 15.

41. Pierce, "Earning Their Wings," 116. Military flight historian Rebecca Hancock Cameron neatly sums up factors that compounded the risks of preparing fliers for battle: "In many ways, training was a valiant but impossible attempt to impose order, control, and predictability on an inherently fierce enterprise of chance and luck, experimentation, fury, uncertainty, and desperation. It would not easily or immediately produce either the level of competence needed of combat crews or the special requirements of the different theaters of operation." See *Training to Fly: Military Flight Training 1907–1945*, 381.

42. United States Army Air Forces, *Office of Flying Safety: Safety as a Factor in the Future of Aviation*, 4, quoted in Pierce, "Earning Their Wings," 208.

43. A record showing seventy-eight AAF aircraft known to be missing stateside (Mireles, *Fatal Army Air Forces Aviation Accidents*, vol. 3, appendix 3, 1, 192) appears thorough though not exhaustive, as it does not include *Getaway Gertie*. My analysis of a data set kept by the Defense POW/MIA Accounting Agency tallies 249 World War II Army Air Forces crew still missing in the United States. This analysis also lacks totality, as it lists only six of the eight crew known to be missing with *Gertie*.

44. Bond, interviewed by Stekel sixty years later, told of the watch piece, the shoe, "various pieces of aluminum, one of them scrunched up like an accordion," and "shreds of human flesh." Stekel, *Final Flight*, 47. According to the AAF accident file, "The wreckage was widely scattered in the upper portion of the glacier and frozen in the ice with only a small portions of metal protruding," including the nose section of one engine, from which a tag was removed. Additionally, "a small piece of frozen flesh was found on the spur of a rock at the upper edge of the glacier," with "small pieces of clothing and a blank navigation log." Edward W. Lynch, "Final Mission Report," October 3, 1947, *Aircraft Accident and Incident Reports 1940–48*, file no. 54, REEL 16141, National Archives and Record Service.

45. Suzanne Herel, "Families Hope Sixty-Three-Year Mystery Finally Solved," SFGate, November 12, 2005, https://www.sfgate.com/news/article/Families-hope-63-year-mystery-finally-solved-2561293.php.

46. Bill Ralston, phone interview with the author, July 28, 2020.

47. *Aircraft Accident and Incident Reports*, file no. 54.

48. "Remove Bodies of Airmen Lost on Peak for Six Years," *Iowa Muscatine Journal*, September 11, 1948.

49. Nanette Asimov, "Army Flier Lost 65 Years Found and Identified," SFGate, March 11, 2008, www.sfgate.com/bayarea/article/Army-flier-lost-65-years-found-and-IDd-3222830.php; also, Stekel, *Final Flight*, 63.

50. Surviving Army records contain no update of the second search. However, Julia Sulzbacher—the widow of Captain Roy F. Sulzbacher, the officer who led the mission—said her husband "went up to find some bodies but he was not able to finding anything." Stekel, *Final Flight*, 65.

51. Stekel, 64. The author was, reasonably, referring to pain and distress of families. But one wonders whether the actions were also intended to spare the Army itself certain hardship. It wouldn't be the first or last deceit along these lines. Long after World War II ended, the Department of Defense was given to choreographing high-profile "arrival ceremonies" for remains of American MIAs purportedly returning from overseas battlefields to Hickam Air Force Base in Honolulu. In reality, the caskets—more technically, transfer cases—were delivered from a nearby military forensic lab to the hangar, covered with flags, and loaded onto a decommissioned C-17 transport plane towed into position for the ceremony. With props set, the public and media arrived to witness a show of homecoming following decades of uncertainty and loss. When the pretense was exposed by NBC News in 2013, Pentagon sources maintained that the caskets did contain remains of MIAs from the lab, if not newly arrived from overseas. Yet the spell was broken. The fraud drew a crush of objection, most vividly summed up in a statement by American Legion National Commander Daniel Dellinger: "Symbolic honors are one thing, but deception is quite another. The so-called 'Big Lie' does not honor our war dead. Instead, it misleads and insults the living." See Bill Dedman, "Pentagon Unit Held Phony Ceremonies for MIAs, Using Planes That Can't Fly," *NBC News*, October 10, 2013, https://www.nbcnews.com/news/world/pentagon-unit-held-phony-ceremonies-mias-using-planes-cant-fly-flna8C11367190; Matthew M. Burke, "American Legion Demands JPAC Reforms over Fake Ceremonies," *Stars and Stripes*, October 15, 2013, https://www.stripes.com/news/american-legion-demands-jpac-reforms-over-fake-ceremonies-1.247183.

52. A recollection of Marjorie Freeman reported by Thelma Gutierrez, "Frozen WWII Airman Identified," CNN, February 4, 2006, https://www.cnn.com/2006/US/02/03/airman.identified/.

53. Associated Press, "Six Decades Later, Family Buries Remains of WWII Airman," *St. Cloud (MN) Times*, March 25, 2006.

54. Marc Benjamin, "Body Found by Seattle Author Identified as WWII Airman," *Seattle Times*, February 13, 2008, https://www.seattletimes.com/seattle-news/body-found-by-seattle-author-identified-as-wwii-airman/.

55. Generally, those lost in stateside training are not by definition MIAs or POWs. The secretary of defense has discretion in allocating funds to search for missing soldiers, though the focus has been on combat losses. For more on budgets and charters see "Operation and Maintenance Overview, FY 2021 Budget Estimates," Office of the Under Secretary of Defense, February 2020, 140–42, https://comptroller.defense.gov/Portals/45/Documents/defbudget/fy2021/fy2021_OM_Overview.pdf.

56. Email response to my query from Sintia C. Kawasaki-Yee, public affairs officer, Sequoia and Kings Canyon National Parks, August 31, 2020.

57. Peter Stekel, phone interview with the author, August 14, 2020.

58. Stekel interview. Also, Stekel, *Final Flight*, 83–84.

59. Stekel interview.

60. Daniel Malloy, "Long Lost Soldier Comes Home," *Pittsburgh Post-Gazette*, May 15, 2008, https://www.post-gazette.com/local/neighborhoods/2008/05/15/Long-lost-soldier-comes-home/stories/200805150449.

61. Stekel, *Final Flight*, 11, 112. Also, "Blond Bomber Comes Home" (interview with Munn's sisters), WBNS-TV, Columbus, May 16, 2008, www.finalflightthebook.com/Final_Flight_Press_TV.htm.

62. Asimov, "Army Flier Lost 65 Years Found and Identified"; Stekel, *Final Flight*, 153, 154.

7. Seekers

1. Caza was yet to upgrade his system to enable coordinates to be digitally cataloged and easily recalled.

2. Cussler's interest in lost planes extended beyond fiction. The late author backed an extensive and fruitless search for Northwest Flight 2501, which disappeared with fifty-eight passengers and crew over Lake Michigan in 1950. V. O. van Heest, *Fatal Crossing: The Mysterious Disappearance of NWA Flight 2501 and the Quest for Answers* (Holland, MI: In-Depth Editions, 2013).

3. The rumor stems from a letter to the editor by Clair Chamberlain published in the *Syracuse (NY) Herald-Journal* on September 26, 1982, claiming "a skeleton, believed to be from the wreck, washed up on Southwick Beach" in "1953 or 1954." Follow-up investigations by Coffed, McLaughlin, and myself found nothing to substantiate the claim. It's possible Chamberlain was remembering reports of Air Force pilot David Lachelt being found, still strapped to his seat, floating near Galloo Island in 1963 after his jet crashed in Lake Ontario. The navigator, Jerry L. Larson, was not immediately found. See "Pilot's Body Found after Lake Ontario Jet Crash," *Schenectady (NY) Gazette*, May 21, 1963. Other reports over the years document the eventual recovery of bodies on the lake's east end after boating and swimming accidents.

4. Antiaircraft exercises over the lake are described more fully in chapter 9.

5. Subsequent analyses support Currelly's assessment. See *America's Lost Vikings*, S01E03, "War in the New World," Discovery Channel, 2019, www.imdb.com/title/tt9680558/episodes?ref_=tt_ep_epl. For an account of Hoffman's find see James Curran, *Here Was Vinland* (Sault Ste. Marie, ON: *Sault Daily Star*, 1939); also, Larry Ann Evans, "Way Back When in Wayne County: Spearhead Is Norse in Origin," *Finger Lakes Times* (Geneva, NY), March 10, 2013, https://www.fltimes.com/lifestyle/local_history/way-back-when-in-wayne-county-spearhead-is-norse-in-origin/article_6f55884a-874d-11e2-8cdc-0019bb2963f4.html.

6. Though conclusive archaeological evidence exists of a settlement at L'Anse aux Meadows at the northern entry to the Gulf of Saint Lawrence, there is little consensus regarding how far the Vikings traveled inland, to a place in Norse epic literature called Vinland.

7. Jim Kennard, phone interview with the author, October 18, 2020.

8. On the western end of the lake, a crew building a waterworks tunnel in Toronto Bay in 1908 uncovered a trail of footprints in a submerged layer of blue clay. A prevailing theory holds that the prints were made eleven thousand years ago, when the lake immediately off Toronto was tundra and spruce forest. See Leslie Scrivener, "The Enigma of Lake Ontario's 11,000-Year-Old Footprints," *Toronto Star*, November 23, 2008, https://www.thestar.com/news/insight/2008/11/23/the_enigma_of_lake_ontarios_11000yearold_footprints.html. For more on the status of paleo-American populations around Lake Ontario during deglaciation see Arthur Roberts, "Paleo Indian on the North Shore of Lake Ontario," *Archaeology of Eastern North America* 12 (Fall 1984): 248–65, www.jstor.org/stable/40914242.

9. Information from Phil Church is from interviews with the author in Oswego, New York, on April 16, 2017, and October 19, 2020, email correspondence spanning those dates,

and newspaper articles where noted. Information from Dale Currier is from phone interviews with author on February 15, 2019, and November 1, 2020.

10. Associated Press, August 19, 1994.

11. Divers were active in the Great Lakes in the nineteenth and early twentieth centuries, though their numbers were few, and their methods were relatively primitive. See Jerry Kuntz, *The Heroic Age of Diving: America's Underwater Pioneers and the Great Wrecks of Lake Erie* (Albany: SUNY Press, 2016).

12. The moral victory and economic rewards the US reaped from the defeat of Germany and Japan are broadly represented throughout literature, with reference here to titles authored by Pulitzer Prize–winning correspondent Studs Terkel and NBC newsman Tom Brokaw, respectively.

13. Bob Weber, "Two Charged after Raising WWII Bomber from Lake," Canadian Press, *Toronto Star*, June 5, 2009, https://www.thestar.com/news/canada/2009/06/05/two_charged_after_raising_wwii_bomber_from_lake.html.

14. Without doubt, the search for *Gertie* was partly motivated by popular perception shaped by hearsay. One local news story cited a diver reporting "a standing offer of $100,000 for rare B-24 parts" from an unnamed Florida museum. See Dick Case, "Mysteries and Stories of Lost Bomber Linger," *Syracuse (NY) Post-Standard*, February 22, 2004.

15. What these sums amounted to depended on multiple factors. Wrecks are often worth less than imagined, owing to their poor condition, high recovery costs, and limited markets. "It's a very old mind-set that every museum will want that plane found in pieces at the bottom of a water body," Megan Lickliter-Mundon, the aviation archaeologist, told me. "There is a very serious disconnect between 'we found this wreck,' and 'it will end up in a museum.'" There are exceptions. One investigation found "wealthy American collectors" behind "a multimillion-dollar frenzy that rivals the most feverish art trend or real estate boom." See Kevin Baron, "Wreck Hunters Race to Find WWII Planes," *Boston Globe*, May 31, 2009, www.sfgate.com/news/article/U-S-wreck-hunters-race-to-find-WWII-planes-3229178.phpl. In one instance, a group of war veterans, with the Navy's permission, set about to recover a Douglas SBD Dauntless from the bottom of Lake Michigan, only to find that a civilian treasure hunter had gotten there first. The wreck (which was not a grave site) was later recovered by the FBI in a barn in Gaithersburg, Maryland, and returned to the sanctioned group. The aircraft, which had been raised in a sling buoyed by fifty-five-gallon drums, had potential value of $1.2 million in today's dollars after restoration, though the US Attorney's Office ruled its "unauthorized recovery" to be "a technical violation" that would be hard to prosecute. See Ben A. Franklin, "Highly Prized 40's Plane Stolen from Lake Michigan Is Recovered by F.B.I.," *New York Times*, September 18, 1982, https://www.nytimes.com/1982/09/19/us/highly-prized-40-s-plane-stolen-from-lake-michigan-is-recovered-by-fbi.html.

16. Coffed's files include detailed reports by eight members of the Finger Lakes Dowsers who sought *Gertie*'s whereabouts. The divinations range from "twenty-one to twenty-three miles offshore northwest of Chimney Bluffs, on an underwater ridge" to "eighteen miles south of Little Galloo Island." Several suggest specific locations directly off Oswego.

17. Highlights of Duell's military career are on file at the town of New Haven (NY) historian's office. Also, "Bails Out over Germany before Plane Explodes," *Mexico (NY) Independent*, June 14, 1945.

18. Suzanne Frangia, "Retired Bombardier Seeks WWII Aircraft in Lake Ontario," *Watertown (NY) Daily Times*, August 19, 1990.

19. Frangia, "Retired Bombardier Seeks WWII Aircraft."

20. Frangia, "Retired Bombardier Seeks WWII Aircraft."

21. Mike McGourty, phone interview with the author, January 19, 2021.

22. Jim Kennard, the famed Great Lakes shipwreck hunter who is a bit older than Currier, recalls, "Back then, divers were like locusts. They hit a wreck and took everything that moved and some stuff that didn't."

23. Associated Press, "Volunteers Search Lake Ontario for B-24 War Bomber," *Watertown Daily Times*, July 12, 1996.

24. Dennis Gerber, phone interview with the author, January 5, 2021.

25. The *Cormorant* was originally found in 1988 by Bill Woodworth, Kirk Marshall, and Rick Ferguson (who were also looking for *Gertie*), though its location was not generally known. See "Sunken Tugboat Rediscovered," *Oswego Palladium-Times*, August 17, 1996.

26. "Kingfisher Will Search for Long-Lost Bomber," *Rochester (NY) Democrat and Chronicle*, July 28, 2000.

27. Dola L. Deloff, "Kingfisher Doesn't Find Plane, but Perhaps Narrows Search," *Oswego Palladium-Times*, July 29, 2000.

28. Some seventeen hundred souls were lost in the Battle of the Atlantic. Those wrecks are being explored and cataloged by archaeologists and soon to be promoted as a public attraction. See "Proposed Sanctuary Expansion," Monitor National Marine Sanctuary, NOAA, https://monitor.noaa.gov/.

29. "A Chumash Perspective," Channel Islands National Marine Sanctuary, NOAA, https://channelislands.noaa.gov/maritime/chumash.html.

30. The *Fair American*, another ship of the War of 1812, is also thought to rest somewhere in the eastern end of the lake. See "Lake Ontario National Marine Sanctuary, Proposal to NOAA National Marine Sanctuary Program," Great Lake Ontario National Marine Sanctuary Nomination Task Force, 2017, https://nmsnominate.blob.core.windows.net/nominate-prod/media/documents/lake_ontario_nms_nomination_appendix_011717.pdf, and https://nmssanctuaries.blob.core.windows.net/sanctuaries-prod/media/docs/20210701-proposed-lake-ontario-national-marine-sanctuary-draft-environmental-impact-statement.pdf. Two of the lake's more famous 1812 wrecks—the USS *Hamilton* and the USS *Scourge*—sank with their crews off Port Dalhousie in the western part of the lake during a storm in August 1813. Diving on these wrecks is prohibited without a permit from Canadian officials who manage them.

31. Benjamin Kail, "Marine Sanctuary Application for Oswego County Nears Completion," *Oswego Palladium-Times*, April 21, 2016. See also "Thunder Bay National Marine Sanctuary Socioeconomics," NOAA newsletter, 2017, https://sanctuaries.noaa.gov/science/socioeconomic/factsheets/thunderbay.html. Two elements of the preserve alone—the Maritime Heritage Center and Alpena Shipwreck Tours—support 467 jobs and contribute $40 million to the local economy. See "Market Economic Contributions of Recreating Users of the Great Lakes Maritime Heritage Center and Alpena Shipwreck Tours in Thunder Bay National Marine Sanctuary," vol. 1, NOAA, 2018, https://nmssanctuaries.blob.core.windows.net/sanctuaries-prod/media/docs/onms-20-02-thunder-bay-economic-contribution-report-vol-1.pdf.

32. The issue over policy to manage access and preservation of wrecks, with reaction from Caza and Kennard, is discussed in chapter 12.

33. "Phil engineered the most impressive gathering of local, regional and state-wide support for a sanctuary I have seen in my long career in the sanctuary program," Bohne stated in an email to the author on January 18, 2021, shortly after his retirement from NOAA.

8. Hope and Prayer

1. Harland was awarded a Distinguished Flying Cross in May 1944 for his exceptional record. "Today in History," *Windsor Ontario Star*, May 10, 1969, 49.

2. RCAF press release 2912, April 4, 1944. Also, Garnet Harland, "The Last Flight of RCAF Liberator 586," *Them Days* 14, no. 2 (January 1989); "Tell Harrowing Trials of Crew Wrecked in Wilds of Labrador," *Ottawa Journal*, April 3, 1944.

3. "Many Planes on Hunt for Lost Bomber," *Syracuse (NY) Herald-Journal*, February 19, 1944.

4. "Chief of Air Base Checks Results of Air-WAC Drive Here," *Binghamton (NY) Press*, April 21, 1944; "Officers' Visit Concludes Air-WAC Show," *Ithaca (NY) Journal*, April 15, 1944. Also, Todd Dewan, "WACs Served in Rome Army Depot in WW II," *Rome (NY) Daily Sentinel*, September 10, 2017, https://romesentinel.com/stories/wacs-served-at-rome-army-depot-in-wwii,15131.

5. Also referred to as the whispering campaign or the rumor campaign, the slander campaign was "an onslaught of gossip, jokes, slander, and obscenity about the WAAC" promoted by certain media outlets and clergy. It gained traction in 1943 through early 1944 before Army public relations mounted a counter-campaign. Mattie E. Treadwell, *The Women's Army Corps* (Washington, DC: US Army Center for Military History, 1991), 191–216, https://history.army.mil/books/wwii/wac/index.htm.

6. Search-and-rescue methods were still evolving to keep pace with the novel challenges of a war waged from the air. Until late February 1944, when formal policy established a separate unit within the Coast Guard for air-sea rescue, efforts were largely improvised from existing military protocol within various branches. See "The Development of Air Sea Rescue," US Coast Guard Aviation Association, https://cgaviationhistory.org/1943-the-development-of-air-sea-rescue/.

7. "No Sign Is Found of Lost Liberator," *Syracuse (NY) Post-Standard*, February 21, 1944.

8. "Half of New York State Being Searched from Air for Lost Bomber, Eight Fliers," *Rome Daily Sentinel*, February 19, 1944; "Many Planes on Hunt for Lost Bomber," *Syracuse Herald-Journal*, February 19, 1944; "Aircraft of All Types Aid Hunt for Lost Plane," *Syracuse Herald-Journal*, February 19, 1944; Associated Press, "Seek Bomber and Crew of Eight Lost in Storm," *Fitchburg (MA) Sentinel*, February 19, 1944.

9. "Scour Mountain for Lost Bomber," *Rome Daily Sentinel*, February 21, 1944; "CAP Planes Join Search for Missing Bomber," *Syracuse Herald-Journal*, February 22, 1944.

10. "Scour Mountain for Lost Bomber," *Rome Daily Sentinel*, February 21, 1944; "CAP Planes Join Search for Missing Bomber," *Syracuse Herald-Journal*, February 22, 1944.

11. *Flight Manual, B-24 Airplane*, Consolidated Aircraft, 1942, 84.

12. "Coast Guard Reserves Aid Plane Search, Syracuse Flotilla Sending Men to Oswego for Training," *Syracuse Herald-Journal*, March 27, 1944.

13. "Coast Guard Reserves Aid Plane Search."

14. Analysis of weather patterns on the lake in February 1944 prepared by National Weather Service meteorologist Tom Niziol, March 1984. Accessed from Jim Coffed's files, March 23, 2017.

15. "Lost Bomber Search Is On Again Today," *Syracuse Herald American*, February 20, 1944.

16. Wilbur B. Evans, "Cold and Snow Bar Search of Wooded Section," *Syracuse Herald-Journal*, January 20, 1944.

17. Evans, "Cold and Snow Bar Search of Wooded Section."

18. Walter Begland obituary, *Dover (OH) Daily Reporter*, July 1, 1974, 1.

19. "Half of New York State Being Searched from Air for Lost Bomber."

20. "No Sign Is Found of Lost Liberator."

21. "Lost Bomber Search Turned to North," *Syracuse Post-Standard*, February 19, 1944; "Lost Bomber Search Is On Again Today"; "Two Areas Searched for Missing Bomber," *Watertown (NY) Daily Times*, February 21, 1944.

22. "North Is Combed for Missing B-24," *Watertown Daily Times*, February 22, 1944.

23. While some Army troops in northern New York apparently were trained in winter warfare in 1944, they would be unrelated to the Tenth Mountain Division, the famed unit now stationed at Fort Drum in Watertown. During World War II, the Army's main winter and mountain warfare unit, the Tenth Light Division (Alpine), was in Camp Hale, Colorado. Watertown's Fort Drum was then called Pine Camp.

24. "Bomber Hunt Centered at Watertown," *Syracuse Herald-Journal*, February 21, 1944.

25. "Lost Bomber Search Is On Again Today."

26. When news broke of the missing plane, the parameters of the search as originally sourced to Martenstein and reported in various outlets were vast and ill-defined. It became clear in subsequent reports that Skinner, Begland, and Hebert focused on certain areas as information came in.

27. "Half of New York State Being Searched from Air for Lost Bomber."

28. "One-Hundred German Prisoners Arrive for Area Crop Work," *Rochester (NY) Democrat and Chronicle*, June 26, 1944; also, "Nazi Prisoners of War to Help Oswego Farmers," *Oswego (NY) Palladium-Times*, June 30, 1944; Lawrence P. Gooley, "Adirondack World War II POW Labor Camps," *New York Almanack*, December 30, 2019, www.newyorkalmanack.com/2019/12/adirondack-world-war-2-pow-labor-camps/.

29. In addition to a POW camp, local officials also pitched the idea of making the base a "reconstruction hospital" for the returning war wounded prior to Roosevelt's decision to turn it into a refugee camp. See "1,000 War Refugees Will Come to Oswego," *Oswego Palladium-Times*, June 9, 1944.

30. While controversy thwarted prospects of refugee shelters elsewhere in the states, the plan for Fort Ontario was enthusiastically embraced by the Oswego Chamber of Commerce, the Oswego Council of Churches, and other local community groups. See "President Glad That Refugee Plan Pleases Oswego," *Oswego Palladium-Times*, June 24, 1944; "Refugees to Arrive at Fort Saturday," *Oswego Palladium-Times*, August 9, 1944.

31. The story of the truck on Route 29 was told by Elwyn Himes to his oldest son, Leo, who relayed it to me in an interview on February 24, 2018. Though the precise origins of the story and the name of the truck driver are unknown, I assign it to conversations at the Perkins General Store and the church, primary clearinghouses of town news and gossip for the Himeses and their friends and neighbors, the Perkinses.

32. Three other airmen aboard parachuted to safety with minor injuries. Mireles, *Fatal Army Air Forces Aviation Accidents in the United States*, 2:692.

33. Mireles, 2:693.

34. Mireles, 2:692–93.

35. Mireles, 2:693.

36. Mireles, 2:693.

37. Mireles, 2:694.

38. Mireles, 2:693.

9. Discovery

1. Horace Goudie, interview with Janet Dyson, posted on RAFCommands.com, July 4, 2006, http://www.rafcommands.com/archive/08718.php.

2. Garnet Harland, "Last Flight of RCAF Liberator 586," *Them Days* 14, no. 2 (January 1989).

3. RCAF press release 2912, April 4, 1944.

4. Harland, "Last Flight of RCAF Liberator 586."

5. RCAF press release 2912.

6. Charles Neville, "They Lived to Fly Again," *Lincoln Nebraska State Journal*, May 17, 1944.

7. "Tell Harrowing Trials of Crew Wrecked in Wilds of Labrador," *Ottawa Journal*, April 3, 1944.

8. "Tell Harrowing Trials of Crew Wrecked in Wilds of Labrador."

9. RCAF press release 2912.

10. The mushers were veterans of Admiral Richard Byrd's historic South Pole expedition. See RCAF press release.

11. Wilbur B. Evans, "Cold and Snow Bar Search of Wooded Section," *Syracuse (NY) Herald-Journal*, January 20, 1944.

12. Evans, "Cold and Snow Bar Search."

13. While Denmark sits just off the plateau, a weather station in the town of Montague, less than ten miles to the south, recorded 467 inches of snow—nearly forty feet—in the 1976–77 season, and a dump of 77 inches in twenty-four hours in 1997. Robert J. Leffler et al., "A Brief Summary on the Report on Montague, New York's, 77-Inch, 24-Hour, January 11–12, 1997, Lake-Effect Snowfall," *American Meteorological Society*, 1997, https://www.ncdc.noaa.gov/monitoring-content/extremes/ncec/reports/summary-of-montague-ny.pdf.

14. "Lost Bomber Search Is On Again Today," *Syracuse (NY) Herald American*, February 20, 1944.

15. According to an assessment by the Associated Press attributed to McCann after Monday's failed attempt, "the swirling snow cut visibility to nearly zero and the intense cold caused such hardships that penetration of the woods would be delayed until some definite indication was obtained from planes or other means that the bomber had fallen in that section." See "Weather Halts Search for Missing Bomber," *Hartford Courant*, February 20, 1944.

16. Though the news of the RCAF crash would not be publicly reported for several more months, AAF senior commanders would be aware of the search in Labrador, especially considering the coordination and cooperation of American and Canadian search parties for both planes.

17. "Scour Mountain for Lost Bomber," *Rome (NY) Daily Sentinel*, February 21, 1944.

18. This mountain, by the Carry Falls Reservoir near South Colton, is not to be confused with a larger mountain of the same name farther east. For more on the history of the fire tower see William Hill's blog, *Hiking the Trail to Yesterday*, https://hikingthetrailtoyesterday.wordpress.com/2018/01/17/catamount-mt-on-carry-falls-reservoir/.

19. "Watertown Area Search Fails to Uncover Bomber," *Syracuse (NY) Post-Standard*, February 22, 1944.

20. "Watertown Area Search Fails to Uncover Bomber."

21. "Rumor Bomber Found Is Denied by Army Officers," *Syracuse Post-Standard*, February 24, 1944.

22. "No Sign Is Found of Lost Liberator," *Syracuse Post-Standard*, February 21, 1944; "Bomber Hunt Centered at Watertown," *Syracuse Herald-Journal*, February 21, 1944.

23. Evans, "Cold and Snow Bar Search of Wooded Section."

24. "Lost Bomber Search Is On Again Today."

25. "Weather Curbs Search for Lost B-24 Bomber," *Syracuse Post-Standard*, February 22, 1944.

26. Aeronautical maps from the period show beams emanating north from Syracuse and northeast from Rome extending over Oswego County.

27. Disoriented by the snow and with no frame of reference, Ponder and Bickel at first might have confused what little they could see of Lake Ontario with Oneida Lake, a much smaller water body directly northeast of the landing field at the Syracuse base, now Hancock International Airport.

28. "Weather Curbs Search for Lost B-24 Bomber."

29. Evans, "Cold and Snow Bar Search of Wooded Section."

30. Any reference to coastal artillery training in Oswego County warrants noting the all-black 369th Regiment from Harlem in 1941. At the time discrimination was rampant, the military segregated, and the 369th (aka the "Harlem Hell Fighters") with eighteen hundred men presented a stark demographic outlier in what one member aptly characterized as "lily white" Oswego. The record, at least the one penned by the Oswego Historical Society in 1946, portrays a positive outcome: "These troops conducted themselves in a highly exemplary fashion. Cut off as they were from association with people of their own race, because up to that time, Oswego had practically no Negro population, they nevertheless, maintained a system of politeness, even of gallantry in their outside contacts." Yet there were tensions. One of the soldiers, accused of raping a white woman, was arrested though ultimately not prosecuted, and the unit subsequently boycotted white businesses in protest of the allegation. Debra J. Groom, "Black Artillery Regiment from Harlem Set Up Camp in Oswego in 1941," *Syracuse Post-Standard*, February 26, 2012, https://www.syracuse.com/news/2012/02/harlem_hellfighters_black_arti.html; John W. O'Connor, "Fort Ontario during the 1940's," *Tenth Publication of the Oswego Historical Society Journal*, 1946, 97–107, http://www.rbhousemuseum.org/wp-content/uploads/2018/07/FortOntario1940sSM.pdf.

31. By 1944, Oswego County antiaircraft installations had been relocated to coastal areas considered more likely targets of attack, though the lakeside site remained functional as an artillery training base off and on until well after the war. In 1962, Niagara Mohawk Power Corporation began purchasing the land for the development of the Nine Mile Point nuclear power plant, which occupies the site today. See O'Connor, "Fort Ontario during the 1940's." Also, "Buy Nearly 1,500 Acres for Nuclear Plant Site," *Oswego Palladium-Times*, April 21, 1962.

32. The practice of towing "sleeve targets" for antiaircraft fire presented obvious hazards to pilots. Drones developed in the early 1940s gained more widespread use as the war developed. Evidence suggests both were employed in Oswego County exercises. Divers search for drones in the lake today. See "Guard Regiment Starts Next Week Firing Practice," *Oswego Palladium-Times*, August 2, 1940; Hugh Maxwell, "When Model Airplanes First Went to War," *Model Aviation Magazine*, July 1992, https://www.ctie.monash.edu.au/hargrave/radioplane_war.html.

10. Recovery

1. "Lost Bomber Search Is On Again Today," *Syracuse (NY) Herald American*, February 20, 1944.

2. "Plane Wing Found in Lake Ontario," *Utica (NY) Daily Press*, February 25, 1944.

3. "Crash Experts to Study Wing in Lake," *Syracuse (NY) Post-Standard*, February 27, 1944.

4. "Wing of Missing Plane Recovered in Lake Ontario," *Oswego (NY) Palladium-Times*, February 25, 1944.

5. "Wing of Missing Plane Recovered in Lake Ontario."

6. While Hebert is referred to as "ensign" in newspaper accounts about *Gertie*, military records and a later news report show him as boatswain's mate—a noncommissioned officer. Either position would qualify him to supervise a Coast Guard station as well as crews and work parties aboard a ship. See "Hebert Takes Over, Heads Coast Guard Station," *Port Huron (MI) Times Herald*, May 29, 1949.

7. "Wing of Missing Plane Recovered in Lake Ontario."

8. "Wing Panel Floating on Lake Is Believed Part of Lost Bomber," *Syracuse (NY) Herald-Journal*, February 25, 1944. Also, "Wing of Missing Plane Recovered in Lake Ontario"; and "Hunt Renewed for Lost Bomber Wreckage," *Mexico (NY) Independent*, March 2, 1944.

9. Participants in the hearing and their quotes are from "Statement of Capt. Paul L. Mathison," *Aircraft Accidents and Incident Reports 1940 thru 1948*. Interpretation of the scene is helped by the analysis of F. Lee Reynolds, public affairs officer at the US Army Center of Military History.

10. "Chamberlin Gibe at Air Rules May Be Costly Joke," *Brooklyn (NY) Daily Eagle*, March 27, 1931.

11. "Description of Accident," *Aircraft Accidents and Incident Reports 1940 thru 1948*.

12. "Report of Aircraft Accident," *Aircraft Accidents and Incident Reports 1940 thru 1948*. A handwritten note on the cover sheet for the thirty-three-page transcript of flight communications on the night *Gertie* disappeared stated, "Very sloppy operation at Westover Field. If all such unnecessary contacts were removed from the interphone and radio circuits, the communication problem would be less acute."

13. US Headstone and Interment Records for US Military Cemeteries on Foreign Soil, 1942–1949, Ancestry.com; Netherlands American Cemetery, American Battle Monuments Commission, www.abmc.gov/Netherlands.

14. "Hunt Renewed by Planes for Lost Bomber Wreckage," *Oswego Palladium-Times*, February 26, 1944.

15. The number of working women increased by a third during the war years, with nearly 50 percent of all women employed at some point during 1944 in response to the labor demand. They took jobs in many fields traditionally held by men. Allan Winkler, *Home Front USA: America during World War II*, American History Series (Wheeling, IL: Harlan Davidson, 2012), 58.

16. "Missing Bomber Believed Found Near Oswego," *Syracuse Post-Standard*, February 25, 1944.

17. A searchlight might have been a viable means of probing the lakebed on a calm night when ambient reflections off the surface were minimized, though its range would be questionable. The depth at the reported location would be between thirty and forty feet.

18. "Lost Bomber Is Found in Lake," *Watertown (NY) Daily Times*, February 25, 1944.

19. "Wing of Missing Plane Recovered in Lake Ontario."

20. The US Office of Censorship issued a Code of Wartime Practices generally embraced and voluntarily enforced by the press establishment. Restrictions included reporting on troop movements, battle casualties, and other military matters—limitations that might be far-reaching. Interestingly, domestic weather reports could serve as critical intelligence for Axis powers weighing conditions for attack, and forecasts were limited to rudimentary blurbs in local papers and not generally broadcast at all. See Polenberg, *War and Society*, 51; Harper, *World War II and the American Home Front*, 6, 30, 174.

21. "Salvagers Seek to Bring Wing Section Ashore," *Syracuse Post-Standard*, February 26, 1944.

22. Reporters would be in short of supply for the same reason as factory workers and police. Many were overseas or preparing to go overseas. Women would have filled some positions, although it's difficult to know who or how many, as local stories tended to lack bylines. Also, journalism paid poorly and, for women especially, held slim opportunities for advancement. Still, the fictional female comic-book reporters Brenda Starr and Lois Lane, and Hildy Johnson of movie fame, flourished in 1940s pop culture, glamorizing and perhaps inspiring women in the profession.

23. "Salvagers Seek to Bring Wing Section Ashore." Variations of the quote, along with Hebert's oft-noted observation that the Coast Guard needed powerboats for the search, appeared in numerous local and regional newspapers, most likely plucked from local coverage and distributed by a wire service. See also "Lost Bomber Hunt Centers near Oswego, Searchers May Get Stored Power Boats Out to Scour Lake," *Syracuse Herald-Journal*, February 28, 1944; "Power Boat Sought for Plane Hunt," *Syracuse Herald-Journal*, March 1, 1944.

24. "Power Boat Sought for Plane Hunt"; also, "Hunt Renewed for Lost Bomber Wreckage."

25. "Ice in Lake Leads to Report More of Bomber Located," *Syracuse Post-Standard*, February 29, 1944.

26. The operation was officially under the command of Colonel D. D. Arnold, head of maintenance at the Rome base, although there is nothing in newspaper articles that suggests Arnold was on-site for any sustained period.

27. "Wing Is Checked for Identification," *Rome (NY) Daily Sentinel*, February 28, 1944.

28. Charles and Louise Himes, interviews with the author, December 1, 2017, and July 18, 2021; Leo Himes, interview with the author, February 24, 2017.

29. Charles and Louise Himes interviews; Leo Himes interview.

30. Correspondence between Marion Himes and parents of the airmen remains lost, leaving me to extrapolate from summaries of the letters and photos referenced in various newspaper accounts. See "Coast Guard Has Found Submerged Object in Lake," *Oswego Palladium-Times*, Thursday, June 15, 1944; social briefs by town, *Mexico Independent*, June 22, 1944, 4. The exception is a note Marion penciled on a newspaper clip found in Lucy Ponder's scrapbook. The note explains that Mrs. Perkins—featured in the corresponding article as a resident who reported a "plane in distress" to police the night it was heard low over Oswego—was a neighbor. See chapter 5.

31. In addition, Lucy Ponder likely received clips from upstate New York papers from Amos, Keith's older brother, stationed in New York City with the Navy. See chapter 11.

32. The text of the article reported only that "Army officials have not given up hope that the eight crew members of the big bomber may have parachuted and landed in a remote section." See "Lost Bomber Search over Lake Pressed," *Syracuse Herald-Journal*, February 26, 1944. In addition to being vague, assessments on whether the crew bailed out were sometimes conflicting, possibly reflecting a degree of bias or intuition by the reporters themselves and their unnamed sources. A competing Syracuse daily reported "Army officers have all but abandoned the possibility that some of the men bailed out." See "Crash Experts to Study Wing in Lake," *Syracuse Post-Standard*, February 27, 1944.

33. Joseph Zebo's sister, Josephine Zebo, provided this letter, dated March 15, 1944, to Jim Coffed on December 29, 1995; accessed from Coffed's files on May 23, 2017. See chapter 11.

11. Misplaced Memory

1. "Father of Flier Lost in Lake Plunge, Dead," *Oswego (NY) Palladium-Times*, June 28, 1944.

2. Himes interviews.

3. As with *Gertie*, the RCAF plane lost January 8, 1942, in bad weather is yet to be found. Missing are Alexander McDonald Morgan, Cy Rutherford, Bede Bernard Sutton, and John Witts. See "Believe Wreck RCAF Plane, Bits Found on Shore in N.Y. Linked to January Crash," *Windsor Ontario Daily Star*, April 8, 1942. Also, *Proposed Lake Ontario National Marine Sanctuary Draft Environmental Impact Statement and Draft Management Plan*, NOAA, July 2021, 36, https://nmssanctuaries.blob.core.windows.net/sanctuaries-prod/media/docs/20210701-proposed-lake-ontario-national-marine-sanctuary-draft-environmental-impact-statement.pdf.

4. Six days of daily dispatches from the Westover base in Massachusetts to the Office of Flying Safety in North Carolina merely noted "attempts to identify wing panel and landing gear . . . unsuccessful to date." On March 3, Colonel Jones sent two briefings concerning the status of *Gertie*. Both informed "search abandoned." One also reported "attempt to identify wing and landing gear . . . unsuccessful to date." The second memo stated, "wing section identified as that of B-24 4–29047," that is, *Gateway Gertie*. See "Incoming Message, Headquarters Army Air Forces, Office of Flying Safety," February 26–March 3, *Aircraft Accidents and Incident Reports. . . .* Also, "Lost Bomber's Wing Identified," *Rochester (NY) Times Union*, March 4, 1944.

5. A farmer found a wheel "believed to be part of the landing gear" of the lost aircraft in April 1944 while walking along a remote stretch of shoreline in Wayne County, about thirty-five miles west of Oswego. Wayne County officials reported the find to the Army base in Rome, although there is no record of a follow-up investigation. "Discover Part of Plane upon Shore of Lake, Wheel at Sodus May Be from Landing Gear of Bomber," *Oswego Palladium-Times*, April 15, 1944.

6. "Incoming Message, Headquarters Army Air Forces, Office of Flying Safety."

7. "Wing Found in Lake Was from Missing Bomber," *Oswego Palladium-Times*, March 4, 1944.

8. Potential Operating Budget, appendix A, *Proposed Lake Ontario National Marine Sanctuary*.

9. Executive Summary, *Proposed Lake Ontario National Marine Sanctuary*.

10. Buckley, phone interview with the author, October 3, 2019. Ray Bickel Jr.'s name had been changed to Ray Buckley, as explained in subsequent section.

11. Amber Simmons shared her family's story in multiple phone interviews and text messages with the author in September and October 2021.

12. The story of the falling out is corroborated by both sides of the family. The families' version holds that the copilot's mother, Mae Bickel, was the beneficiary of her son's policy. Army records list Marion as the beneficiary. Regardless, family members from both sides agree that seemingly unjustified ill will toward Marion led to the estrangement.

13. Jean Vanasek shared her family's story in multiple phone interviews and email correspondence with the author in September, October, and November 2021.

14. The Department of Defense and its adjuncts are tasked with archaeological recovery of remains of battle casualties overseas. The remains of *Gertie*'s crew, if found, would initially fall under the jurisdiction of local law-enforcement officials. Since the sunken plane fuselage is already considered a war grave by state and federal governments, it is unlikely that agencies would pursue recovery of remains without strong justification.

15. Ray Vanasek, phone interview with the author, November 15, 2021.

16. The *Jackson (MS) Clarion-Ledger* and *Syracuse (NY) Post-Standard* were among the few newspapers that identified the plane as *Gateway Gertie*.

17. *Syracuse Post-Standard*, June 17, 1944.

12. Recognition

1. See chapter 7, note 16.

2. The exception is a letter from the mother of Kenneth Jonen to the mother of Joseph Zebo, March 15, 1944, noted in chapter 10. Coffed received the letter from Zebo's sister, Josephine Zebo, in December 1995.

3. Cheryl Allen, phone interview with the author, January 18, 2022.

4. "Nine Lives Lost as Steamer Sinks," *New York Times*, November 26, 1921.

5. See *Shipwrecks of Upstate New York*, www.sonarguy.com.

6. For all of Amelia Earhart's remarkable accomplishments, the aviation pioneer remains a household name largely owing to her lasting disappearance and the imperfect knowledge base to explain it.

7. Kennard's team for both discoveries included Roger Pawlowski and Roland Stevens. "Explorers Find Second-Oldest Confirmed Shipwreck in Great Lakes," *Chicago Tribune*, August 17, 2016, https://www.chicagotribune.com/news/breaking/ct-sloop-shipwreck-great-lakes-20160817-story.html. Also, "US Air Force Plane Abandoned in Flight in 1952 Discovered in Lake Ontario," Syracuse.com, https://www.syracuse.com/news/2014/07/us_air_force_aircraft_abandoned_in_flight_in_1952_discovered_in_lake_ontario.html.

8. Ellen Brody, phone interview with author, April 20, 2022.

9. Phil Church, interview with the author, October 19, 2020.

10. Jim Kennard, phone interview with the author, October 31, 2021.

11. For more on this technology and plans to employ it in Lake Ontario see "Maritime Heritage in American's Inland Seas: A Multi-tiered Autonomous Vehicle–Based Survey of Two Proposed Great Lake Maritime Sanctuaries," NOAA, 2021, https://oceanexplorer.noaa.gov/explorations/21greatlakes/welcome.html.

INDEX

Figures and notes are indicated by f and n following the page number.